Excel

T0359323

Revise in a Month

Years 5–6
Selective Schools
and Scholarship Tests

Get the Results You Want!

**Lyn Baker
Kristine Brown
Sharon Dalgleish
Tanya Dalgleish
& Allyn Jones**

PASCAL
PRESS

Completely new edition incorporating late 2020 Selective School test changes

Reprinted 2023, 2024

ISBN 978 1 74125 699 4

Pascal Press
PO Box 250
Glebe NSW 2037
(02) 9198 1748
www.pascalpress.com.au

Publisher: Vivienne Joannou
Project editor: Mark Dixon
Edited by Mark Dixon and Rosemary Peers
Answers checked by Peter Little and Dale Little
Typeset by Grizzly Graphics (Leanne Richters)
Cover and page design by DiZign Pty Ltd
Printed by Vivar Printing/Green Giant Press

Acknowledgements
The publisher wishes to thank the people and organisations who gave their kind permission to reproduce copyright material. Specific acknowledgements appear under each text. The publisher would particularly like to thank Cameron Little for the use of 'The Race' and James Athanasou for the use of some materials.

All efforts have been made to gain permission for the copyright material reproduced in this book but we have not been successful in contacting all copyright holders. The publisher welcomes any information that will enable rectification of any reference or credit in subsequent editions.

Contents

About the tests

The NSW Selective High School Placement Test consists of four test papers containing questions from the four areas of Reading, Mathematical Reasoning, Thinking Skills and Writing. The first three tests each last for 40 minutes and the Writing Test lasts for 30 minutes. Victoria has selective entry to some schools, and while the Victorian Selective Entry High Schools Examination has a slightly different structure, it covers similar general content to the NSW test.

The ACER Scholarship Tests (Secondary Level 1) have a slightly different format to the NSW Selective High School Placement Test. They contain a Reading test (under the name 'Humanities—Comprehension and Interpretation', 40 minutes), a Mathematics Test (40 minutes) and a Written Expression Test (two tests of 25 minutes each). More specific information about the different test components follows below.

Note: You will receive detailed information about the particular test you are sitting; it is important you read it carefully. Supervising teachers should be able to clarify any points causing concern.

Reading test

The NSW Selective High School Placement Test and all scholarship tests include a Reading comprehension component that asks you to read a number of texts and then answer questions to show how well you understood them.

The NSW Selective High School Placement Test calls this section 'Reading'. The ACER Scholarship Tests call it 'Humanities—Comprehension and Interpretation'.

The question format for the Selective Schools Test varies from subsection to subsection. At the time of writing, the question format is as follows for the four subsections:

◎ Literary prose text—multiple-choice questions about two different texts or about different stages of one text
◎ Poetry—multiple-choice questions about one poem
◎ Factual text—a task which asks you to place sentences or phrases into an information text in a way that makes sense (a cloze task)
◎ Varied short texts—matching descriptive statements to four short texts on the same theme but with different content and written in different styles or from different perspectives.

What kinds of questions will be in the test?

All tests, except Writing, use multiple-choice questions. This means you are given a question and have to choose the best answer from four or five possibilities. However, in the Selective Schools Test you will also have to do a cloze task and a matching task. The tests vary in the way you record your answers but most ask you to mark your answers on a separate answer sheet. You don't have to write any words.

What kinds of texts will I have to read and understand?

All tests include a variety of types of texts. For example, you are likely to have to answer questions about narrative fiction, poems, factual descriptions, information reports, explanations, biographies, literary recounts and/or texts including some visual information.

What will the texts be about?

The texts are usually on a wide range of topics, including personal feelings and experiences, different cultures, animals and plants, history, the environment, science and technology, art and music, and family life.

Do I have to study these areas before the test?

No. The topics will be general interest and all the information you need to answer the questions will be in the texts. The questions test **how** you read, not how much you know. Sometimes, however, you will need to figure things out from the information in the text.

What kinds of questions will I be asked?

The questions cover a range of reading skills and strategies. You will be familiar with most question types from classroom work and from other tests you have done.

Some questions will ask you to find particular facts. Others will ask you to work out the main idea or ideas. Some questions will ask you to work out the meaning of a word or phrase. Others will ask you to draw a conclusion based on what you have read—the answer won't be clearly given to you in the text and you will have to use the text to work out the answer (for example, to predict what is going to happen). Sometimes the question might involve a personal judgement or evaluation.

Some questions could ask you to look more at the way the text is written (for example, to identify the tone of a piece, or words that express emotion and opinion).

Do I have to answer all the questions?

Yes, you should try to answer every question. However, it is quite possible that you will not have time to do them all. You will have to work quite quickly to read all the texts and answer all the questions. Many students don't manage to do this.

How can I make the best use of my time?

Here are a few tips to help you get through the test and make the best use of your time. You probably have some of your own test techniques and strategies. If so, use them too. In fact, use anything that works for you!

◎ Quickly skim the text to get a general idea of the topic and type of text and then quickly look at the questions.

◎ Next read the text carefully but quickly.

◎ Attempt the questions one at a time and choose the answer you think is best. There are often one or two answers that are obviously wrong, so it can help to cross these out as soon as you see them.

◎ Be sure to look back at the text to answer the questions. Don't just answer them from memory! Also, look again at the question to make sure you have not made a silly mistake when reading it.

◎ Don't waste too much time on any one question. If you are not sure, guess the answer but mark it so you can come back to it later (if you have time). If it seems impossible to choose, choose the answer you first thought was right.

◎ Answer every question. Don't leave any out. You will have a chance of getting the right answer, even if you guess.

◎ If you do have some time to spare, go over your answers. Sometimes you will realise the correct answer to a question after answering other questions.

Thinking Skills test

Many of the standardised tests include a Thinking Skills test component. This is different to testing knowledge: it tests your reasoning ability—how well you can think through problems. All tests are generally of the same format.

How much time will I have?

The test time and paper length may vary from test to test and from year to year. Expect around 40 questions to answer in 40 minutes.

What kinds of questions will be in the test?

All tests use multiple-choice questions. This means you are given a question and have to choose the best answer from four or five possibilities. The tests vary in the way you record your answers but most ask you to mark your answers on a separate answer sheet. You don't have to write any words.

What do I need to bring to the test?

As the tests are multiple choice, you will need soft leaded pencils and erasers to answer paper-based tests. Apart from this, you will not need to bring anything except your well-prepared self!

What topics will be covered in the test?

The tests include questions that involve both verbal and non-verbal reasoning skills (critical thinking and problem solving). You may be familiar with the topics covered in the test, although sometimes questions might involve something new or unusual.

Do I have to study these areas before the test?

No. The best preparation is to know what to expect on the day of the test and to practise the types of questions in the test.

What kinds of questions will I be asked?

You will be familiar with some question types from classroom work. Some of the questions will test your understanding of language and grammar and some will test your numeracy skills. The questions may be more difficult or of a type you haven't seen before. You will need to be logical and think carefully about your answers.

Where can I do my working?

You will be able to write on the question booklet if you need to do some working.

Do I have to answer all the questions?

Yes, you should try to answer every question. However, it is possible that you will not have time to do them all. Some questions will take less than one minute to answer, while others will take longer. You will have to work quite quickly to answer all the questions. Many students don't manage to do this.

How can I make the best use of my time?

Here are a few tips to help you get through the test and make the best use of your time.

◎ Don't waste too much time on any one question. If you are not sure, guess the answer but mark it so you can come back to it later (if you have time). If it seems impossible to choose, select the answer you first thought was right.

◎ Answer every question. Don't leave any out. You'll have a one in four (or five) chance of getting the right answer, even if you guess.

◎ If you do have some time to spare, go over your answers. Sometimes you will realise the correct answer to a question after answering other questions.

Mathematical Reasoning test

The NSW Selective High School Placement Test and the ACER Scholarship Tests include a Mathematical Reasoning test component.

All tests are generally of the same format. Mostly you will be given information and asked one question about it. Sometimes you might get more than one question.

What kinds of questions will be in the test?

All tests use multiple-choice questions. This means you are given a question and have to choose the best answer from four or five possibilities. The tests vary in the way you record your answers but most ask you to mark your answers on a separate answer sheet. You don't have to write any words.

What do I need to bring to the test?

As the tests are multiple choice, you will need pencils and erasers. Calculators, rulers and geometrical instruments are not allowed, so you need to be good at mental calculations and estimating length and angles.

What mathematics topics will be covered in the test?

The tests include questions involving Number, Measurement, Data, Patterns and Algebra, Space and Geometry, and Working Mathematically. This means you will be familiar with the topics covered in the test but the questions may be more difficult or of a type you may not have seen before.

Do I have to study these areas before the test?

No. The best preparation is to know what to expect on the day of the test and to practise the types of questions in the test.

What kinds of questions will I be asked?

You will be given some information and asked one question about it. The information might be given in words or might involve a diagram, graph or table.

You will be familiar with most question types from classroom work and from other tests you have done, such as the NAPLAN tests.

Where can I do my working?

Most tests have a question booklet and a separate answer sheet. Many of the questions are so difficult you will need to write down some working to help you find your answer. You can use space on the booklet near the question.

Do I have to answer all the questions?

Yes, you should try to answer every question. However, it is possible you will not have time to do them all. Some questions will take less than one minute to answer, while others will take longer. You will have to work quite quickly to answer all the questions. Many students don't manage to do this.

How can I make the best use of my time?

Here are a few tips to help you get through the test, and to make the best use of your time.

◎ Don't waste too much time on any one question. If you are not sure, guess the answer but mark it so that you can come back to it later (if you have time). If it seems impossible to choose, select the answer you first thought was right.

◎ Answer every question. Don't leave any out. You'll have a one in four (or five) chance of getting the right answer, even if you guess.

◎ If you do have some time to spare, go over your answers. Sometimes you will realise the correct answer to a question after answering other questions.

Writing test

The NSW Selective High School Placement Test and the ACER Scholarship Tests include a Writing component that asks you to complete one or two pieces of writing. The NSW Selective High School Placement Test asks you to write one piece. The ACER Scholarship Tests ask you to write two pieces. You need to find out exactly what is required in your test.

How much time will I have?

The NSW Selective High School Placement Test gives you 30 minutes to write one piece, while the ACER Scholarship Tests give you 25 minutes per piece. Again, you need to find out about your test. Whichever test you are doing, your usual method of preparing, drafting, revising and proofreading is not practical for these tests because there is not enough time.

How much should I write?

There is no set length but, as a general guide, aim to write about one and a half pages of an A4 booklet—about 200 to 250 words. The important thing is the quality of what you write, not the quantity.

How will I know what to write?

You will be given stimulus material to respond to. This might be words or pictures. For example, you might be asked to respond to a photograph, a drawing, a quote or comment, a question, or an extract from a story or other text.

Will I have a choice of what to write?

Generally there is only one question or topic. However, some questions give you a completely free choice of how to respond to the question—you can choose which type and form of text you write (e.g. a narrative, a diary, a description, a poem, a letter or an essay).

Other questions might tell you the way you should respond. You might be told to write a newspaper report or an advice sheet, for example. Some might suggest or tell you a type of text (e.g. an opinion or persuasive text), but will allow you to choose in which form to write that opinion (e.g. as a letter to a newspaper editor, as a speech to your classmates or as an essay).

There is never only one way to respond and so, in a way, you always have a choice of what to write. You could write about something completely different from the next student and in a completely different way—and both of you could do well. Look at the question below:

Use this picture as the basis for a piece of writing.

This question might lead one student to write a description of what the stadium looked like minutes before. Another student might write a letter to a friend telling them about the football match his team has just won. Another might write a newspaper article about how the stadium was built. All would be acceptable.

How can I make the best use of my time?

◎ Read or look at the stimulus material very carefully.

◎ Brainstorm some ideas on the topic, including ideas about which type of text to use if you have a choice. Don't waste time thinking of a million different possibilities. Think of two or three at most and then choose one.

- Organise your ideas into a logical plan—for many texts this is an introduction, body and conclusion. You may not stick to your plan but it helps to have one.
- Start writing and keep going!
- If you have time, read through your writing to make quick improvements to wording and to proofread for spelling, grammar and punctuation.

How will the markers judge my writing?

The markers are looking for clear, lively and interesting writing. They are looking for:

- the quality of your ideas—how well you develop something interesting from the question
- the way you organise your ideas—how well you shape them to make a whole text
- the language you use—how clearly and effectively you express yourself.

Try to make your writing as interesting as possible. Don't try to rewrite something you have prepared or something you have copied or adapted from a book like this one, or from a website. The markers will pick up on this. One more very important thing: if you are sitting a handwritten test, write legibly—that is, in a way that can actually be read! It does not matter how brilliant your ideas are if the markers cannot read your handwriting—they will not be able to give you a good mark. So, if you know your handwriting is not always clear, take time now to improve it. If you are sitting an online test, do all the things you would do normally to craft and check your writing. In this situation, the only thing you won't have to worry about is your handwriting!

> **Important!**
>
> This information was correct at the time of writing but make sure you check the information you get about your particular test. It is possible that changes might be made to test names, length, and so on.

Follow this plan to revise for the Selective Schools and Scholarship Tests!

Introduction

The content of this book is organised into days of the week—four days each week. Each day covers the maximum you should do on one day. You do not necessarily need to do every section, topic or task. You should focus on the parts you need to practise. Of course you can do all sections, topics and tasks if you wish to.

Times are **suggested** for each section. These are **guides only.** You may take more or less time than other students.

In each week

Day 1

On Day 1, you will practise one Reading comprehension topic. Each topic covers a different category of text. For example, in Week 1 Day 1 you will look at literary prose texts.

Each topic will have the following parts:

◎ **Key Points** give you an overview of these types of texts, common types of questions asked, and tips and clues on answering questions.

◎ **Practice Tasks** give you practice reading and answering questions about these types of texts and questions of the kind you will meet in your test. Read the texts and answer the questions. Then go to the answer section at the back of the book for the answers and the explanations of why a particular answer is correct. While there is time set, this is just a guide. You do not have to complete the task in that time.

◎ **Real Test** allows you to practise answering questions similar to those in the real test under a strict time limit. Answers and explanations are given at the back of the book.

Day 2

On Day 2, you will cover three topics from the Thinking Skills test. For example, in Week 1 Day 2 you will cover:

◎ Critical thinking—Identifying the main idea

◎ Critical thinking—Assessing the impact of further evidence to strengthen an argument

◎ Critical thinking—Assessing the impact of further evidence to weaken an argument.

Each topic will have the following parts:

◎ **Key Points** gives a summary of the topic, as well as examples and sample questions.

◎ **Real Test** allows you to answer questions like those in the real test. Time yourself doing these questions. Answers are given at the back of the book.

Day 3

On Day 3, you will cover two topics from the Mathematical Reasoning test. For example, in Week 1 Day 3 you will cover:

◎ Whole numbers and place value

◎ Fractions.

Each topic will have the following parts:
- ◎ **Key Points** gives a summary of the topic, as well as examples and sample questions.
- ◎ **Real Test** allows you to answer questions like those in the real test. Time yourself doing these questions. Answers are given at the back of the book.

Day 4

On Day 4, you will practise one Writing topic. Each topic covers a different type of text: description, recount, narrative and persuasive text. For example, in Week 1 Day 4 you will cover descriptive response. The four types of texts chosen are the most useful to revise and practise before the tests. However, there is always more than one way to shape these basic types of texts. Some possible forms are:

- ◎ a letter to the editor
- ◎ a letter to a person in authority
- ◎ a personal letter
- ◎ a diary entry
- ◎ an advertisement
- ◎ a magazine or newspaper article
- ◎ an information report
- ◎ instructions and rules

- ◎ an essay
- ◎ a poem
- ◎ a speech
- ◎ a conversation
- ◎ an interview
- ◎ an imaginative recount
- ◎ a personal recount.

Each of the four topics will have the following parts:

- ◎ **Key Points** give you a summary of the type of text, common types of questions, and tips and clues on answering questions for that type of text.
- ◎ **Sample Tasks** give you a model question and response for the type of text. The model response has clear notes showing you the appropriate structure and language for that type of text.
- ◎ **Practice Tasks** give you a variety of tasks to allow you to develop skills for writing the type of text. Follow the instructions to complete the tasks. Answers and explanations for many of the tasks are given at the back of the book.
- ◎ **Real Test** allows you to practise answering questions similar to those in the real test under a strict time limit. A checklist for each type of text is given at the back of the book.

Sample Test Paper

- ◎ **A Sample Test Paper** appears at the end of the book. It is very similar to the actual NSW Selective High School Placement Test.
- ◎ Before attempting the Sample Test Paper, make sure you have done the **Real Test** for any topic you were unsure of and that you have worked through the answers for any questions you answered incorrectly.
- ◎ Set aside the **time allowed** for each part and complete the Sample Test Paper under **test conditions**—no sneaking a look at your earlier work or class books! That way you will be better prepared for the real tests.
- ◎ **Answers and explanations** for the Sample Test Paper are given at the back of the book on pages 221–231.

Let's start to revise!

Week 1

This is what we cover this week:

Day 1   **Reading:** Literary prose texts

Day 2   **Thinking Skills:**
- ◎ Critical thinking—Identifying the main idea
- ◎ Critical thinking—Assessing the impact of further evidence to strengthen an argument
- ◎ Critical thinking—Assessing the impact of further evidence to weaken an argument

Day 3   **Mathematical Reasoning:**
- ◎ Whole numbers and place value
- ◎ Fractions

Day 4   **Writing:** Descriptive response

- Literary texts are **imaginative or creative texts**. They are usually about people and events that are invented by the writer. They aim to make us respond in a particular way—to make us laugh or cry, to make us frightened or concerned, or to make us more aware of our world.

- **Literary prose texts** are texts written in normal sentences and paragraphs. We use this term to distinguish this kind of writing from the kind of writing used in poetry. In your test, you might be asked, for example, to answer questions about short stories, novels, folk tales, fables, or even play scripts. These are all examples of literary prose texts.

- Some texts might be mostly **descriptive**, while others focus more on **action and events**. Others might be mostly about what people say or think and contain a lot of **dialogue**.

- Always **read a literary text right through** before answering any questions about it (unless you run out of time). This is because you often have to search for meanings in different parts of the text. Ideas about a person, an event or an experience may be spread across one paragraph, many paragraphs, or even the whole text. You may have to pull these ideas together to come up with one main idea.

- Sometimes the answer will not be obvious—the writer will not have given it to you in black and white. Instead you will have to **search for hints and clues** here and there to work out the answer— to draw a conclusion or make a judgement or prediction.

- You might be asked about, for example:
  - the **theme**—the main concern or issue expressed in the writing or part of the writing (e.g. family relationships, freedom, prejudice)
  - the **characters**—what they did or said, and how they felt
  - the **setting**—where the events take place and how they are described
  - the **atmosphere**—the feeling or mood created in the writing (gloomy, tense, exciting, hopeful, depressing, frantic)
  - the **plot**—what actually happened in the story, or the order in which the events happened
  - the **writer's feelings and attitudes** towards what he or she is writing about—sometimes called the tone of the writing (humorous, sarcastic, sympathetic, respectful, light-hearted)
  - the **meanings of words**—perhaps words you have not seen before. Writers of literary texts often use unusual words, and you will have to really use your brains to work out the most likely meaning. You will mainly need to use contextual clues hiding in the words and sentences before and after the unfamiliar word.

Practice Task 1

Use this first practice task as a guide. Read the text below carefully and then read the eight questions on the next page. Circle the option which best answers each question. Then look at the answers to get tips about how to answer the questions correctly and also to get explanations about why one answer was right. Don't worry if you don't get every question right. The aim is to give you practice with the type of texts and questions you will find in the test. Don't worry too much about the time limit in this first practice task. In this task there is only one text. The paragraphs are clearly numbered and some questions will ask you to look closely at particular paragraphs.

Extract: from 'Mr Pemberley Checks the Gates' by Morris Lurie

1. In the high stone vaulted entrance hall before the great door, the great door of oldest oak stronger than any iron that had once protected an ancient castle and borne witness to the coming and goings of many kings, Mr Pemberley tallied the time on his gold fobwatch with that on the face of the old grandfather clock by the far wall, nodded, good, excellent, eleven o'clock precisely, eleven o'clock on the dot, donned his overcoat and his muffle and his favourite soft tweed cap, and then took up, first, in his left hand, his flashlight, tested it— yes, all in order, the beam strong and sharp and true—and then, in his right hand, his stout stick of black mahogany with the carved white ivory grip in the shape of a crouched tiger, and then, thus dressed and prepared and equipped, stepped out as he did every night at exactly this time, to check the gate. The great door closed behind him with a sound of banks. The stick was for the bears.

2. Mr Pemberley stood stock-still outside in the night.

3. And first, as he did every night, Mr Pemberley sniffed, a great deep sniff filling his sharp nose with the smell of trees and lawns and flowers and bushes, of thick leaf mould and rich black soil, of things wet, of things growing, and all his, every single leaf, every single spot of soil, every single bud and blade of grass, Pemberley property, Pemberley land, the rich smell of ownership, mine, all mine.

4. 'Ah!' said Mr Pemberley.

5. And then, as he did every night, Mr Pemberley stared, a great deep stare filling his sharp eyes with the canopy of the sky vast overhead, the clear night sky unsullied by fumes of industry or traffic, by smokes, by smogs, the sky rich with stars and ablaze with moon, and all beaming down just for him staring up, Pemberley heavens, Pemberley lights, the rich blaze of ownership, mine, all mine.

6. Ah!' said Mr Pemberley.

7. Now Mr Pemberley pointed his sharp nose and his sharp eyes straight ahead, and with his grip firm on his flashlight in one hand and on his stout stick in the other he stepped out onto the white gravel of the long driveway to the gate lit by the blazing moon like a white road through his gardens dark on either side, and with his stout stick stabbing the gravel too at every second step crunch! crunch! he began.

8. Mr Pemberley, it should be said, was rich. He was very rich.

From *Dream Time*, ed. Gascoigne et al., Penguin Group (Australia), Melbourne, 1990; reproduced with permission

Practice Task 1

1 The door of Mr Pemberley's house is described as
   A a door from an ancient king's castle.
   B a door made of the strongest iron.
   C an oak door reinforced with iron.
   D a door which is stronger than a door from an ancient king's castle.

2 Mr Pemberley was pleased that his watch showed eleven o'clock because
   A he was on time to meet someone.
   B the watch was keeping excellent time.
   C he was on time for his nightly routine.
   D it was not too late for his evening walk.

3 Why does the writer use the expression 'a sound of banks' in paragraph 1?
   A because Mr Pemberley owned and lived in a bank
   B because the house was as securely locked as a bank
   C because the house contained money or valuables
   D because Mr Pemberley lived in a bank

4 Which paragraph shows that Mr Pemberley believes he owns the entire universe?
   A Paragraph 1   B Paragraph 3   C Paragraph 5   D Paragraph 8

5 Which of the words below is closest in meaning to 'unsullied' as used in paragraph 5?
   A coloured   B darkened   C illuminated   D unspoilt

6 As he progresses from the house to the gates, Mr Pemberley shows
   A a fixed satisfied attitude to his place in the world as a rich man.
   B a change in his attitude to his place in the world as a rich man.
   C a decrease in satisfaction with his place in the world as a rich man.
   D an increase in satisfaction with his place in the world as a rich man.

7 What does the use of the four single-line paragraphs in the extract help to do?
   A mark the different stages of Mr Pemberley's walk
   B build up the sense of drama as Mr Pemberley walks towards his gates
   C both A and B
   D neither A nor B

8 On the basis of the information in the text, Mr Pemberley seems to be
   A a rich man who only cares about his wealth.
   B a rich but kind man who likes to share his wealth.
   C a rich man who does not care about his wealth.
   D a rich man who does not know how wealthy he is.

☞ **Answers and explanations on page 186**

Practice Task 2

READING
Literary prose texts

In this task there are two texts to read because you may be asked to work across two texts in the actual test. Read the text carefully and answer the questions. Circle the answers you think are correct. When you finish, check your answers. If you did not choose the correct answer or if you were unsure about it, read the answer explanation. Again, don't worry if you don't get every question right—the aim is to give you practice. Try to work more quickly and finish in close to 15 minutes. You will have to work very quickly in the real test.

Extract A: from 'Roaches' by Isobelle Carmody

The day was bright and cold, casting sharp-edged shadows over the crumbling city. Framed in a sagging doorway, the boy stood motionless, with pale, wary eyes skimming along slabbed grey surfaces, alert for movement.

But that alone was not enough to be sure.

He listened with ears so attuned to the noises of the dead city that he did not register the gritty hiss of the wind, or the rustle it caused at the fringe of great sodden banks of debris on the cracked footpath.

His eyes rested on a spiral dance of leaves, a voice inside his thoughts warning of the danger that lay in moving around in the daylight: Gordy's voice speaking to him out of the past, stiff with warning.

'Day is dangerous because you might be seen, and night is dangerous because you can't see who might be watching.'

But the scrapers fell when they willed. The boy sniffed at the air, ripe with the rain smell, knowing anything exposed would be ruined. But he noticed the way the sun shone fair on the ruins. You could be seen for miles out in the open like that.

He chewed his knuckle, trying to decide.

The Carnies living in that part of the city had passed by that morning as he watched unseen from his high window.

Usually they stayed away all day. But you had to act as if they might be back at any moment.

'Don't expect the Carnies to be like us,' the Gordy voice said. 'Their brains are scrambled. They don't think like us no more. Don't try to out-think them. If you let them see you or guess you are there, they will hunt until they find you, and then they will eat you.'

From *Into the Future*, ed. Gascoigne et al., Penguin Group (Australia), Melbourne, 1992; reproduced with permission

---

Extract B: adapted from *War of the Worlds* by HG Wells

For my own part, I remember nothing of my flight except the stress of blundering against trees and stumbling through the heather. All about me gathered the invisible terrors of the Martians.

At last I could go no further; I was exhausted with the violence of my emotion and of my flight, and I staggered and fell by the wayside. That was near the bridge that crosses the canal by the gasworks. I fell and lay still.

I must have remained there some time.

I sat up, strangely perplexed. For a moment, perhaps, I could not clearly understand how I came there. My terror had fallen from me like a garment. A few minutes before, there had only been three real things before me—the immensity of the night and space and nature, my own feebleness and anguish, and the near approach of death. Now it was as if something turned over, and the point of view altered abruptly. I was immediately the self of every day again—a decent, ordinary citizen. The silent common, the impulse of my flight, the starting flames, were as if they had been in a dream. I asked myself had these latter things indeed happened? I could not credit it.

I rose and walked unsteadily up the steep incline of the bridge. My mind was blank wonder. My muscles and nerves seemed drained of their strength. I dare say I staggered drunkenly. A head rose over the arch, and the figure of a workman carrying a basket appeared. Beside him ran a little boy. He passed me, wishing me good night. I was minded to speak to him, but did not. I answered his greeting with a meaningless mumble and went on over the bridge.

Over the Maybury arch a train, a billowing tumult of white, firelit smoke, and a long caterpillar of lighted windows, went flying south—clatter, clatter, clap, rap, and it had gone. A dim group of people talked in the gate of one of the houses in the pretty little row of gables that was called Oriental Terrace. It was all so real and so familiar. And that behind me! It was frantic, fantastic! Such things, I told myself, could not be.

First published in 1898

Practice Task 2

1 Both extracts describe someone
A stumbling along unfamiliar streets.
B struggling to understand a situation.
C searching for hiding places.
D fleeing an unseen enemy.

2 In which extract does the main character show a change from fear to disbelief?
A Extract A   B Extract B   C Both   D Neither

3 In Extract A, the city scene could best be described as
A shabby and neglected.
B clean and bright.
C almost totally destroyed.
D cheap and dirty.

4 In Extract A, where is the main character?
A in a hole in the ground
B in a tall building
C on the street
D in a basement

5 Which of the words below is closest in meaning to 'register' as it is used in Extract A?
A resist   B get frightened by   C react to   D hear

6 In Extract B the mention of the workman and the little boy signifies that
A the main character is almost home.
B the main character is imagining things.
C some people are unaware of what the main character has seen.
D some people want normal life to go on.

7 The impression given in Extract A is that the main character is trying to decide
A whether or not to go for a walk.
B whether or not to hunt for food.
C whether or not to fight the Carnies.
D whether or not to go home.

8 The impression given in Extract B is that the main character does not share his experiences with others because
A they would not believe them.
B they do not want to hear about them.
C he hopes they won't ever have such experiences.
D he is only thinking of his own needs.

☞ **Answers and explanations on page 187**

Practice Task 3

READING
Literary prose texts

15 min

As with the last practice task, you have two texts to read in this task. Read and answer the questions, working as quickly as you can and aiming to finish in 15 minutes. When you finish, check the answers and read the answer explanation if needed. Again, don't worry if you don't get every question right—the aim is to give you practice with the types of texts and questions you will find in the test.

Extract A: from *Night of the Muttonbirds* by Mary Small

The storm lasted three days. Harsh icy winds blew keenly in from the south. People kept to their houses, warming themselves by wood stoves and fires, while the islands smothered by clouds and battered by angry seas waited for the storm to pass.

As evening approached on the third day there was a sudden lull in the wind and the grey clouds dispersed, revealing a pale watery sun over the western horizon. A broad belt of glistening white light spread across the swollen sea and, one by one, each rain-blurred, wave-beaten island stood out in sharp relief.

As the sun dipped, there appeared on the eastern horizon a cloud, darker and more definite than the wind-torn fragments still lacing the evening sky. It moved close to the face of the sea; a strange rising then falling undulation that grew increasingly larger and denser as it came closer. Within this cloud flew millions of shearwaters skimming the surface of the waves, making full use of the up-draughts and currents to bank, then glide on their sickle-shaped wings. They flew with an urgency, an urgency that had propelled them from half a world away over limitless horizons towards these Bass Strait islands, their summer breeding grounds. Many were exhausted, and some had been lost on the way through battling strong headwinds.

Night came early as the bird cloud curtained the rising moon and converged landwards. Over granite outcrops and sandhills, dark forms flitted and swept low as each bird circled, then recircled to locate its burrow from the previous year, the only sound being the whispering swish-swish of wings stroking the air. Gradually, the dark cloud disintegrated as, one by one, small shadows folded their wings and dropped, plummeting awkwardly into the thick spiny tussock grass that for centuries had hidden and protected their homes.

Harcourt Brace Jovanovich, Sydney, 1992

☞ **Answers and explanations on page 188**

Practice Task 3

Extract B: adapted from *White Fang* by Jack London

Dark spruce forest frowned on either side the frozen waterway. The trees had been stripped by a recent wind of their white covering of frost, and they seemed to lean towards each other, black and ominous, in the fading light. A vast silence reigned over the land. The land itself was a desolation, lifeless, without movement. It was the Wild, the savage, frozen-hearted Northland Wild.

But there was life, abroad in the land and defiant. Down the frozen waterway toiled a string of wolfish dogs. Their bristly fur was rimed with frost. Their breath froze in the air as it left their mouths, spouting forth in spumes of vapour that settled upon the hair of their bodies and formed into crystals of frost. Leather harness was on the dogs, and leather traces attached them to a sled which dragged along behind. On the sled, securely lashed, was a long and narrow oblong box. There were other things on the sled—blankets, an axe, and a coffee-pot and frying-pan; but prominent, occupying most of the space, was the long and narrow oblong box.

In advance of the dogs, on wide snowshoes, toiled a man. At the rear of the sled toiled a second man. On the sled, in the box, lay a third man whose toil was over,—a man whom the Wild had conquered and beaten down until he would never move nor struggle again. It is not the way of the Wild to like movement. Life is an offence to it, for life is movement; and the Wild aims always to destroy movement. It freezes the water to prevent it running to the sea; it drives the sap out of the trees till they are frozen to their mighty hearts; and most ferociously and terribly of all does the Wild harry and crush into submission man.

But at front and rear, unawed and indomitable, toiled the two men who were not yet dead. Their bodies were covered with fur and soft-tanned leather. Eyelashes and cheeks and lips were so coated with the crystals from their frozen breath that their faces were not discernible. This gave them the seeming of ghostly masques, undertakers in a spectral world at the funeral of some ghost. But under it all they were men, penetrating the land of desolation and mockery and silence, puny adventurers bent on colossal adventure, pitting themselves against the might of a world as remote and alien and pulseless as the abysses of space.

First published in 1906

Practice Task 3

1 Both extracts refer to
   A the movement of human beings across the landscape.
   B a change in very severe weather.
   C animals serving human beings.
   D the powerful impact of nature on living things.

2 In which extract do the animals follow a familiar route?
   A Extract A   B Extract B   C Both   D Neither

3 In Extract A, why did night come early?
   A because it was the middle of winter
   B because it was a stormy night
   C because the birds covered the light from the sun
   D because the birds covered the light from the moon

4 In Extract A, which statement is true?
   A The birds changed height as they flew.
   B The birds flew in a straight, level line until they reached the land.
   C Some birds flew straight and level while other birds changed height.
   D The birds gradually flew nearer and nearer to sea level.

5 In which extract is nature or the landscape presented as a living creature?
   A Extract A   B Extract B   C Both   D Neither

6 The writer of Extract B mentions a 'long and narrow oblong box' twice at the end of paragraph 2
   A to make sure the reader knows the box is on the sled.
   B to add necessary detail to the description of the sled.
   C to make the reader think about what is in the box.
   D to show the box takes up most of the space on the sled.

7 In Extract B, what would be the best word to replace 'discernible'?
   A visible
   B moving
   C unable to show expression
   D in shadow

8 There is evidence that the writer of Extract B
   A thinks the men are stupid for trying to exist in such a cold harsh land.
   B is envious of the men's adventure in the wilderness.
   C has respect for the men as they fight against the wilderness.
   D believes they will be beaten by the wilderness.

☞ **Answers and explanations on pages 188–189**

You only have to read one text in this Real Test. The paragraphs are clearly numbered and some questions will ask you to look closely at specific paragraphs. Read and answer the questions, working as quickly as you can and stop at 15 minutes. When you finish, check the answers and read the answer explanations if needed.

Extract: adapted from *Hard Times* by Charles Dickens

1. 'Now, what I want is, Facts. Teach these boys and girls nothing but Facts. Facts alone are wanted in life. Plant nothing else, and root out everything else. You can only form the minds of reasoning animals upon Facts: nothing else will ever be of any service to them. This is the principle on which I bring up my own children, and this is the principle on which I bring up these children. Stick to Facts, sir!'

2. The scene was a plain, bare, monotonous vault of a school-room, and the speaker's square forefinger emphasised his observations by underscoring every sentence with a line on the schoolmaster's sleeve. The emphasis was helped by the speaker's square wall of a forehead, which had his eyebrows for its base, while his eyes found commodious cellarage in two dark caves, overshadowed by the wall. The emphasis was helped by the speaker's mouth, which was wide, thin, and hard set. The emphasis was helped by the speaker's voice, which was inflexible, dry, and dictatorial. The emphasis was helped by the speaker's hair, which bristled on the skirts of his bald head, a plantation of firs to keep the wind from its shining surface, all covered with knobs, like the crust of a plum pie, as if the head had scarcely warehouse-room for the hard facts stored inside. The speaker's obstinate carriage, square coat, square legs, square shoulders,—nay, his very neckcloth, trained to take him by the throat with an unaccommodating grasp, like a stubborn fact, as it was,—all helped the emphasis.

3. 'In this life, we want nothing but Facts, sir; nothing but Facts!'

4. The speaker, and the schoolmaster, and the third grown person present, all backed a little, and swept with their eyes the inclined plane of little vessels then and there arranged in order, ready to have imperial gallons of facts poured into them until they were full to the brim.

5. Thomas Gradgrind, sir. A man of realities. A man of facts and calculations. A man who proceeds upon the principle that two and two are four, and nothing over, and who is not to be talked into allowing for anything over. With a rule and a pair of scales, and the multiplication table always in his pocket, sir, ready to weigh and measure any parcel of human nature, and tell you exactly what it comes to. It is a mere question of figures, a case of simple arithmetic.

6. In such terms Mr Gradgrind always mentally introduced himself, whether to his private circle of acquaintance, or to the public in general. In such terms, no doubt, substituting the words 'boys and girls', for 'sir', Thomas Gradgrind now presented Thomas Gradgrind to the little pitchers before him, who were to be filled so full of facts.

7. Indeed, as he eagerly sparkled at them from the cellarage before mentioned, he seemed a kind of cannon loaded to the muzzle with facts, and prepared to blow them clean out of the regions of childhood at one discharge. He seemed a galvanising apparatus, too, charged with a grim mechanical substitute for the tender young imaginations that were to be stormed away.

8. 'Girl number twenty,' said Mr Gradgrind, squarely pointing with his square forefinger, 'I don't know that girl. Who is that girl?'

9. 'Sissy Jupe, sir,' explained number twenty, blushing, standing up, and curtseying.

First published in 1854

Real Test

1 Why is the word 'Facts' written with a capital F?
   A because 'Facts' is a proper noun
   B because all nouns were written with capital letters when this book was written
   C because 'Facts' are very special to the speaker
   D because it is an error

2 In the first paragraph the speaker is asking for a system of education where
   A the children memorise information.
   B the feelings of the children are considered.
   C the children's learning interests are engaged.
   D the children are well behaved.

3 The schoolroom described is
   A large and empty.
   B cluttered and interesting.
   C small and cramped.
   D dirty and bare.

4 In paragraph 2 the speaker's eyes are said to find 'commodious cellarage'. What does this phrase mean in this text?
   A His eyes showed the effects of heavy drinking.
   B His eyes were staring and frightening.
   C His eyes were sunk deeply in his head.
   D His eyes were dark and red.

5 How would you describe the author's description of the speaker in paragraph 2?
   A abusing
   B flattering
   C respectful
   D mocking

6 Thinking now only of the speaker's speaking style, which word would best describe it?
   A loud   B emphatic   C longwinded   D hesitant

7 Why were the children labelled as 'vessels' in paragraph 4?
   A because the children were sitting in orderly rows
   B because the children were considered to be empty of knowledge and simply needed filling up
   C because the children were considered to be thirsty for knowledge
   D because the children were like ships waiting for cargo

8 Which paragraph refers to Mr Gradgrind's approach to teaching children as something that might happen on a battlefield?
   A Paragraph 1   B Paragraph 2   C Paragraph 5   D Paragraph 7

☞ **Answers and explanations on page 189**

The main idea:

● is the **conclusion** that the creator of the text wants you to accept

● can be **anywhere** in the text

● will be **supported** by the rest of the text.

Example

Instead of students bringing their own packed lunch to school each day, schools should provide all students with a healthy lunch. This would ensure that all students receive the same healthy lunch. Such a uniform delivery of food to all students would bring many benefits to health and learning. Research shows that children provided with a healthy lunch concentrate better in the classroom, which in turn leads to better learning outcomes.

Which of the following best expresses the main idea of the text?

A   There are many benefits to health and learning from eating a healthy lunch.

B   Schools should provide all students with a healthy lunch each day.

C   New infrastructure would be needed to deliver healthy lunches.

D   Children who eat a healthy lunch concentrate better in class.

Steps to work out the answer

1   Read the text carefully. Ask yourself: What does the creator of the text want me to accept?

2   Underline the sentence you think is the main idea: <u>Instead of students bringing their own packed lunch to school each day, schools should provide all students with a healthy lunch.</u>

3   Check: Does the rest of the text give you reason to believe this underlined sentence?

4   Decide which of the statements listed in the question best expresses the main idea you found.

B is correct. The creator of the text wants you to accept that instead of students bringing their own packed lunch to school each day, schools should provide all students with a healthy lunch. You can check this is the main idea by seeing if the rest of the text gives you reason to believe it. In this case, the rest of the text gives information about the health and learning benefits of all children receiving the same healthy lunch each day. So that confirms the main idea and B is the statement in the list that best expresses it.

Incorrect answers

A is incorrect because it supports, or is a reason to believe, the main idea that schools should provide all students with a healthy lunch each day.

C is incorrect because it is extra information not stated in the text, so it cannot be the main idea of the text.

D is incorrect because it supports, or is a reason to believe, the main idea that schools should provide all students with a healthy lunch each day.

Checklist

Can you:

1 *read a text carefully and think about what the creator of the text wants you to accept?*

2 *underline the sentence you think is the main idea?*

3 *check that the rest of the text gives you reason to believe this main idea?*

4 *from a list of statements given, find the one that best expresses this main idea?*

Real Test 1

THINKING SKILLS
Critical thinking—Identifying the main idea

1 Hens are hard workers. All gardens need some. With hens in the garden, you can grow more in a smaller space and use less water. Hens will scratch and dig to till the soil ready for planting. Once you plant, hens love to eat the pests that can destroy your precious plants. Even the old bedding from the coop is helpful. It can be added to compost bins to make better fertiliser. Don't miss out on all the wonderful benefits of these feathered helpers. Get yours today!

Which of the following best expresses the main idea of the text?

A Every garden needs to have hens.
B Hens are hard workers.
C Hens are feathered helpers.
D Chickens make great pets and are fun to watch.

2 A letter to the editor said: 'It's time to stop wasting money on space exploration. It costs billions of dollars every year when there are people right here on Earth who need help, and problems with the environment on this planet that need solving. We should spend money helping those people and solving those problems before we spend money sending robots to other planets.'

Which of the following best expresses the main idea of the letter?

A Earth has many problems that need solving.
B It costs money to send robots to other planets.
C We should not waste money on space exploration.
D People who write letters to the editor do not like space exploration.

3 Many movies are based on books, but it's more relaxing to sit and watch a movie than read the book it is based on. With a movie, you can see everything happening without having to think. A movie is also much faster. What can take hours to read in a book can be delivered in an 80-minute movie. Watching a movie is much better than reading a book!

Which of the following best expresses the main idea of the text?

A Movies are fast and easy to watch.
B Movie directors can put their own interpretation on a book.
C Many movies are based on books.
D Watching a movie based on a book is better than reading the book.

4 Zoos play an important role in animal conservation. Scientists study animals in zoos and learn more about protecting animals in the wild. Zoos also have breeding programs for endangered animals. Without these programs the animals would become extinct. Plus seeing animals in zoos makes people more aware of the animals and more likely to want to protect animals in the wild.

Which of the following best expresses the main idea of the text?

A Awareness and understanding of animals makes people more likely to protect them.
B Zoo animals help scientists learn about protecting wild animals.
C Zoos have an important role to play in animal conservation.
D Wild animals in captivity can suffer health problems.

☞ **Answers and explanations on pages 189-190**

5 When a giraffe begins to feast on the leaves from an umbrella thorn acacia, it only takes a few minutes for the tree to notice. As soon as it does, it pumps poison into its leaves. This makes the giraffe move to another tree. But the giraffe doesn't move to the tree next door. It moves to a tree upwind. That's because while pumping poison to protect itself, the acacia tree also gives off a gas to warn its neighbours about the giraffe. So, the neighbouring trees start pumping poison into their leaves as well. The hungry giraffe must move far enough away to trees that haven't received the message. Trees talk to help each other out!

Which of the following best expresses the main idea of the text?

A Umbrella thorn acacia trees notice when giraffes eat their leaves.

B Trees communicate with each other.

C Giraffes can only eat a few leaves from each tree they come to.

D Giraffes know when leaves are poisonous.

6 The 'bee's knees', 'cat's whiskers' and 'ant's pants' are expressions that carry a figurative, not literal, meaning. The technical term for these kinds of expression is idiom. When you say something or someone is the bee's knees you are not literally referring to a bee's knees. You are using the expression figuratively to mean that someone or something is terrific or admirable. Idioms make English more colourful and interesting but they can also make it more difficult to understand, especially for people whose first language is not English.

Which of the following best expresses the main idea of the text?

A Idioms can appeal to your senses.

B Idioms carry a depth of meaning that can't be conveyed as readily when using other words.

C Another idiom is to call something good the cat's pyjamas.

D Idioms make language more colourful and interesting but they can also make it more difficult to understand.

7 A 'whistleblower' is a word used to describe someone who exposes wrongdoing. A whistleblower figuratively blows a whistle to alert others to an illegal, corrupt, unsafe or fraudulent activity to instigate positive change. A whistleblower sometimes takes great risks to blow the whistle if the wrongdoing is so entrenched in a company, an organisation or a government department that the whistleblower is viewed by others as a traitor. Whistleblowers do a great public service. The rights of the whistleblower are protected by law in many countries because we need to support people who come forward and draw attention to wrongdoing.

Which of the following best expresses the main idea of the text?

A In many countries whistleblowers are protected by law.

B A whistleblower sometimes takes great risks to blow the whistle.

C Whistleblowers do a great public service.

D Whistleblower is a term used to describe someone who exposes wrongdoing.

☞ **Answers and explanations on pages 189-190**

8 Some scientists believe it is possible to fold space-time and therefore shorten the distance between two locations. The two locations are connected in space by an invisible tunnel or channel that's called a wormhole. In the future scientists might be able to work out a way that humans can create wormholes and travel through them in space-time. It's an exciting prospect.

Which of the following best expresses the main idea of the text?

A The prospect of time travel in the future is exciting.

B Some scientists believe it is possible to fold space-time.

C Wormholes are like invisible tunnels connecting two locations in space-time.

D Some scientists believe that time travel might be possible in the future.

9 The Great Barrier Reef is the largest living marine organism in the world. It's beautiful, it can be seen from space and its biodiversity is extraordinary, but it is under threat. The reef's survival is under threat because of problems such as climate change, the impact of coastal development and agricultural run-off. The Great Barrier Reef is a designated World Heritage Site and the majority of Australians agree that it needs to be protected from threats caused by humans.

Which of the following best expresses the main idea of the text?

A The Great Barrier Reef is the largest living marine organism in the world.

B The Great Barrier Reef needs to be protected.

C It needs to be protected from threats caused by humans.

D The Great Barrier Reef is under threat.

10 'An apple a day keeps the doctor away' is a proverb that can be traced back to at least 1866. It literally means that eating an apple is good for your health. Apples are good for your health but it's best to eat a range of fruit to get the most vitamins and minerals. If you had to pick just one fruit to eat every day instead of apples it should probably be one of the berries. Berries are full of important vitamins and minerals as well as antioxidants which help prevent cancer.

Which of the following best expresses the main idea of the text?

A An apple a day keeps the doctor away.

B Eating fruit is good for your health.

C Berries are full of antioxidants as well as other important vitamins and minerals.

D Eat berries every day.

☞ **Answers and explanations on pages 189–190**

THINKING SKILLS
*Critical thinking—Assessing the impact of
further evidence to strengthen an argument*

An argument text:

● presents a **point of view** or makes a **claim**

● uses supporting **evidence** to convince others to accept the point of view or claim.

Example

Vet: 'Your dog seems very lethargic and has poor coat quality. I've found the Go Dog brand of dog food to be the most nutritious dog food. I use it with my own dogs and they are very healthy. I recommend Go Dog for your dog. You can buy it through my clinic if that makes things easier for you. Just see Matt at reception and he'll put an order through on your account.'

Which statement most strengthens the vet's argument?

A Dogs need a balanced diet for optimal health.

B I've tried various other brands and they just don't give my dogs the energy they need.

C Go Dog has been designed by animal nutritionists for dogs' optimum health benefits.

D I get a commission on each bag of Go Dog I sell, and I donate that money to the animal shelter.

Steps to work out the answer

1 Identify the argument. The vet wants people to accept that Go Dog is the most nutritious brand of dog food. Note that the vet's opinion may or may not be true.

2 Judge which of the statements most strengthens the vet's argument that Go Dog is the most nutritious brand of dog food. Look for further evidence which supports the vet's claim.

C is correct. The statement that most strengthens the vet's argument is that Go Dog has been designed by animal nutritionists for dogs' optimum health benefits. This statement addresses both of the vet's concerns regarding the dog—lethargy and poor coat quality—and supports the argument that Go Dog is the most nutritious brand of dog food.

Incorrect answers

A is incorrect. This statement might be true but it does not support the argument that Go Dog is the most nutritious brand of dog food.

B is incorrect. The statement that the vet 'has tried various other brands and they just don't give dogs the energy they need' provides additional evidence to support the vet's claim however it only addresses one aspect of a dog's health—lethargy/or lack of energy. The vet has also reported to the dog owner that the dog has poor coat quality. Option B does not address coat quality so B is not the most supportive statement.

D is incorrect. The fact that the vet gets a commission on each bag of Go Dog sold and donates that money to the animal shelter might be an additional reason to buy Go Dog but it is not the most supportive statement for the argument that Go Dog is the most nutritious dog food.

Checklist

Can you:

1 *identify the argument?*

2 *assess the impact of further evidence?*

Real Test 2

10 MIN

1 **Isaac:** 'Most people in Australia eat too much salt (sodium). Too much salt can lead to high blood pressure and other health conditions including heart disease and kidney disease. Salt occurs naturally in foods so we consume enough salt for our needs without adding extra during cooking or at the table. Australians should think about how much hidden salt they are eating, how much salt they add to their food and the consequences for their health.'

Which statement most strengthens Isaac's argument?

A Processed and takeaway foods contain more salt than most of us realise.

B We should all try to cut back on the amount of salt we add to our food.

C It only takes a few weeks for your tastebuds to get used to eating less salt in your foods.

D Salt is an essential nutrient that we need to help regulate the fluids in our bodies.

2 Unit for sale.
Two bedrooms, two bathrooms, one car space.
Great location—quiet street across from a park. Only a short walk to nearby shops.
Low Body Corporate levies.
Auction 26 February if not sold prior. Book an inspection now.
You'd better be quick! This great property won't last.

Which statement most strengthens the argument?

A The park across the street is a great dog exercise park.

B The unit next door recently sold for a record price.

C The owners are moving interstate.

D Don't miss out!

3 **Kelly:** 'One-third of all the homeless people in Australia are under 18 years of age while one in six young people in Australia have been homeless at some time. Homelessness can be caused by family breakdown, poverty, unemployment and other reasons but the main cause in Australia is domestic violence. It's important that Australia works towards ending homelessness as well as eliminating the reasons why people become homeless.'

Which statement most strengthens Kelly's argument?

A Some homeless people live in their cars.

B Safe housing is a basic human right.

C When you have no home it's impossible to eat healthily so that leads to nutritional deficiencies.

D When children are homeless, they fall behind in their studies.

4 **Anna:** 'Captain James Cook is a controversial figure in Australia's history. In some circles he is acknowledged as the man who claimed the continent of Australia in the name of the British crown and therefore deserves the title of "Founder of Australia". On the other hand, Cook's reports to England about the east coast of Australia led the British Crown to declare Australia *terra nullius*. The term *terra nullius* means nobody's land and because Australia was declared *terra nullius* it meant that the British Crown could legally take possession of it. Is it fair to blame Cook for beginning the dispossession of First Nations Australians? Probably not. But should we revere him with the title "Founder of Australia"? Definitely not.'

☞ **Answers and explanations on pages 190-191**

Real
Test 2

THINKING SKILLS
*Critical thinking—Assessing the impact of further
evidence to strengthen an argument*

Which statement most strengthens Anna's argument?

A First Nations Australians have a rich and complex cultural life.

B Australia was not *terra nullius* when Cook visited.

C Cook was a brilliant cartographer and he needs to be honoured as such.

D Many Australians do not accept that we should revere Cook with the title 'Founder of Australia'.

5 Philip: 'Artificial intelligence means that computers and machinery can learn and improve for themselves. I think that is scary because computers can become smarter than people. What's to stop them taking control of everything? Or what's to stop an individual or a country from using AI to take control of everything, including banking and finance, traffic, power grids and communications?'

Which statement most strengthens Philip's argument?

A The use of AI in military applications is also a concern.

B Robot doctors can improve medical outcomes.

C A computer malfunction could prevent people from accessing their money.

D Self-driving cars are safer than cars with human drivers.

6 Anh: 'If pets held Olympics, cats would win gold for the high jump. The average cat can jump 1.5 to 1.8 metres. That's five to six times their own height. Proportionally, that is much higher than humans can jump.'

Which one of these statements most strengthens Anh's argument?

A Cats are flexible and have excellent coordination and balance.

B Cats have powerful hind legs to propel them up and a tail for balance.

C Some cats prefer to laze in the sun.

D Cats like to sit in elevated positions where they can see any dangers.

7 A journalist said: 'It's time to do away with Valentine's Day once and for all. It used to be a simple tradition to honour and celebrate love. Now it is an over-commercialised boon for advertising and an excuse for card companies, florists and restaurants to make money.'

Which one of these statements most strengthens the journalist's argument?

A Valentine's Day is a $14 billion industry.

B Valentine's Day is fun.

C Legend has it that Saint Valentine secretly married couples.

D Commercial marketing is part of society.

☞ **Answers and explanations on pages 190-191**

Real Test 2

8 The Student Council argued: 'Teachers at this school have always been evaluated by how well their students perform in tests. But this does not give a complete picture of what is happening in a classroom. We propose that students complete a survey to evaluate their teachers, so that teachers hear directly from their students. This would allow students to have their voices heard at last, to feel more in control of their lives, and ultimately to be happier and more successful in the classroom.'

Which one of these statements most strengthens the Student Council's argument?

A Student opinions are rarely heard.

B Students don't have enough educational knowledge to judge teachers.

C Discipline is impossible to enforce if job security is tied to how well students like the teacher.

D There is a correlation between a student's happiness in class and their academic success.

9 Sitting for too long is dangerous. Physical inactivity increases your risk of chronic health problems, including heart disease, diabetes and some cancers. Too much sitting is also bad for your mental health. Almost 70 per cent of Australian adults have low levels of physical activity and are at risk.

Which one of these statements most strengthens the argument?

A Breaking up long blocks of sitting to stand and flex your muscles is a wise move.

B Stand up to read emails and reports.

C Six per cent of all deaths can be attributed to physical inactivity.

D Hunching over a computer keyboard can lead to pain and stiffness in the neck.

10 When Luca was in the city, he saw a sign saying that a number of trees were scheduled to be chopped down. He went home and wrote an email to the City Council: 'Trees are important in the city. They provide shade and create cooler air. They also produce oxygen, something our choking city is in need of. We must save the trees in the city centre, not chop them down.'

Which one of these statements most strengthens Luca's argument?

A Cities look nicer with trees growing.

B Trees cool cities down.

C One large tree produces enough oxygen for 20 people to breathe.

D During a storm, tree branches might break and fall on cars.

☞ **Answers and explanations on pages 190-191**

Key Points

THINKING SKILLS
Critical thinking—Assessing the impact of further evidence to weaken an argument

10 MIN

An argument text:

● presents a **point of view** or makes a **claim**
● uses **supporting evidence** to convince others to accept the point of view or claim
● can be **weakened** by any statement that **calls into question any of the ideas** the argument wants you to accept as true.

Example

Lenny: 'Different theories exist about how dinosaurs became extinct and why it seems that their mass extinction 66 million years ago was a sudden event. One of the most accepted claims is that a huge meteor crashed into Earth causing the sky to darken with dust and debris and making the planet unliveable for many years. A crater on the Yucatan Peninsula in Mexico seems the right size to have been the meteor impact site.

Another theory is that a massive volcanic event occurred which darkened the skies with carbon dioxide and other gases and changed the climate.

I personally agree with the meteor theory. The meteor site on the Yucatan Peninsula in Mexico also holds evidence of the metal iridium, which is rare on Earth but common on meteors. So that supports the meteor argument.'

Which statement most weakens Lenny's argument?
A   Climate changes can have a drastic effect on all life on Earth.
B   There is evidence of mass dinosaur die-offs earlier than 66 million years ago.
C   Volcanic activity is common on Earth and a likely cause of other ancient extinctions.
D   When the meteor impact caused the sky to darken, food chains were interrupted and dinosaurs starved to death.

Steps to work out the answer

1   Identify the argument: that a giant meteor was responsible for the sudden mass extinction of dinosaurs.
2   Judge which of the statements weakens the argument. Remember that any statement which undermines or calls into question any of the claims in the argument will weaken the argument.

B is correct. For the argument to hold it can't be true that dinosaurs were experiencing mass die-offs prior to the meteor's arrival. This statement undermines the claim that dinosaur extinction was sudden and therefore it weakens Lenny's argument.

Incorrect answers

A is incorrect. The statement that 'Climate changes can have a drastic effect on all life on Earth' might be true but it does not weaken the argument related to the meteor's impact on dinosaurs.
C is incorrect. The statement that 'Volcanic activity is common on Earth and a likely cause of other ancient extinctions' weakens the argument that meteors are the cause of sudden extinctions because it allows for the claim that volcanic activity could have contributed to dinosaur extinction but it is not the statement that most weakens the argument.
D is incorrect. The claim that a meteor impact caused the sky to darken and food chains to be interrupted so that dinosaurs starved to death supports the argument rather than weakens it.

Checklist

Can you:
1 *identify the argument?*
2 *assess the impact of further evidence to weaken an argument?*

Real Test 3

1 **Genevieve:** 'My netball team is on a losing streak. We have to find ways to improve our game because all the players are feeling really demoralised. I know there are some things we need to do, including accepting responsibility for our own performances and we need to stop blaming the umpires, the weather and other factors for our losses.'

Which statement most weakens Genevieve's argument?

A Players need to look at their individual performances and assess their behaviours.

B Players need to reflect on what is working and what isn't working in the team's strategies.

C Players need praise and encouragement to maintain their motivation.

D Players have lost so often they now expect to lose.

2 Holiday in beautiful tropical Fiji!
Glorious weather all year round.
Perfect for beach-side holidays, swimming, snorkelling, diving, surfing.
Enjoy a warm welcome from the friendly locals.
Experience the natural beauty of waterfalls and rainforests.
Book your trip now!

Which statement most weakens the argument?

A You can relax by the pool in any one of Fiji's lovely resorts or seek out more adventurous activities.

B It's 3215 kilometres from Sydney to Fiji.

C Cyclones can occur between November and April.

D Fijians are considered amongst the happiest people on earth.

3 **Ahmed:** 'We moved to Mudgee six months ago from Katoomba in the Blue Mountains. I much prefer living here because it's close to a wilderness area for hiking. I hike in the Wollemi National Park every weekend.'

Which statement most weakens Ahmed's argument?

A There's thrilling hiking opportunities in Wollemi.

B The Wollemi National Park is part of the Greater Blue Mountains wilderness area.

C Mudgee is further from Sydney than Katoomba.

D Hiking boosts fitness as well as mental health and well-being.

4 **Alyssa:** 'Running shoes can cost a lot of money with so many brands competing for business and it's not true that the more you pay the better the shoe will be. One market research study found that the cheaper shoes had higher ratings for user satisfaction.'

Which statement most weakens Alyssa's argument?

A A person's running form is a better predictor of a potential running injury than the shoes they wear.

B Lighter running shoes are better regardless of price.

C Comfort is more important than style or brand.

D Ten minutes of stretching before running prepares your body for a run.

5 **Jessica:** 'A shark would lose a fight with a dolphin. Dolphins are strategic thinkers. A dolphin can kill a shark by pounding its snout into a shark's stomach from below and causing internal injuries or ramming its snout into a shark's gills. And dolphins travel in pods and support each other, including in times of danger. They wouldn't let a shark capture one of them.'

Which statement most weakens Jessica's argument?

A If a great white shark managed to capture a dolphin its jaws would kill the dolphin.

B Sharks are individuals and don't support each other in times of danger.

C Dolphins are faster swimmers than sharks.

D Dolphins use their brains to outsmart a shark.

☞ **Answers and explanations on pages 191-192**

Real Test 3

6 The town planner said: 'New housing and retail will beautify the area. This proposed development has retail premises, a gym and basement car park—all set within beautiful landscaping. On top of the shops will be 51 modern apartments demonstrating design quality.'

Which statement most weakens the town planner's argument?

A The developer has reduced the number of storeys from three to two.

B The development will replace existing beautiful native rainforest.

C The architect has won numerous awards for developing new town centres.

D There is plenty of parking for cars in the next town.

7 A mining company announced: 'Antarctica is a land of new opportunity for mineral and metal exploitation as resources elsewhere are drying up. It is also a frozen wasteland with no indigenous inhabitants. The value of the minerals to be extracted far outweighs any minor impacts from mining. Therefore, we propose commencing exploration immediately so we can turn Antarctica into the next mining hub.'

Which statement most weakens the mining company's argument?

A Vital supplies of oil are running out in other parts of the world.

B Antarctica is the coldest, driest continent in the world.

C Antarctica has valuable deposits, including coal, gas, copper, gold, zinc and iron ore.

D Antarctica has a critical impact on the world's ocean systems and environment, so any changes there from mining would have a disastrous global impact.

8 Ella's father wants dogs to be allowed to run off-leash at the local beach. He says that the sand dune vegetation along the beach provides a natural fence between the beach and the road, so it would be quite safe for dogs, and no extra fencing would be needed. He also claims that 84 per cent of residents surveyed were in favour of the idea.

Which statement most weakens Ella's father's argument?

A There is an on-leash park nearby.

B Dogs love running free on the sand.

C The sand dune vegetation is habitat for endangered shorebirds.

D The beach is far enough from houses so that noise will not be a problem.

9 Not enough time to cook a healthy meal? Worried you are missing vital vitamins? DILL—dinner in a pill—has the solution! Simply replace one main meal a day with a DILL tablet and you can be sure you are getting all the vitamins and minerals needed to keep you healthy and active.

Which statement most weakens the argument?

A Swallowing a tablet is faster and easier than preparing and eating fresh food.

B Fresh food is delicious.

C Research shows that vitamins in fresh food are more effective.

D Market surveys prove that fresh food is more expensive than a DILL tablet.

10 A consumer organisation said: 'Consumers demand products that are built to last. Too many products are built to break. They break too soon and cost too much to repair. Repairs, spare parts, software updates and recycling options should be easily available. And there should be penalties for companies that mislead consumers about the availability of these things.'

Which statement most weakens the consumer organisation's argument?

A Consumers want to have the latest model and prefer to buy new products.

B People want to choose products that last longer because it is better for the planet.

C A survey shows that one in four people had an issue with a product that stopped working or broke in the first year.

D Companies make more money by superseding old models and selling new models.

☞ **Answers and explanations on pages 191-192**

MATHEMATICAL REASONING
Whole numbers and place value

- **The place or position of a digit** in a number determines its value.

  Example: What is the place value of 7 in the number 376 809?
  A   7 hundred-thousands
  B   7 ten-thousands
  C   7 thousands
  D   7 hundreds
  E   7 tens
  The correct answer is **B**, as the number is three hundred and seventy-six thousand, eight hundred and nine.

- **One million** is one thousand thousands and is written as 1 000 000.
  One billion is one thousand million and is written as 1 000 000 000.
  One trillion is one thousand billion and is written as 1 000 000 000 000.

  Example: What is the place value of 5 in the number 150 008 490?
  A   5 ten-billions
  B   5 billions
  C   5 hundred-millions
  D   5 ten-millions
  E   5 millions
  The correct answer is **D**, as the number is one hundred and fifty million, eight thousand, four hundred and ninety.

- **Numbers can be rewritten in expanded form** by recognising place value.

  Example: Which of these is fifty-seven million, three hundred and six thousand and twenty in expanded form?
  A $5 \times 10\,000 + 7 \times 1000 + 3 \times 100 + 6 \times 10 + 2 \times 1$
  B $5 \times 1\,000\,000 + 7 \times 100\,000 + 3 \times 100\,000 + 6 \times 10\,000 + 2 \times 1$
  C $5 \times 10\,000\,000 + 7 \times 1\,000\,000 + 3 \times 10\,000 + 6 \times 1000 + 2 \times 10$
  D $5 \times 10\,000\,000 + 7 \times 1\,000\,000 + 3 \times 100\,000 + 6 \times 10\,000 + 2 \times 10$
  E $5 \times 10\,000\,000 + 7 \times 1\,000\,000 + 3 \times 100\,000 + 6 \times 1000 + 2 \times 10$
  The correct answer is **E**, as the number is 50 million + 7 million + 300 thousand + 6 thousand + 20.

- A **prime number** has exactly two factors. A **composite number** has more than two factors.

  Example: How many numbers from 1 and 20 are not composite?
  A 5   B 6   C 7   D 9   E 10

The correct answer is **D**, as the numbers are 1, 2, 3, 5, 7, 11, 13, 17 and 19. Remember: 1 is neither prime nor composite.

- **A simple number puzzle involves** a single mathematical operation.

  Example: If the pattern in the first three boxes is repeated in the second group of boxes, find X.

8	4

2

12	3

X

  A 6   B 4   C 9   D 15   E 18

  💡 *Tip:* Try different combinations of operations.
  The correct answer is **B**, as 8 ÷ 4 = 2, then 12 ÷ 3 = 4.

- **Consecutive numbers can be placed into a shape** so that particular sequences of numbers add to the same total.

  Example: Each of the numbers 1, 2, 3, 4, 5, 6, 7 are written into the squares so that all lines add to the same number. The number to replace X is
  A 1   B 2   C 4   D 7   E 3

  💡 *Tip:* Guess and check.
  The correct answer is **C**. If X = 4, then the total is 12. This means the vertical is 6, 4, 2 and the other diagonal is 7, 4, 1 and each line adds to 12.

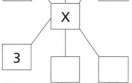

- **A magic square is a pattern** of numbers where every row, column and diagonal adds to the same total.

  Example: Find the value of X in the magic square.
  A 7   B 10   C 9
  D 50   E 15

  💡 *Tip:* Start with the completed diagonal.
  The correct answer is **C**, as the total is 50, and after further calculations, X = 9.

5			17
19	10	14	
		11	6
8	13	X	

- **Letters can replace numbers** in simple mathematical problems.

  Example: If M and N represent digits and MN + N = NM, then N equals
  A 9   B 8   C 3   D 6   E 7

  The correct answer is **A**. N is more than 5, and by guessing and checking, 89 + 9 = 98. This means N is 9.

Checklist
Can you:
1 *recognise the digits in large numbers greater than one million?*
2 *express very large numbers in expanded form?*
3 *solve problems involving prime and composite numbers?*
4 *solve simple number patterns involving a single mathematical operation?*
5 *place consecutive numbers around a number puzzle?*
6 *find missing numbers in a magic square?*
7 *find the value of a letter that is standing for a number in a mathematical problem?*

Real Test 1

MATHEMATICAL REASONING
Whole numbers and place value

10 min

1 Oliver multiplies the largest four-digit number by the smallest three-digit number.

What is her answer?

A	999 000	B	999 900
C	9 900 999	D	9 999 000
E	9 999 999		

2 Emily and Chloe are thinking of numbers between 1 and 50.

Emily thinks of the largest possible odd number that is a multiple of 5.

Chloe thinks of the smallest possible even number that is a multiple of 9.

Which of these is the difference between the girls' numbers?

27	29	31	33	35
A	B	C	D	E

3 William and Lucas both round the number 24 508 329.

William rounds the number to the nearest million.

Lucas rounds the number to the nearest ten thousand.

What is the difference between the boys' numbers?

A	472 000	B	482 000
C	490 000	D	572 000
E	582 000		

4 Two positive numbers differ by 2.

Their product is 48.

What is the sum of the squares of the two numbers?

64	72	80	100	196
A	B	C	D	E

5 The numbers 1, 3, 6, 9, 10 and 20 are written on cards. Four cards are chosen which have a product of 180.

Which of these is the sum of the four numbers?

19	20	34	42	45
A	B	C	D	E

6 How many positive two-digit numbers are **not** divisible by 7?

77	78	81	82	83
A	B	C	D	E

7

$$\begin{array}{r} PQ \\ \times\ \ 6 \\ \hline QQQ \end{array}$$

The number for PQ is

58	62	32	82	74
A	B	C	D	E

8 Complete the magic square to find the value of X.

10	X	
	7	
5		4

8	2	5	6	9
A	B	C	D	E

9 The two 'mathsmen' follow the same patterns. Find the value of X.

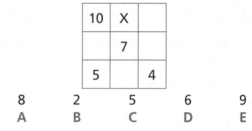

22	31	14	18	19
A	B	C	D	E

10 Complete the magic square to find the value of X.

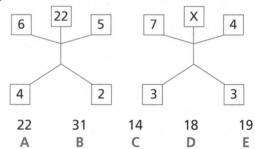

		2	13
5	10	11	
	6	X	
4	15		1

A 7
B 9
C 16
D 3
E 14

☞ **Answers and explanations on pages 192-193**

Real Test 2

MATHEMATICAL REASONING
Whole numbers and place value

10 MIN

1 Liam wrote the number 138 002 406.

How many times larger is the value of the 8 than the value of the 4?

100	1000	2000	10 000	20 000
A	B	C	D	E

2 Scarlett picks five consecutive positive numbers.

She divides each of the numbers by 5 and adds the remainders together.

Which of these is her total?

8	10	13	14	15
A	B	C	D	E

3 What is the number represented by * in this magic square?

13	8	
14		
9		*

A 7
B 10
C 11
D 15
E 16

4 The digits 3, 4, 5, 6, 7 and 8 are used once to create two three-digit even numbers.

What is the largest possible difference between the two numbers?

512	522	530	540	542
A	B	C	D	E

5 When two positive numbers are multiplied the result is 56. When these two numbers are subtracted the result is 10.

Which of these is the result when the two numbers are added?

18	19	20	22	24
A	B	C	D	E

6 There are four times as many girls in the hall as there are boys.

Five girls and five boys leave the hall. There are now seven times as many girls in a hall as boys.

How many students were in the hall at the start?

25	30	35	40	50
A	B	C	D	E

7

```
 YYYY
+   X
XZZZZ
```

The number for Z is

0	1	2	3	5
A	B	C	D	E

8 The numbers 1 to 13 are to be placed in the squares so that each straight line adds to the same number. The value of X is

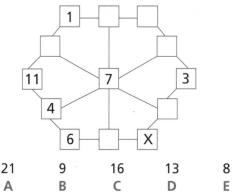

21	9	16	13	8
A	B	C	D	E

9 The two 'mathsmen' follow the same patterns. Find the value of X.

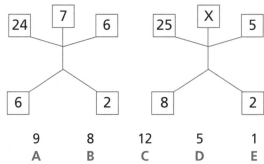

9	8	12	5	1
A	B	C	D	E

10 Complete the magic square to find the value of X.

14		X
13	11	9
	19	

5	11	14	16	6
A	B	C	D	E

☞ **Answers and explanations on page 193**

MATHEMATICAL REASONING
Fractions

- In a fraction, the top number is called the **numerator** and the bottom number the **denominator**. In an **improper fraction** the numerator is larger than the denominator, and these improper fractions are often rewritten as **mixed numerals**.

  Example: Rewrite $\frac{16}{5}$.

  A $2\frac{1}{5}$ B $3\frac{1}{5}$ C $3\frac{2}{5}$ D $5\frac{1}{3}$ E $6\frac{1}{5}$

  The correct answer is **B**, as 5 divides into 16 three times with a remainder of 1.

- A **fraction can be expressed** in many different but equal ways: $\frac{1}{2} = \frac{3}{6} = \frac{7}{14} = \ldots$ Fractions are **simplified** by dividing the numerator and the denominator by the same number.

  Example: Which of these does not simplify to $\frac{2}{3}$?

  A $\frac{20}{30}$ B $\frac{212}{313}$ C $\frac{12}{18}$ D $\frac{14}{21}$ E $\frac{222}{333}$

  The correct answer is **B**. $\frac{20}{30} = \frac{2 \times 10}{3 \times 10} = \frac{2}{3}$, $\frac{12}{18} = \frac{2 \times 6}{3 \times 6} = \frac{2}{3}$, $\frac{14}{21} = \frac{2 \times 7}{3 \times 7} = \frac{2}{3}$, $\frac{222}{333} = \frac{2 \times 111}{3 \times 111} = \frac{2}{3}$.

  $\frac{212}{313}$ does not simplify to $\frac{2}{3}$.

- Fractions can be **compared** easily if they have the same denominator. Use **related denominators** to rewrite the fractions with a different denominator.

  Example: Brayden compared these four fractions: $\frac{7}{12}, \frac{3}{4}, \frac{5}{6}, \frac{12}{18}$.
  Brayden wrote these three statements:

  1. The smallest fraction is $\frac{3}{4}$.

  2. The largest fraction is $\frac{5}{6}$.

  3. $\frac{3}{4}$ is between $\frac{7}{12}$ and $\frac{5}{6}$.

  Which is/are correct?

  A statement 1 only
  B statement 2 only
  C statement 3 only
  D statements 1 and 3 only
  E statements 2 and 3 only

  The correct answer is **E**. First, $\frac{12}{18} = \frac{2 \times 6}{3 \times 6} = \frac{2}{3}$. As 12, 4, 6 and 3 are factors of 12, rewrite each fraction with a denominator of 12. $\frac{7}{12}, \frac{3}{4} = \frac{9}{12}, \frac{5}{6} = \frac{10}{12}, \frac{12}{18} = \frac{2}{3} = \frac{8}{12}$. The order is $\frac{7}{12}, \frac{12}{18}, \frac{3}{4}, \frac{5}{6}$.

  This means statements 2 and 3 are correct.

- To find a **fraction of a quantity** you can divide the quantity by the denominator and multiply by the numerator.

  Example: There are 20 objects in a box. Three-quarters of the objects are balls. Two-thirds of the balls are red. How many red balls are in the box?

  A 5   B 19   C 10   D 15   E 16

  The correct answer is **C**. $\frac{3}{4}$ of 20 is $20 \div 4 \times 3 = 15$. There are 15 balls in the box. Now, $\frac{2}{3}$ of 15 is $15 \div 3 \times 2 = 10$. There are 10 red balls in the box.

- **Fractions can be added or subtracted** when the denominators are the same.

  Example: Erica cut her birthday cake into equal slices. She gave half to her friends and a quarter to her workmates. What fraction remained?

  A $\frac{1}{8}$ B $\frac{1}{4}$ C $\frac{1}{3}$ D $\frac{3}{4}$ E $\frac{2}{3}$

  The correct answer is **B**. As $1 = \frac{4}{4}$ and $\frac{1}{2} = \frac{2}{4}$ then $1 - \frac{1}{2} - \frac{1}{4} = \frac{4}{4} - \frac{2}{4} - \frac{1}{4} = \frac{1}{4}$. This means $\frac{1}{4}$ of the cake remains.

- **The rules for order of operations** are applied to calculations involving fractions. Multiplication and division are performed before addition and subtraction and in order from left to right.

  Example: There are 45 students in Year 6. $\frac{3}{5}$ of the students are boys and $\frac{2}{3}$ of the girls catch a bus to school. How many girls in Year 6 do **not** catch a bus to school?

  A 6   B 8   C 12   D 15   E 16

  The correct answer is **A**. As $1 - \frac{3}{5}$ is $\frac{2}{5}$, and $45 \div 5 \times 2$ is 18, there are 18 girls in Year 6. As $1 - \frac{2}{3} = \frac{1}{3}$, and $18 \div 3 = 6$, there are 6 girls who do not catch a bus.

- **The unitary method finds the value** of one unit and then uses multiplication to find the necessary value.

  Example: Three-quarters of the students in a class watched a grand final on television on the weekend. A third of the students in the class play the sport themselves. If 18 students watched the game, how many students play the sport?

  A 3   B 4   C 6   D 8   E 12

  The correct answer is **D**. If $\frac{3}{4}$ of the class = 18, then $\frac{1}{4}$ of the class = $18 \div 3 = 6$, and so all the class ($\frac{4}{4}$) = $6 \times 4 = 24$. There are 24 students in the class. As $\frac{1}{3}$ of 24 is $24 \div 3 = 8$, there are 8 students who play the sport.

Checklist

Can you:

1 *understand terms such as numerator, denominator, improper fractions and mixed numerals?*

2 *find equivalent fractions by simplifying?*

3 *compare and order fractions?*

4 *find a fraction of a quantity?*

5 *add and subtract fractions?*

6 *apply order of operation rules to number sentences involving fractions?*

7 *use the unitary method to solve problems involving fractions?*

Real Test 3

MATHEMATICAL REASONING
Fractions

10 min

1 A ball is dropped from a window 24 metres above the ground. The ball bounces off the ground and rises to a height half the previous height before bouncing again. The ball continues this pattern. When it hits the ground on the third occasion, how far has the ball travelled since leaving the window?

36 m	42 m	30 m	60 m	39 m
A	B	C	D	E

2 Here is a rectangle made from identical squares.

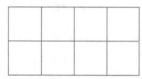

Amrit shades $\frac{1}{2}$ of the squares. Annona then shades $\frac{1}{4}$ of the remaining squares.

How many squares are still unshaded?

1	2	3	4	6
A	B	C	D	E

3 Keeley wrote these fractions: $\frac{3}{4}$, $\frac{7}{10}$, $\frac{4}{5}$, $\frac{13}{20}$.
She made three statements:

1. The smallest fraction is $\frac{13}{20}$.

2. The largest fraction is $\frac{7}{10}$.

3. $\frac{3}{4}$ is between $\frac{7}{10}$ and $\frac{4}{5}$.

Which is/are correct?

A statement 1 only
B statement 2 only
C statement 3 only
D statements 1 and 3 only
E statements 2 and 3 only

4 There are 24 biscuits in a jar. Elijah was given $\frac{3}{4}$ of the biscuits and he ate $\frac{2}{3}$ of his biscuits. How many biscuits did he eat?

8	9	12	15	16
A	B	C	D	E

5 Asha has a long piece of string. He cuts the string into six equal pieces. He then cuts each piece into two equal lengths. He uses four of these lengths to tie a project together. What fraction of the original length has Asha **not** used?

$\frac{2}{3}$	$\frac{3}{8}$	$\frac{1}{6}$	$\frac{1}{3}$	$\frac{3}{4}$
A	B	C	D	E

6 Two-thirds of the audience at a movie screening are children. A quarter of the adults are male. How many women are watching the movie if there are 120 children?

36	40	42	45	50
A	B	C	D	E

7 The cost of a pencil is $\frac{3}{5}$ the cost of a pen. Charlie has enough money to buy 15 pens. He decides instead to buy pencils. How many pencils can Charlie buy?

9	12	18	21	25
A	B	C	D	E

8 Colton has two-thirds as many stickers as Nolan. Colton gives half his stickers to Nolan. If Nolan now has 60 stickers, how many has Colton?

15	16	24	30	36
A	B	C	D	E

9 Delilah and Madeline both collect spoons. Delilah had four times as many spoons as Madeline. Delilah decided to give Madeline two-fifths of her spoons, but still kept 36 spoons. How many spoons did Madeline originally have?

10	12	15	18	24
A	B	C	D	E

10 There are 28 students in a class. $\frac{4}{7}$ of the students are girls. If $\frac{1}{3}$ of the boys were born overseas, how many boys were born in Australia?

6	8	9	12	15
A	B	C	D	E

☞ **Answers and explanations on pages 193-194**

Real Test 4

MATHEMATICAL REASONING
Fractions

10 MIN

1 The larger cube has sides twice the length of the smaller cube. The smaller cube is filled with water and the water poured into the empty larger cube. What fraction of the larger cube is filled?

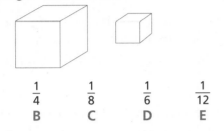

$\frac{1}{2}$	$\frac{1}{4}$	$\frac{1}{8}$	$\frac{1}{6}$	$\frac{1}{12}$
A	B	C	D	E

2 A petrol tank is $\frac{3}{8}$ full and contains 24 litres. How much petrol will the tank contain when it is half full?

A 8 litres   B 27 litres   C 30 litres
D 32 litres   E 36 litres

3 What fraction is halfway between a quarter and a half?

$\frac{1}{3}$	$\frac{3}{8}$	$\frac{1}{5}$	$\frac{3}{4}$	$\frac{5}{16}$
A	B	C	D	E

4 The shape is made up of identical squares.

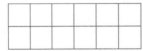

Jacob shades $\frac{1}{3}$ of the squares. Henry shades $\frac{3}{4}$ of the remaining squares.

How many squares are now shaded?

6	8	9	10	12
A	B	C	D	E

5 Grace, Lilley, Riley and Leah are participating in a charity fun run. Grace has completed $\frac{5}{8}$ of the course, Lilley $\frac{2}{3}$, Riley $\frac{3}{4}$ and Leah $\frac{7}{12}$. Which of the following statements is/are correct?

1. Lilley is ahead of Leah.
2. Grace is behind Riley.
3. Lilley is in front of the other three girls.

A statement 1 only
B statement 2 only

C statement 3 only
D statements 1 and 2 only
E statements 2 and 3 only

6 Savannah bought three pizzas to share with her friends. Naomi ate $\frac{1}{2}$ of a pizza. Ethan ate $\frac{3}{4}$ of a pizza. Logan ate a whole pizza. Savannah ate the rest of the pizza. How much more pizza did Savannah eat than Naomi?

$\frac{1}{8}$	$\frac{1}{4}$	$\frac{1}{2}$	$\frac{3}{8}$	$\frac{3}{4}$
A	B	C	D	E

7 *P* is one-fifth of 40. *Q* is three-quarters of 20. *R* is two-thirds of 36. What does *P* + *Q* + *R* equal?

24	18	35	47	48
A	B	C	D	E

8 Josiah is following a recipe that requires 6 cups of flour and $1\frac{1}{2}$ cups of sugar. He only has one cup of sugar and uses all of it. How much flour should he use to keep the ingredients in the same proportion as called for in the recipe?

2	$2\frac{1}{2}$	3	$3\frac{1}{2}$	4
A	B	C	D	E

9 A box of apples is to be shared between three families. The Stonehouse family took $\frac{2}{5}$ of the apples. The Thong family took $\frac{2}{3}$ of the remaining apples. The Aldrich family took the rest. If there were 60 apples in the box, how many apples were taken by the Aldrich family?

12	18	20	24	27
A	B	C	D	E

10 Emma had a collection of 160 beads. She gave $\frac{3}{8}$ of the beads to Layla. She gave 40 beads to Grace and $\frac{2}{3}$ of the remaining beads to Sofia. How many beads did Emma have left?

20	30	32	36	48
A	B	C	D	E

☞ **Answers and explanations on pages 194–195**

- A description is a **picture in words of a person, thing, place or scene**. When you describe something, you aim to give your readers a clear and vivid picture in their minds of what you are describing. After reading your description, they should be able to close their eyes and picture your subject, even though they cannot see it.

- Descriptions **always include some facts**. For example, a description of a building might say how high the building is, how old it is and what it is made of, and perhaps describe the doors, windows and other features. Some descriptions might consist **only** of facts: a description written as part of an information report, for example.

- Many descriptions, however, also include **expressions of the writer's feelings and reactions**. These are the kinds of imaginative descriptions you find in story books and poetry. When describing the building, you might say that it looks gloomy or unwelcoming, or that it reminds you of another place or experience. You might give it a personal characteristic, for example, comparing its windows to eyes.

- Descriptions are useful types of texts to practise before your test. They can be the easiest type of text to write when you are given a free choice. This is because they **don't take as much planning and organisation** as other texts, such as narratives. This means that you can get started on them quite quickly and use up your time well. Of course, you won't **always** be able to write a description. It will depend on what stimulus material you are given and what you are instructed to do.

- Another reason to practise writing descriptions is that you will often have to describe something or somebody **as part of another kind of writing**—for example, a personal recount, a narrative or a newspaper report.

- A very important part of descriptions is the **language**. The language is what helps to paint a detailed, interesting picture. If you simply describe what you can see in the picture on the page in a general way, it will be dull and boring. If you pick up on the **interesting detail**, and describe it precisely, it will come alive for the reader.

- On the next page is an example of a description written in response to a test question, though not under test conditions. In your test, you **might not have time** to produce a polished piece of writing like this. However, if you are **well prepared**, you will be able to aim for this standard.

Sample

10 MIN

Question

Use this picture as the basis for a piece of writing. You can choose which way to write. You could write a description, a story, a poem, a letter, a newspaper article or other kind of writing.

Response

Structure

Title—adding a title gives the description a focus

Orientation to the topic immediately tells your reader about *who, what, when, where*. Orientation might set up a persona (character) for the writer

Description
- what you can see (things, people, activity)
- imagined sounds, smells
- atmosphere
- your feelings and reactions to the scene

Paragraphs separate parts of description

Concluding comment

Language

Present tense verbs to describe the scene (although descriptions can be written in the past or future if that suits the ideas)

Phrases and clauses that add interesting detail

Adjectives to describe things in the scene

Verbs and **adverbs** that accurately describe activity

Correct **spelling, grammar** and **punctuation**

Thinking and **feeling verbs**

Home Sweet Home

The house stands alone below us, in a gully between two steep hills. It looks welcoming and warm inside. I imagine sleeping in one of the brightly lit rooms while the winds rage outside.

The house is a blue colour although it does not look as if it has been painted for a very long time. It is quite small and perfectly square. Next to one corner is an old, very rusty water tank partly covered by brightly coloured creepers. Gardening tools and pots are scattered on the grass nearby.

At the back of the house there is a barn or a garage. I can see the heavy double doors—paint peeling off them and hanging rather crookedly across the grass. There is not much in the garden except for two kids' bikes and a fringed swing chair, now creaking as it moves back and forth in the wind.

The house looks larger than it really is because of the wide verandah that runs around all four sides. On the front side there is a cane table and chairs, and a big old lounge covered with colourful cushions and rugs. Around the corner there is a narrow bed and a child's swing. How lucky that child is, I think. Even though the house does not look especially well cared for, it looks comfortable and cosy and full of love.

The doors and windows are closed but the lights make me think that at least someone is home. I can just smell the smoke puffing up from the small back chimney—and am I imagining it or can I hear music?

Oh, how I want to be inside that house instead of out here in the cold.

Practice Tasks

WRITING
Descriptive response—Getting started

50 MIN

These practice tasks will give you some ideas about how to get writing quickly and complete an interesting description in the short time you have in the test.

You will have to look back at *Home Sweet Home* to answer some questions, and then do some descriptive writing yourself based on the practice question below.

Look at the question now before you start the tasks.

Practice writing question

Write a description of this scene. You may choose to write your description as part of a story, as a newspaper article, a letter, a poem or another form of text.

- Descriptions don't take much planning. Your plan should really be just a quick brainstorm of the things you could describe. Of course, once you start writing, you might leave out some of these ideas or add extra ones. Look at the brainstorming the student writer did for *Home Sweet Home*. Notice she did not cover all these ideas in her writing. She also added extra ideas that came to her as she wrote.

  ○ setting, gully, hills, sunset
  ○ house and garden—roof, colour, shape, paint, window shutters, tank, garage, bikes, plants, seat
  ○ verandah—table, chairs, lounge, bed, swing, railing
  ○ signs of life—boots, lights, smoke, music

Practice Tasks

- Use this brainstorming checklist when you are **describing scenes**:
  - ○ location—landscape (e.g. hill, river, track) or street scene (e.g. shops, traffic)
  - ○ things—what they are and how they look (e.g. buildings, plants, furniture)
  - ○ people—what they look like, how they seem (e.g. happy, sad, angry)
  - ○ activity—what is happening, what people are doing
  - ○ sounds and smells that you imagine might be coming from the scene
  - ○ atmosphere—the feeling or mood of the scene (e.g. spooky, calm, busy, happy)
  - ○ feelings and reactions—what you think and feel as you look at the scene.

- If you are **describing people**, think about:
  - ○ their facial features
  - ○ their facial expressions
  - ○ their age
  - ○ their size and build
  - ○ their dress
  - ○ their actions
  - ○ the way they are sitting or standing
  - ○ where they are looking
  - ○ whether they look rich, poor, well-cared for, and so on.

- After your brainstorm, you need to think quickly about the **best order** for your ideas.

Task 1

Look closely at the circus picture in the practice writing question on page 34 and quickly brainstorm the parts of the scene you could describe (use the brainstorming checklist above). Then number your ideas in the order you think best for writing. Give yourself about three minutes.

Practice Tasks

● You usually start a description with one or two sentences to **orient** the reader to the scene you are describing. You answer the questions in the reader's mind about **who, what, where and when**.

● A good orientation will also suggest the **persona** (imagined character) who is writing the description and why they are writing it.

● A great way to add interest to your description is to write it in an interesting form—for example, as a letter, a newspaper article, an advertisement, a diary entry, an interview, or as part of a narrative. Your orientation will show which form you have chosen. *Home Sweet Home* is written as part of a narrative.

💡 *Tip:* Try to make your opening sentences **interesting**. Don't just write 'I can see a ...' or 'There is a ...' or 'This picture shows ...'.

Task 2

1 Look at the orientation from *Home Sweet Home.* Tick the persona that the writer adopts.

☐ an old man looking back at the house he used to live in

☐ a child who lives in the house

☐ a child who is in hiding for some reason and unable to enter the house

2 The writer could have begun the house description in other ways. Which of the writing forms below is used in the following two extracts? Write your answer on the line after each.

> a letter   a newspaper article   an advertisement   a diary entry   an information report

a 26 June: camped last night on a hill about 300 metres from a small farmhouse. The house looked warm and cosy and made me think ... _____

b Police last night surrounded a small farmhouse in the hills west of the town, lying in wait for the escaped convict who had taken a young family hostage earlier that morning. The scene looked peaceful ... _____

Task 3

Write an orientation for your description of the circus scene (page 34). Think about which form you will use. Give yourself about five minutes.

_____

_____

_____

_____

_____

☞ **Answers and explanations on page 195**

Practice Tasks

WRITING
Descriptive response—Describing what you see

- Descriptions in the tests are generally in response to an illustration or photograph, so they will mostly be about **what you can see** and **how things look**.

- You will need to use some **adjectives** to help you paint a picture of what you see. Sometimes you will only need simple, common adjectives. For example, the house in *Home Sweet Home* is described as 'a blue colour', 'small' and 'square'. At other times, it will be better to use unusual adjectives to describe the scene more precisely (e.g. steep, welcoming).

- If the picture includes people, animals or things doing something, use interesting and unusual **verbs and adverbs** to describe what they are doing. Remember: Verbs are doing words; adverbs add extra detail to the verb.

  For example, the writer of *Home Sweet Home* writes that the 'heavy double doors [were] hanging rather crookedly across the grass' (hanging = a form of verb; crookedly = adverb).

- Your description will be more interesting if you add **phrases and clauses** to give **details**. These will make the scene come alive and give the impression that you were actually at the scene. In *Home Sweet Home*, for example, the writer says the house 'did not look as if it had been painted for a very long time'.

🔆 *Tip:* Don't overload your description with adjectives and adverbs. Think about whether or not they really help to paint the picture of the scene. Avoid very common words such as nice, lovely, fantastic, cool and beautiful.

Task 4

1 Underline one adjective used in *Home Sweet Home* to describe the following:
  a the house   b the water tank
  c the bed   d the verandah

2 Underline the verbs (and adverbs, if applicable) the writer uses to describe the following:
  a what the winds are doing   b what the chair is doing

3 Underline the details the writer gives about the following:
  a the water tank   b the garage doors   c the lounge

4 Look at the circus picture on page 34 and brainstorm some words you could use to describe the scene.

_____

_____

_____

_____

_____

_____

_____

☞ **Answers and explanations on page 195**

Practice Tasks

WRITING
Descriptive response—Imagining sounds and smells

You shouldn't only write about what you can see in the picture. Use your imagination to write about other senses besides sight—about what you imagine you can hear, smell, and even taste and touch. This will add a special, realistic element to your description and make it seem as if you are really at the scene, not just describing a picture on the page.

Task 5

1 What two things does the writer of *Home Sweet Home* say she can hear?

_____

_____

2 What does she say she can smell?

_____

_____

Task 6

Look back at the circus picture on page 34, and write two (only) short paragraphs to describe the scene. Remember to describe the action and to write about imagined sounds, smells and so on. Give yourself about 10 minutes.

_____

_____

_____

_____

_____

_____

_____

_____

_____

_____

_____

☞ **Answers and explanations on page 195**

Practice Tasks

WRITING

Descriptive response—Expressing your thoughts and feelings

- Your description will be more interesting if you do more than write down what you see. The best descriptions also give a sense of what the writer **feels and thinks** about the scene.
- One way to express your thoughts and feelings is to **comment on the atmosphere** (e.g. frightening, eerie, spooky, mysterious, calm, peaceful, busy, frantic, cheerful, joyous). The writer of *Home Sweet Home* tells us the house looks 'welcoming', 'warm', 'comfortable' and 'filled with love'.

- *Tip:* Use some of these verbs to express your feelings and reactions: think, suspect, hope, expect, upsets, feel sorry, feel angry, fear, envy, love, hate, makes me think of, reminds me of.

Task 7

Underline the sentences in paragraphs 1, 4 and 6 of *Home Sweet Home* that express the writer's thoughts and feelings.

Task 8

Write one or two sentences to express your feelings and reaction to the circus picture on page 34. Try to include words that comment on the atmosphere. Give yourself about three minutes.

_____

_____

_____

_____

_____

_____

Note: If you like, you can work on the circus description some more, refining what you have written so far and writing it out again on your own paper. Use the checklist below to review your writing.

Checklist for writing a description

Have you:

1 *oriented the reader to the scene and suggested a persona for the writer?*
2 *given some details about the scene using vivid adjectives or other language?*
3 *included imagined sounds and smells as well as sights?*
4 *expressed your own thoughts and feelings about the scene?*
5 *commented on the atmosphere of the scene?*
6 *checked your grammar, punctuation and spelling?*

Remember: In the test you won't have time to revise thoroughly and make big changes. You may have time to change a few words, but you will really be aiming to do a good piece of writing in one draft.

☞ **Answers and explanations on page 195**

Real Test

WRITING
Descriptive response

30 MIN

- Choose **one** of the writing tests below to do now. The first test question tells you to write a description. The second question gives you the opportunity to write in many different ways. If you choose the second question, write a description to practise all the points you have just revised.

- Use your own paper. You are encouraged to use two or three sheets of paper. Use the first one for planning and rough work, and do your response on the second and third sheets.

- If you prefer, you may do both tests. However, it would be better to do them on different days. For extra practice, you could use the tests again, writing in different ways each time.

- Set yourself a time limit of 25 or 30 minutes (depending on the test you will be taking). Use the checklist on page 39 to guide your writing and to give it a quick review.

---

1 Describe a person you know very well or who you see very often. It may be a member of your family, a friend or just a person you pass by each morning on the way to school.

OR

2 Use this picture as the basis for your writing. You may write in any form you like—for example, a description, a narrative story, a diary, a report or a newspaper article.

EMERALD PRIMARY SCHOOL

PRINCIPAL FERGUS Bloom

☞ **Checklist on page 39**

What's next?

Week 2

This is what we cover this week:

Day 1 **Reading:** Poetry

Day 2 **Thinking Skills:** ◎ Critical thinking—Drawing a conclusion

◎ Critical thinking—Identifying an assumption

◎ Critical thinking—Checking reasoning to detect errors

Day 3 **Mathematical Reasoning:** ◎ Decimals, percentages and money

◎ Patterns and algebra

Day 4 **Writing:** Recount response

- Poetry is a **special kind of literary text**. It expresses ideas and feelings about our human experiences through imagery, sounds and special use of language.

- Poetry can be more difficult to understand than other kinds of writing. **Words are used in unusual ways and with different meanings.** Even punctuation is used differently.

- Poetry is usually written to be read out loud, but of course you can't do this in a test. However, it can help to **'say it aloud' in your head**, and imagine the rhythm and beat of the poem.

- Always **read the poem right through** once before answering the questions (unless you run out of time). However, you will probably need to read it right through more than once to really understand it.

- Think about the **overall meaning of the poem** as you read—don't just focus on a line at a time. What is it saying about the subject?

- Mostly you will be asked about:

  ○ the **meaning of a word, a line, a stanza (verse) or the whole poem**—poets sometimes choose words that are not often used in everyday conversation, or use everyday words in unusual ways

  ○ the poet's use of **imagery**—this is how the poet has created an image in our minds about how something looks, sounds, tastes, feels, smells, moves, and so on

  ○ how the poet has compared one thing to another through **metaphor and simile**—a metaphor is when one thing is said to be another (e.g. the sky is a thick blanket); a simile is when one thing is said to be like another (e.g. as green as the sea; green like the sea)

  ○ the poet's use of **symbols**—for example, the colour red might symbolise anger, a forked road might symbolise a choice

  ○ the poet's use of **personification**—this is where the poet gives the non-human subject of the poem a human characteristic (e.g. the dry land yearned for rain)

  ○ the poet's use of **alliteration**—this is the repetition of consonant sounds in words near each other (e.g. slid silently; whistled and whooped)

  ○ why the poet **repeated lines** or made **rhymes**

  ○ who the **persona** is—this is the character adopted by the poet to write the poem (e.g. a farmer, a mother, a child, an old person, a lonely person)

  ○ how **the poet feels** or would feel about something.

Note: A stanza is a group of lines in the poem that form a unit of thought or feeling, similar to a paragraph in other kinds of texts.

Practice Task 1

READING
Poetry

15 MIN

Use this first practice task as a guide. Read the poem below carefully and answer the questions. Then look at the answers to get tips about how to answer the questions correctly and also to get explanations about why one answer was right. Don't worry if you don't get every question right. The aim is to give you practice with some types of poetry and questions you might find in the test. Don't worry too much about the time limit in this first practice task but try to improve your speed over the next practice tasks.

The Sea

The sea is a hungry dog,
Giant and grey.
He rolls on the beach all day.
With his clashing teeth and shaggy jaws
5   Hour upon hour he gnaws
The rumbling, tumbling stones,
And 'Bones, bones, bones, bones!'
The giant sea-dog moans,
Licking his greasy paws.

10   And when the night wind roars
And the moon rocks in the stormy cloud,
He bounds to his feet and snuffs and sniffs,
Shaking his wet sides over the cliffs,
And howls and hollos long and loud.

15   But on quiet days in May or June,
When even the grasses on the dune
Play no more their reedy tune,
With his head between his paws
He lies on the sandy shores,
20   So quiet, so quiet, he scarcely snores.

James Reeves

Practice Task 1

1 The sea is compared to a dog throughout the whole poem. What kind of dog do you think the poet has in mind?

A a small stray dog

B a small pet dog

C a large pet dog

D a large stray dog

2 What characteristic of the sea is emphasised in stanza 1?

A how it constantly crashes against the shore

B how it can be dangerous and threatening

C how its mood changes from day to day

D how big and deep it is

3 This poem was written in the Northern Hemisphere. Keeping that in mind, what characteristic of the sea is emphasised in stanza 3?

A its calmness and stillness in warm weather

B its calmness and stillness during the day

C the noise it makes as it comes ashore

D the tides ebbing and flowing

4 In stanza 1, the dog moans

A with pain.

B with hunger.

C with anger.

D with satisfaction.

5 What does 'reedy tune' (line 17) refer to?

A the sound of the sea

B the sound of the wind in the grass in winter

C the sound of the wind in the grass in summer

D the sound the dog makes when he rests

6 'Hollos' in stanza 2 is an unusual word. What more common word would be closest in meaning to 'hollos' as it is used in the poem?

A growls

B yaps

C barks

D calls

☞ **Answers and explanations on pages 195-196**

In this task there are two poems to read because you may be asked to work across two poems in the actual test. Read the poems carefully and answer the questions. Circle the answers you think correct. When you finish, check the answers. If you did not choose the correct answer or if you were unsure about it, read the answer explanation. Again, don't worry if you don't get every question right—the aim is to give you practice. Try to work more quickly and finish in close to 15 minutes. You will have to work very quickly in the real test.

The Great Snake

Into a hole in the ground he went,
Into a hole and the darkness before him;
Into the hole he went, and the dark
About him; into the hole he went
5 And the dark behind him.

No light of moon or sun
Was with him there;
Then with a rock the earth closed him in.

10 Forever he sleeps, save that
Sometimes in dreams he turns.
Then the mountains are shaken

Mary Gilmore

Relatively Speaking

Suddenly the grass before my feet
shakes and becomes alive.
The snake
twists, almost leaps,
5 graceful even in terror,
smoothness looping back over smoothness,
slithers away, disappears.
And the grass is again still.

And surely,
10 by whatever means of communication
is available to snakes,
the word is passed:
'Hey, I just met a man, a monster, too:
must have been, oh, seven feet tall.
15 So keep away from the long grass,
it's dangerous there.'

Ian Mudie

1 Which feature of snakes is described in both 'The Great Snake' and 'Relatively Speaking'?
A how they communicate
B how they move
C how we fear them
D how they sleep

2 In the first poem 'The Great Snake', in stanza 1, the poet writes either 'into a hole' or 'into the hole' four times. Do you think she did this to suggest
A the length of the snake?
B the speed of the snake?
C the length of the hole?
D how often the snake uses the hole?

3 In 'The Great Snake', why does the poet say 'then the mountains are shaken'?
A to show that even though the snake is asleep, he is still powerful and dangerous.
B to show that even though the snake is asleep, it is only a light sleep
C to show that you should always be careful around snakes
D to show that snakes have dreams just like we do

4 The second poem is called 'Relatively Speaking' because it shows that
A snakes and humans are relatives.
B from the snake's point of view we are dangerous.
C we shouldn't think that snakes are dangerous.
D snakes can communicate with each other just as humans do.

5 In 'Relatively Speaking', Stanza 1 contains one line that makes us realise that the poem is about the feeling of snakes towards humans, and not the other way around.
A line 1
B line 4
C line 5
D line 8

6 Why does the poet have the snake say 'oh, seven feet tall'?
A to show how tall we look to snakes
B to show how we sometimes exaggerate the length of snakes
C because that is how tall the poet is
D both A and B

☞ **Answers and explanations on page 196**

Practice Task 3

READING
Poetry

15 MIN

This poem is short but you still have to read carefully. Read and answer the questions, working as quickly as you can and aiming to finish in15 minutes. When you finish, check the answers and read the answer explanation if needed. Again, don't worry if you don't get every question right—the aim is to give you practice with what you might be asked in the test.

> **Lake**
>
> I can't hold it, keep it.
> It's full of mountains fluttering down,
> And trees—or rather their other selves.
>
> I can break it with a stone,
> 5 My foot: and I can almost see
> Just what it's thinking. I'm certain it's thinking.
>
> A fisherman unpacks himself gently
> On a ledge, and soon his line
> Is holding the lake exactly.
>
> *RA Simpson*
>
> Reproduced with the permission of Pam Simpson for the estate of RA Simpson

1 We don't usually talk of mountains 'fluttering' (line 2). Why do you think they are described this way?
   A because the wind is whipping snow off the mountains
   B because the reflection of the mountains in the lake is moving slightly
   C because there are so many birds around the lake
   D because there are noises in the treetops

2 What are the 'other selves' of the trees?
   A the trees in a different season   B the trees on each side of the lake
   C the reflection of the trees in the water D the roots of the trees

3 Which line most clearly represents the lake as a human being?
   A line 1   B line 3   C line 6   D line 7

4 Why does it look like the fisherman 'is holding the lake exactly'?
   A because the fishing line is straight and taut and looks like it is attached to the lake
   B because the fisherman looks strong enough to hold the lake
   C because the fisherman behaves quietly and carefully
   D because the fishing line has the chance to go deep into the lake

5 How would you describe the feeling of the poet for the fisherman?
   A anger   B envy   C hate   D love

☞ Answers and explanations on page 197

Real Test

Read the poem carefully and answer the questions, working as quickly as you can and finishing it in 15 minutes. When you finish, check the answers and read the answer explanation if needed.

Lone Dog

I'm a lean dog, a keen dog, a wild dog and lone,
I'm a rough dog, a tough dog, hunting on my own!
I'm a bad dog, a mad dog, teasing silly sheep;
I love to sit and bay the moon and keep fat souls from sleep.

5   I'll never be a lap dog, licking dirty feet,
A sleek dog, a meek dog, cringing for my meat.
Not for me the fireside, the well-filled plate,
But shut door and sharp stone and cuff and kick and hate.

Not for me the other dogs, running by my side,
10 Some have run a short while, but none of them would bide.
O mine is still the lone trail, the hard trail, the best,
Wide wind and wild stars and the hunger of the quest.

Irene McLeod

---

1 What kind of dog does the poet describe?
A a wild dog   B a sheepdog   C a pet dog   D a hunter's dog

2 What does 'keep fat souls from sleep' (line 4) tell us about the dog's attitude to humans?
A annoyance   B lack of interest   C affection   D disgust

3 What is the 'quest' (line 12)?
A search for a good master   B search for prey
C search for a mate   D search for other dogs

4 What does 'meek' (line 6) mean?
A brave   B hungry   C timid   D greedy

5 What happens whenever the dog goes near a house?
A He gets a good feed.
B He is treated badly.
C He is welcomed inside.
D He is given a bed for the night.

6 What is the dog's attitude to domestic dogs?
A disgust   B envy   C affection   D disinterest

☞ **Answers and explanations on page 197**

In order to draw a conclusion:

● **read and assess** the information and evidence provided
● make sure the conclusion holds up as true by checking the **supporting evidence**.

Example

In a survey of people who watched the most recent Olympics on television, it was found that everyone who liked to watch basketball also liked to watch the hockey. Everyone who liked watching the hockey liked to watch soccer, but no one who liked watching the hockey liked to watch the weightlifting events.

Zoi, Sahara, Nils and Max took part in the survey.

Based on the information above, which of the following must be true?

A   If Nils did not like watching hockey, he did not like watching the basketball.
B   If Max liked to watch the hockey, he also liked to watch the basketball.
C   If Zoi liked watching the soccer, she also liked watching the basketball.
D   If Sahara liked watching hockey, she did not like watching the weightlifting.

Steps to work out the answer

1   Read the information in the text.
2   Read the suggested conclusions.
3   Judge which conclusion must be true based on the evidence in the text.

D is correct. The text tells you that no one who liked hockey liked to watch the weightlifting events so it must be true that if Sahara liked watching hockey, she did not like the weightlifting.

Incorrect answers

A is incorrect. The text tells you that everyone who liked to watch basketball also liked hockey but there is no evidence to suggest that anyone who did not watch hockey also did not watch basketball.

B is incorrect. Just because everyone who liked to watch the basketball liked to watch the hockey does not mean that if they liked to watch the hockey they automatically liked to watch the basketball.

C is incorrect. It might be true that Zoi liked the soccer and she also liked basketball but there is no evidence in the survey results to support this conclusion.

Checklist

Can you:
1   *read a text and draw a conclusion from the evidence presented?*
2   *assess whether conclusions are supported by evidence?*
3   *assess whether conclusions are disproved because there is evidence that refutes them?*
4   *assess when conclusions are neither proven nor disproved because the evidence is incomplete or unavailable?*

Real Test 1

THINKING SKILLS
Critical thinking—Drawing a conclusion

10 MIN

1 The hospital wanted to find out how different colours affect people's level of calmness. They asked patients to rate how they felt in rooms painted different colours.

This is what they found:
- The most calming shades of purple (lilac and lavender) were more calming than any shades of blue.
- All shades of green were more calming than some of the deeper shades of purple.
- All the shades of blue were more calming than all the shades of greens.

Based on the information above, which of the following cannot be true?

A The best colours to paint the rooms to bring a sense of calm to patients were lilac and lavender.

B The greatest range between most calming and least calming was found in shades of purple.

C Deeper purple shades were more calming than shades of blue.

D Shades of green were less useful at calming patients than shades of blue.

2 Before placing an order to purchase new books, the librarian did a survey of the types of books Year 6 students preferred to read.

He found that:
- everyone preferred historical fiction to non-fiction
- comics are more popular than mystery novels
- non-fiction was preferred over comics or mystery novels
- horror was more popular than historical fiction.

The librarian only has the budget to order books from the two most popular categories.

Based on the information above, which of the following must be true?

A The librarian will order more horror novels and historical fiction.

B The librarian will order more comics than non-fiction.

C The librarian will not place an order for horror novels.

D The librarian will order historical fiction and mystery novels.

3 Regarding school canteen lunch orders:
- Alok and Shukufa prefer pita bread wrap-style sandwiches
- Eddy and Airen only ever order multigrain sandwiches
- Alok and Airen always have avocado with their salad sandwiches
- Eddy and Alok always add cheese to their salad sandwiches
- Shukufa is allergic to dairy and Airen is vegan so won't eat cheese.

Based on the information above, which conclusion must be true?

A Airen is the one most likely to order cheese and salad on multigrain.

B Eddy is the one most likely to order cheese and salad on pita bread.

C Alok is the one most likely to order a pita sandwich with cheese and avocado.

D Shukufa is the one who is likely to order cheese on her pita bread wrap.

☞ **Answers and explanations on pages 197-198**

4 Extreme heat causes heat stroke, which can cause death as well as mental health issues. Older people are particularly at risk of heat stroke as well as people who engage in manual labour or who work outdoors. Extreme heat costs more and more lives globally every year.

Based on the information above, which of the following must be true?

A Action to mitigate climate change is needed urgently.

B Air conditioning further contributes to climate change if it is run by electricity made using fossil fuels.

C Extreme heat worsens other climate challenges such as wildfires.

D Extreme heat is a growing health issue.

5 Ali, Willis and Timur live in a share house where each person buys their own food. Ali left her fruit salad in the fridge, but it went missing overnight. The housemate who took Ali's fruit salad must have had both an opportunity and a reason.

Based on the information above, which of the following must be true?

A If Willis had both an opportunity and a reason, he must have taken the fruit salad.

B If Timur had neither an opportunity nor a reason he cannot have taken the fruit salad.

C If Willis did not take the fruit salad, he must have had a reason to take it.

D If Timur took the fruit salad he must not have had an opportunity.

6 Oliver's school was selecting students to represent the school at a young leaders' convention. As well as considering the leadership positions students already held in the school, the school set students a community service challenge and a debating challenge.

If a student held at least one leadership position in the school, then they only had to pass the community service challenge. If they held no leadership positions, then they either needed an excellent result in the community service challenge or to do well in both the community service challenge and the debating challenge.

Oliver has two leadership positions in the school but failed to be selected to attend the convention.

Based on the information above, which conclusion must be true?

A Oliver did not hold enough leadership positions in the school.

B Oliver did badly in the debating challenge.

C Oliver did well in the community service challenge but badly in the debating challenge.

D Oliver failed the community service challenge.

☞ **Answers and explanations on pages 197-198**

Real Test 1

THINKING SKILLS
Critical thinking—Drawing a conclusion

7 **Sho:** 'Let's go to the basketball courts after school.'

Lily: 'No I can't. I have to practise my solo. If I don't practise, I will likely fail the audition tomorrow.'

Sho: 'If you fail the audition then you will not be given the solo for the concert.'

Lily: 'Yes—and if I do well in the audition I might get the solo in the concert. Otherwise, there is no way I will get it.'

Based on the information above, which of the following cannot be true?

A Lily did not practise, but she got the solo in the concert.

B Lily practised, but she did not get the solo in the concert.

C Lily did not do well in the audition, but she got the solo in the concert.

D Lily did well in the audition, but she did not get the solo in the concert.

8 Five friends entered a readathon challenge. Lucia read more books than Grace. Joe read fewer books than Jim who read two fewer books than Grace and four fewer than Lucia. Alex read more books than Grace but fewer than Lucia.

Based on the information above, which conclusion must be true?

A Jim read more books than Grace.

B Of the five friends Joe read the fewest books.

C Alex read fewer books than Jim.

D Grace and Jim read the same number of books.

9 Ms Lin's class was discussing which planet students would most like to travel to if they could go there for a holiday. The class found that anyone who would definitely go to Pluto also liked the idea of a holiday on Mars. Plus, anyone who would definitely go to Mars liked the idea of travelling to Venus, but no one who liked the idea of going to Mars wanted to go to Jupiter.

Based on the information above, which conclusion must be true?

A If Louise would definitely go to Pluto, she does not want to go to Jupiter.

B If Ying does not want a holiday on Pluto, she does not want to go to Venus.

C If Finn likes the idea of traveling to Venus, he would also definitely go to Mars.

D If Carlos does not want to go to Jupiter, he does not like the idea of a holiday on Venus.

10 Whoever won the local community art prize must have been a paid-up member of the local art society when they entered the competition and also must have attended the exhibition on opening night.

Based on the information above, which conclusion must be true?

A If Wei both attended the opening night and was a paid up-member of the art society when he entered the competition, he must have won the art prize.

B If Wei did not win the art prize, he must not have attended the opening night.

C If Wei did not win the art prize, he must not have been a paid-up member of the art society when he entered the competition.

D If Wei did not attend the opening night, he cannot have won the art prize.

☞ **Answers and explanations on pages 197-198**

THINKING SKILLS
Critical thinking—Identifying an assumption

An assumption:

● is information that is **not stated** in a text
● is **assumed** or taken for granted in order to draw a conclusion
● is **not always tru**e
● can lead to **incorrect conclusions**.

Example

Ash walks into the hallway and notices that Breno's hat is not on the hat rack.

Ash: 'Breno must have gone out.'

Which assumption has Ash made in order to draw her conclusion?

A   Breno likes his hat.
B   Breno is Alice's brother.
C   Someone has stolen Breno's hat.
D   Breno always takes his hat when he goes out.

Steps to work out the answer

1   Identify the conclusion: Breno has gone out.
2   Identify the evidence given to support this conclusion: Breno's hat is not on the rack.
3   Ask yourself: What important point (not stated in this evidence) would need to be assumed for the conclusion to hold?

D is correct. Ash's conclusion is that Breno has gone out. She based this conclusion on the evidence that his hat is not on the rack. So, for her conclusion to hold, it must be assumed that Breno always takes his hat when he goes out.

EVIDENCE	+	ASSUMPTION	=	CONCLUSION

Breno's hat is not on the rack + Breno always takes his hat when he goes out = Breno has gone out.

Incorrect answers

A is incorrect because it is not necessary to the conclusion. It does not have to be true that Breno likes his hat for the conclusion that he has gone out to hold.

B is incorrect because it is not necessary to the conclusion. It does not have to be true that Breno is Alice's brother for the conclusion that he has gone out to hold.

C is incorrect because it does not support Alice's conclusion. She could have assumed that the hat was not on the rack because it was stolen, but that assumption would not lead to the conclusion that Breno had gone out.

Checklist

Can you:

1 *identify a conclusion?*
2 *identify the reasoning or evidence given to support this conclusion?*
3 *identify something that was not stated in the evidence that would need to be assumed or taken for granted if this conclusion is to hold?*

Real Test 2

THINKING SKILLS
Critical thinking—Identifying an assumption

10 MIN

1 **Joe:** 'Did you get an invitation to Tom's party?'
Gemma: 'Yes, but I'm not going.'
Joe: 'You don't like parties!'

Which assumption has Joe made in order to draw his conclusion?

A Gemma will be out of town on the night of the party.
B Tom and Gemma are not good friends.
C Anyone who says no to a party invitation must not like parties.
D Gemma does not like parties.

2 **James:** 'You could ask for a bird for your birthday. Cages are on special at the pet store.'
Santi: 'Birds should not be kept in cages. It is exploitation for the purpose of entertaining people.'

Which assumption has Santi made in order to draw her conclusion?

A It is entertaining to watch birds in cages.
B Bird cages are expensive.
C It is a lot of work to look after birds in cages.
D Exploitation is wrong.

3 **Aviana:** 'You must be allergic to peanuts.'
Conner: 'No, I'm not.'
Aviana: 'So why don't you ever have peanut butter on your sandwich?'
Conner: 'Because I hate peanut butter!'

Which assumption has Aviana made in order to draw her conclusion?

A Anyone who doesn't eat peanut butter sandwiches is allergic to peanuts.
B Conner does not like peanut butter sandwiches.
C Conner never eats peanut butter sandwiches.
D Conner is allergic to peanuts.

4 **Suma:** 'Mum has a big report to finish this weekend, so we must not do anything to upset her.'
Ramesh: 'I'd better not lose my new soccer ball then.'

Which assumption has Ramesh made in order to draw his conclusion?

A Anyone who is busy gets upset.
B Losing the new soccer ball will upset Mum.
C Mum is very busy.
D Suma wants to borrow his new soccer ball.

5 David is in the kitchen baking a cake when his friend Mari arrives.
Mari: 'You love baking!'
David: 'No, I don't but it's Mum's birthday and I want to surprise her.'

Which assumption has Mari made in order to draw her conclusion?

A David loves baking.
B David's mum loves birthday cake.
C Everyone who eats cake loves baking.
D Everyone who bakes cake loves baking.

☞ **Answers and explanations on pages 198-199**

6 **Brittany:** 'Colin cycles at least 50 kilometres a day.'
Sven: 'He must be in very good health.'

Which assumption has Sven made in order to draw his conclusion?
A Cycling 50 kilometres a day requires a good level of fitness.
B Cycling is a challenging sport.
C Only a person in good health could cycle 50 kilometres a day.
D Colin is very fit.

7 **Antoine:** 'My finished manuscript is due at the publisher in three weeks.'
Hannah: 'Congratulations. You must be excited.'

Which assumption has Hannah made in order to draw her conclusion?
A Antoine has nearly finished writing her book.
B Antoine must be excited.
C Antoine's book will be a bestseller.
D It's exciting that the manuscript is due in three weeks.

8 Yutaka works for a landscaping company.
Yutaka: 'I know it's not company policy to allow staff to use equipment for personal reasons but may I take the mower home on Friday?'
Yutaka's employer: 'I'll bend the rules and allow you to borrow what you need this one time, Yutaka.'

Which assumption has Yutaka's employer made in order to draw his/her conclusion?
A Yutaka will use the mower on the weekend.
B Yutaka's own mower must be broken.
C Yutaka's backyard must be huge.
D Yutaka has not accepted company policy.

9 **Ingrid:** 'I nearly stepped on a grasshopper and squashed it on my walk today. It was just sitting on the footpath.'
Stavros: 'Lucky you noticed it in time.'

Which assumption has Stavros made in order to draw his conclusion?
A Grasshoppers play an important role in the environment.
B Ingrid nearly squashed a grasshopper on the footpath.
C The grasshopper should not have been sitting on the footpath.
D Ingrid would not want to kill a grasshopper.

10 **Courtney:** 'I've requested another cookbook from the library. This one is on Vietnamese cooking.'
Kiera: 'Your cooking must be improving.'

Which assumption has Kiera made in order to draw her conclusion?
A Courtney borrows cookbooks from the library to improve her cooking.
B Courtney loves eating Vietnamese food.
C Courtney is learning from the cookbooks.
D Courtney will cook a meal for Kiera.

☞ **Answers and explanations on pages 198–199**

A reasoning error:

● is a **flaw in an argument**

● is something that **has not been thought of**, or that has been assumed, when drawing the conclusion.

Example

> To be a successful dentist, you need good manual dexterity and problem-solving skills, as well as excellent communication skills and the ability to work under pressure.

Zara: 'Felicity always does well in problem-solving challenges and loves making tiny models. She also has excellent communication skills—she's even president of the debating club. Plus, she loves the challenge of working under pressure. She says it's exciting! She'll definitely be a successful dentist.'

Leon: 'Hank is in the robotics club. He loves making the robots and collaborating to figure out complex problems. But he likes to take his time to think them through. He might not be good at working under pressure—so he definitely wouldn't be a successful dentist.'

If the information in the box is true, whose reasoning is correct?

A   Zara only

B   Leon only

C   Both Zara and Leon

D   Neither Zara nor Leon

Steps to work out the answer

1   Identify the conclusion made by each child.

2   Identify the evidence given to support each conclusion.

3   Ask yourself: Does the conclusion follow from the evidence? If it doesn't follow from the evidence, why doesn't it? There must be a flaw in the argument. What has been assumed or not thought of?

D is correct. Neither Zara nor Leon's reasoning is correct.

Incorrect answers

A is incorrect because Zara says that Felicity will definitely be a successful dentist, and she does appear to have the skills and qualities needed. However, the information does not say that someone with those skills and qualities will **definitely** be a successful dentist. Zara's reasoning is therefore flawed.

B is incorrect because Leon says that Hank definitely would not be a successful dentist. Hank appears to have the skills and qualities needed, except for the ability to work under pressure. Leon says Hank *might* not be good at this, but that does not mean he is **definitely** not good at it. So Leon's reasoning that Hank **definitely** wouldn't be a successful dentist is flawed.

C is incorrect by a process of elimination.

Checklist

Can you:

1   *identify a conclusion?*

2   *identify the reasoning or evidence given to support this conclusion?*

3   *detect any reasoning errors or flaws in the argument?*

Real Test 3

THINKING SKILLS
Critical thinking—Checking reasoning to detect errors

10 min

1 The tour guide led the guests through the new resort on Mars. He told them that the resort was on the site of the very first garden geodome on Mars. He said garden geodomes were the only type of geodome with tri-layered panels. He also said that garden geodomes are still in use today to grow food for the resort.

Uma: 'If you see a geodome with tri-layered panels then you know it must be a garden geodome growing food for the resort.'

Noah: 'If you see a geodome and it doesn't have tri-layered panels, then it can't be a garden geodome.'

If the information in the box is true, whose reasoning is correct?

A Uma

B Noah

C Both Uma and Noah

D Neither Uma nor Noah

2 Tim's neighbour's dog, Muttley, barks whenever a postie delivers a parcel to the neighbour.

Tim: 'Muttley is barking now. There must be a parcel.'

Aanya: 'I heard Muttley barking yesterday. Maybe the neighbour got a parcel yesterday.'

If the information in the box is true, whose reasoning is correct?

A Tim

B Aanya

C Both Tim and Aanya

D Neither Tim nor Aanya

3 Arlo's teacher said that any student who does not return all their library books by the last day of term would not be able to go to the end-of-term party.

Arlo: 'I've returned all my books already. I'll definitely be able to go to the end-of-term party.'

Which one of the following sentences shows the mistake Arlo has made?

A Arlo did not return all his books in time.

B There may be another reason Arlo is not able to go to the party.

C Arlo might deserve to go the party even if he did not return his books.

D We do not know how many students can go to the party.

4 The music teacher said that any students who did not get a chance to audition for a solo in last term's concert will definitely be offered an audition this term.

Jun: 'I didn't get a chance to audition last term. I hope I get a solo this term.'

Melia: 'Oh no, I really wanted a solo, but I auditioned last term. That means I won't be offered an audition this term.'

If the information in the box is true, whose reasoning is correct?

A Jun

B Melia

C Both Jun and Melia

D Neither Jun nor Melia

☞ **Answers and explanations on pages 199-200**

Real Test 3

 5

The local garden shop has a special offer. With every large herb planter box, customers get a bag of soil plus a packet of seeds of the customer's own choice. Customers can choose to upgrade the offer by paying an extra five dollars to then also include either: an extra bag of soil and a watering can; or two extra packets of seeds and a red or green garden gnome.

Paul: 'I'd like the large herb planter box with the upgrade offer please. I'd like the red garden gnome. And I'll have basil seeds and parsley seeds.'

Which one of the following sentences shows the mistake Paul has made?

A Paul does not have enough money to pay for the upgrade offer.

B Paul is not eligible for the red garden gnome.

C Paul has not chosen enough packets of seeds.

D The upgrade offer is only available on Saturdays.

 6

To successfully win the cooking competition you have to follow a recipe exactly so that you produce a replica of the original item. To do that you need to have good reading comprehension, an ability to follow instructions and you need to pay attention to detail.

Hamish: 'Greta is a great cook. Everything she cooks is delicious and looks fabulous. She embellishes on recipes and improves them. She has a flair and passion for cooking. I'm sure she'll win the competition.'

Mia: 'Jesper follows recipes exactly as long as they are vegetarian. He won't cook meat but he can follow instructions and he pays great attention to detail. He is a perfectionist in his cooking. He's sure to win the cooking competition.'

If the information in the box is true, whose reasoning is correct?

A Hamish only   B Mia only

C Both Mia and Hamish   D Neither Mia nor Hamish

 7

Jed: 'I am learning some conversational French so I can go to the new French restaurant in town and be able to read the menu to order dinner.'

Brianna: 'The language you use in conversation is not the language you'd need to read to be able to choose items from a French menu. I think Jed will struggle with his reading task.'

Karolina: 'Conversational French would include things like, "Hello. My name is Fred. What is your name? Excuse me, please. Thank you. How are you today? I'm well, thank you. Where is the nearest supermarket?" Conversational French will be useless to Jed in the French restaurant.'

If the information in the box is true, whose reasoning is correct?

A Brianna   B Karolina

C Both Karolina and Brianna   D Neither Karolina nor Brianna

☞ **Answers and explanations on pages 199-200**

 8 The theme park assures users on its website that it did all the safety checks required to open and operate the new ride. The park did a rigorous pre-open test and they advised that they do regular maintenance and engineering inspections. They've also installed controlled-stop sensors so the ride operator can stop the ride if anything unexpected happens, such as wildlife obstruction or poor guest behaviour.

Ollie: 'The theme park is doing all the safety checks it needs to do. The new ride is perfectly safe.'

Amanda: 'The new ride is as safe as possible but accidents can happen.'

If the information in the box is true, whose reasoning is correct?

A Ollie
B Amanda
C Ollie and Amanda
D Neither Ollie nor Amanda

9 Whenever Peyton gets a message on her phone that she is almost out of storage space it means she has to go through her photos urgently and delete all the unwanted ones to clear as much storage space as she can or, instead of deleting the photos, she can transfer them to a back-up device.

Peyton: 'The warning message on my phone is not on display at the moment so I must still have plenty of storage available.'

Which one of the following sentences shows the mistake Peyton has made?

A The warning message indicates that storage space is limited.
B Photos can take up a lot of storage space.
C There may not be plenty of space left because the warning message only comes up when storage is almost full.
D When storage is almost full space has to be created for new photos.

 10 There are nine subspecies of giraffe. One of the subspecies is the Rothschild's giraffe, also called the Baringo giraffe after Lake Baringo in Kenya, or the Ugandan giraffe because all Rothschild's giraffes in the wild live in Kenya or Uganda. You can tell a Rothschild's giraffe from other giraffes because it has five fur-covered ossicones rather than three but you can hardly see the two smaller ossicones behind its ears. Also, its patches are orange-brown on a cream-coloured background rather than brown on a brighter whitish background.

Hiromichi and Aria are looking at a giraffe at the zoo.

Hiromichi: 'That giraffe has brown patches on a light background and I can't see five ossicones so it can't be a Rothschild's giraffe.'

Aria: 'That giraffe is too far away to see if it has ossicones behind its ears but its patches are orange-brown so it's more likely a Rothschild's giraffe.'

If the information in the box is true, whose reasoning is correct?

A Hiromichi
B Aria
C Both Hiromichi and Aria
D Neither Hiromichi nor Aria

☞ **Answers and explanations on pages 199-200**

Key Points

MATHEMATICAL REASONING
Decimals, percentages and money

10 MIN

- When **decimals are multiplied, the number of decimal places is maintained**.
  Example: 0.8 × 0.03 = ?
  A 0.024   B 0.24   C 2.4   D 24   E 240
  Tip: Multiply 8 by 3, then decide about the decimal point.
  The correct answer is **A**, as 8 × 3 = 24, and as there are 3 decimal places in the question there will be 3 decimal places in the answer. This means 0.8 × 0.03 = 0.024.

- You should know some common **conversions**:
  $\frac{1}{2}$ = 0.5 = 50%; $\frac{1}{4}$ = 0.25 = 25%; $\frac{1}{5}$ = 0.2 = 20%; $\frac{1}{10}$ = 0.1 = 10%; $\frac{1}{100}$ = 0.01 = 1%.
  Remember: A percentage is a fraction with a denominator of 100.
  Example: Grant noticed that 16 out of 20 students on his bus were in Year 6. What percentage of the students were in Year 6?
  A 16%   B 32%   C 45%   D 80%   E 84%
  The correct answer is **D**, as $\frac{16}{20} = \frac{4}{5}$, and as $\frac{1}{5}$ = 0.2 = 20%, then $\frac{4}{5}$ = 80%.

- You should understand the **magnitude of fractions, decimals and percentages**.
  Example: Which of the following are arranged in ascending order?
  A $\frac{3}{4}$, 0.7, 0.076, 80%   B 0.7, $\frac{3}{4}$, 0.076, 80%   C 0.076, 0.7, $\frac{3}{4}$, 80%
  D 80%, 0.076, 0.7, $\frac{3}{4}$ E 0.076, 0.7, 80%, $\frac{3}{4}$
  The correct answer is **C**: 0.076, 0.700, $\frac{3}{4}$ = 0.750, 80% = 0.800.

- Often the word **'of' replaces a 'times'** symbol.
  Example: Find 75% of 80.
  A 60   B 34   C 45   D 75   E 76
  Tip: First find 25%, or a quarter, by dividing by 4.
  The correct answer is **A**. First, 75% = $\frac{3}{4}$, then we can find $\frac{1}{4}$ × 80 = 20, then $\frac{3}{4}$ × 80 = 60.

- One quantity can be **expressed as a percentage** of another.
  Example: What percentage is 30 seconds of 5 minutes?
  A 10%   B 20%   C 30%   D 6%   E 35%
  The correct answer is **A**. First rewrite both with the same units, then express them as fractions before rewriting as a percentage. As 5 minutes is 300 seconds, this means $\frac{30}{300} = \frac{1}{10}$ = 10%.

- The **unitary method** approach helps with some percentage problems.
  Example: In the school choir there are 80 students, which is exactly 40% of the school. How many students attend the school?
  A 160   B 320   C 360   D 400   E 200
  The correct answer is **E**, as 40% of school enrolments = 80 students, then 1% = 2 (by dividing by 40) and 100% = 200 (by multiplying by 100). (The solution could also have been found by 40% = 80, 20% = 40, then 100% = 200.)

Checklist
Can you:
1 *recall common conversions between fractions, decimals and percentages?*
2 *order fractions, decimals and percentages on the basis of size?*
3 *express one quantity as a percentage of another?*
4 *use the unitary method approach to solve problems involving percentages?*

Real Test 1

MATHEMATICAL REASONING
Decimals, percentages and money

1 A survey of students was conducted to find their favourite type of household pet.

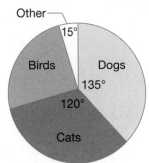

What percentage favoured birds?

45%	20%	25%	15%	30%
A	B	C	D	E

2 Last week Leyton travelled from Tocumweal to Beauty Point and, during the journey, saw this sign.

60 Tocumweal ⋮ Beauty Point 20

What percentage of the journey has Leyton already travelled?

25%	75%	60%	80%	20%
A	B	C	D	E

3 In a test comprising 25 questions, Melena achieves a result of 84%. How many of her answers were incorrect?

16	9	4	21	5
A	B	C	D	E

4 If 90% of an iceberg is below the water surface and 5 metres is above water, the total height of the iceberg is

A 95 metres   B 45 metres
C 10 metres   D 50 metres
E 85 metres

5 When his maths quiz was marked by the teacher, Simon had scored 15 marks out of a possible 20 marks. When he checked the paper, he found an error in the addition. He should have scored another 2 marks. What percentage is added to his result?

2%	20%	17%	15%	10%
A	B	C	D	E

6 The table shows the number of televisions in the households of students in Class 5K.

What percentage of the students has two televisions in their household?

Televisions	Students
1	4
2	6
3	3
4	4
5	3

40%	20%	60%	30%	12%
A	B	C	D	E

7 Sarah had $2000. She gave some of the money to Liana. She then gave half of the remaining money to Cyrus. She then gave half of what she had left to Austin. She gave the remaining $300 to Elizabeth. How much money did she give to Liana?

$400	$500	$600	$700	$800
A	B	C	D	E

8 To hire a bodyboard and a beach towel, there is a fixed fee of $5 for the towel and an hourly rate for the bodyboard. For a towel and 3-hour rental, Taylor paid $41. What is the cost for a towel and a 5-hour rental?

$48	$50	$56	$65	$75
A	B	C	D	E

9 Claire charges $16 to babysit for the first hour. For each additional hour, she charges 25% less than she did for the previous hour. How much money will Claire earn if she babysits for 4 hours?

$40.80	$42.00	$43.75	$48.00	$62.50
A	B	C	D	E

10 A dress costs $\frac{7}{10}$ of the cost of a pair of jeans. If the jeans cost $45 more than the dress, what is the total cost of the dress and a pair of jeans?

$255	$240	$250	$225	$260
A	B	C	D	E

☞ **Answers and explanations on page 201**

Real Test 2

MATHEMATICAL REASONING
Decimals, percentages and money

10 MIN

1 The distance from Frankston to Belldale is 1000 km. If Ross leaves Frankston and travels for 8 hours at 80 km/h, what percentage of the trip to Belldale has he yet to complete?

64%	32%	55%	45%	36%
A	B	C	D	E

2

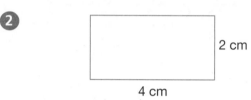

2 cm

4 cm

If the length of the rectangle is doubled and the width remains the same, the area of the rectangle increases by

50%	200%	100%	150%	20%
A	B	C	D	E

3 Which of the following is in ascending order?

A $0.088, 0.7, \frac{3}{4}, 72\%$

B $0.088, 0.7, 72\%, \frac{3}{4}$

C $0.088, \frac{3}{4}, 0.7, 72\%$

D $\frac{3}{4}, 0.088, 0.7, 72\%$

E $\frac{3}{4}, 72\%, 0.7, 0.088$

4 A tub is in the form of a rectangular prism with dimensions 50 cm by 10 cm by 20 cm. If 4 litres of water are poured into the empty tub, what percentage of the tub is filled with water?

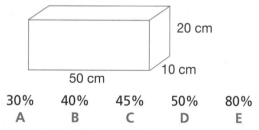

20 cm

10 cm

50 cm

30%	40%	45%	50%	80%
A	B	C	D	E

5 Roy measures the height of a tomato plant in his vegetable garden as 100 cm. A week later it has grown by 10%. By the end of the second week, Roy finds that it has increased in height by another 10%.

How tall is the tomato plant?

A 120 cm	B 111 cm	C 125 cm
D 102 cm	E 121 cm	

6 A 600 mL bottle contains exactly 320 mL. If 130 mL is added to the bottle, what percentage of the bottle has now been filled?

45%	75%	65%	85%	90%
A	B	C	D	E

7 An adult ticket and a child ticket to a concert together costs $280. Two adult tickets and three child tickets costs $670. What is the cost of an adult ticket?

$140	$150	$160	$170	$180
A	B	C	D	E

8 Grandma wanted to give $800 split between each of her grandsons. She gave a quarter of the money to Sebastian. She gave Theodore half the amount she gave to Sebastian. Another grandson Andrew received two-fifths of the total amount given to Sebastian and Theodore. Her fourth grandson Isaac received the remainder of the money. How much more money did Isaac receive than Sebastian?

$180	$200	$380	$240	$420
A	B	C	D	E

9 What is 20% of 20 multiplied by 50% of 50?

10	1000	200	700	100
A	B	C	D	E

10 At a back-to-school sale a shop offers a 'Buy 4 pencils, get the fifth pencil for 40 cents'. James buys 20 pencils and pays a total of $14.40. What is the regular price of one pencil?

$0.40	$0.60	$0.70	$0.80	$0.90
A	B	C	D	E

☞ **Answers and explanations on page 201**

MATHEMATICAL REASONING
Patterns and algebra

- **A number sentence is used** to solve a word problem.

  Example: Tyler packs 355 apples into 14 boxes. Each box contains 24 apples, and there are 19 apples left over. Which number sentence shows this information?

  A $24 \times 14 + 19 = 355$
  B $24 \times 14 - 19 = 355$
  C $24 \times 19 + 14 = 355$
  D $24 \times 19 - 14 = 355$
  E $19 \times 14 + 24 = 355$

  The correct answer is **A**. There are 24 apples in each of the 14 boxes which is 24×14 apples. Now add 19 because these apples remain unboxed. The number sentence is $24 \times 14 + 19 = 355$.

- **Shapes can be used to represent unknown values** in number sentences involving equal signs.

  Example: ■ and ▲ represent numbers. If ■ + 17 = 32 and ■ ÷ ▲ = 3, what is ▲?

2	3	4	5	6
A	B	C	D	E

  The correct answer is **D**. If ■ = 32 − 17 then ■ = 15. Now, 15 ÷ ▲ = 3, then ▲ = 15 ÷ 3 which is 5.

- **A sequence of numbers can be formed** using a rule.

  Example: Here is a sequence of numbers.

  _____, 18, 13, 10.5, 9.25

  What is the missing number?

23	26	28	31	32
A	B	C	D	E

The correct answer is **C**. Look at the differences between the numbers: 5, 2.5, 1.25. The differences are halving, so as $2 \times 5 = 10$ and $18 + 10 = 28$, the missing number is 28.

Example: Jayne completed this **table** using the rule *square the top number and subtract the middle row number* to find the bottom number.

Top	3	4	6	?
Middle	7	3	16	27
Bottom	2	13	20	37

What is the missing number?

7	8	9	10	11
A	B	C	D	E

The correct answer is **B**. To find the missing number, use the inverse operations. $37 + 27$ is 64. Now take the square root of 64 which is 8.

- **A two-pan balance, or balance scale,** can be used to find the number represented by a shape.

  Example: Using a two-pan balance, if ■ balances ●●●● and ●● balances ▲, which of these would balance

  A ■■   B ■▲   C ■▲●●
  D ■●▲   E ■■▲

The correct answer is **E**. Suppose ● = 1. This means ■ = 4 and ▲ = 2. Now, ●●●●●●▲▲ is $6 \times 1 + 2 \times 2$ which is 10. Looking through the options, ■■▲ is $2 \times 4 + 2$ which is 10.

Checklist
Can you:
1 *write a number sentence and use it to solve a word problem?*
2 *find the missing number in a number sentence involving an equals sign?*
3 *use a rule that has generated a sequence to find a missing number?*
4 *find the number represented by a specified shape used in a two-pan balance?*

Real Test 3

MATHEMATICAL REASONING
Patterns and algebra

10 MIN

1 Merryll has 85 books she wants to place in a bookcase which has four shelves. There is space for 16 large books or 24 small books on each shelf. Merryll places her large books on three shelves and her small books on the other shelf. When she fills the shelves Merryll has 13 books that do not fit. Which number sentence shows this information?

A 24 + 16 + 13 × 3 = 85
B 16 + 24 × 3 + 13 = 85
C (16 + 24) × 3 + 13 = 85
D 24 × 3 + (16 − 13) = 85
E 24 + 16 × 3 + 13 = 85

2 Ella has 67 balls. She places 8 balls in each of 5 boxes. She then places 4 balls in each of 6 boxes and has 3 balls remaining. Which number sentence shows this information?

A 8 × 5 + 4 × 6 − 3 = 67
B 8 × (5 + 4) × 6 − 3 = 67
C 8 × 5 + 4 × 6 + 3 = 67
D 8 × 5 × 4 + 6 + 3 = 67
E 8 × 5 + 4 × (6 + 3) = 67

3 ■ and ▲ represent numbers.
If 42 − ■ = 26 and ■ ÷ ▲ = 2, what is ▲?

5	6	7	8	9
A	B	C	D	E

4 ▲ and ★ represent numbers.
If 14 − (▲ + ★) = 8 and ★ + ★ + 3 = 13, what is the value of ▲?

1	2	4	5	10
A	B	C	D	E

5 Here is a sequence of numbers:

6, 11, 16, 21, 26, 31 …

What is the sum of the tenth and twelfth numbers in the sequence?

22	102	112	121	122
A	B	C	D	E

6 Kalyn writes out a sequence where he counts by 7s starting at 5. The resulting sequence is 5, 12, 19, 26, and so on. Which of these will appear in Kalyn's sequence?

58	65	68	77	78
A	B	C	D	E

7 In an increasing list of consecutive numbers, the fifth and sixth numbers in the list add to 17. What is the tenth number on the list?

12	13	14	15	28
A	B	C	D	E

8 This year, Zoe's age is a multiple of 6. Next year her age will be a multiple of 7. In how many years will Zoe be 60 years old if she is more than 10 years old now?

11	12	24	25	27
A	B	C	D	E

9 Lucy wrote the numbers 1 to 50 on a sheet of paper. She crossed out all the multiples of 4, 5 and 6. How many numbers have **not** been crossed out?

24	25	26	27	28
A	B	C	D	E

10 Theo uses a set of two-pan balance scales to compare the mass of solids.

If ▲ balances ●●● and ●● balances ■, which of these would balance ▲■●■?

A ■■▲
B ■▲
C ■■●●
D ■■■
E ▲▲■

☞ **Answers and explanations on pages 201–202**

Real Test 4

MATHEMATICAL REASONING
Patterns and algebra

10 MIN

1 Bill uses four pieces of firewood every night. There are 34 pieces of firewood in his stack. After a week he buys another five bags each containing 10 pieces. Which number sentence is used to calculate the number of nights from today his firewood will last?

A $34 - 4 \times 7 + 5 \times 10 \div 4$
B $(34 - 4 \times 7 + 5 \times 10) \div 4$
C $34 - 4 \times (7 + 5) \times 10 \div 4$
D $(34 - 4 \times 7 + 5) \times 10 \div 4$
E $34 - 4 \times (7 + 5 \times 10) \div 4$

2 Mrs Judd has 150 stickers. She has 26 students in her class. Twelve of her students are to be given three stickers each, nine students are to receive four stickers each and the rest of her students need to be given six stickers. Which number sentence can be used to find the number of stickers remaining?

A $150 - 26 \times 3 + 4 + 6$
B $150 - 12 \times 3 + 9 \times 4 + 5$
C $150 - (12 \times 3 - 9 \times 4 - 5 \times 6)$
D $150 + (12 \times 3 - 9 \times 4 - 5 \times 6)$
E $150 - (12 \times 3 + 9 \times 4 + 5 \times 6)$

3 ● and ■ represent numbers.
If $4 + 6 \times ■ = 40$ and $(3 + ■) \times ● = 63$, what is the value of ● ?

2	3	7	9	27
A	B	C	D	E

4 Each of ▲, ◣ and ● represent numbers. It is known that $▲ + ◣ \times ● = 28$ and $▲ + ◣ = 7$. If $▲ \times ▲ = 16$, what is the value of ●?

4	5	6	7	8
A	B	C	D	E

5 Here is a pattern of numbers.

53, 49, 45, 41, 37 …

What is the product of the tenth and thirteenth numbers in the pattern?

75	85	95	105	115
A	B	C	D	E

6 A sequence of numbers is changing by the same amount each time. The fourth, fifth and sixth numbers are 9, 3, –3.

What is the sum of the first 10 numbers in the sequence?

48	24	9	3	0
A	B	C	D	E

7 The symbols ⃠ and ▲ represent two different positive odd whole numbers less than 30.
If $⃠ \times ⃠ \times ⃠ = ▲$, what is the value of $▲ \div ⃠$?

2	3	4	6	9
A	B	C	D	E

8 Emilio completed this table using the rule *square the top number and subtract twice the middle row number* to find the bottom number.

Top	5	8	9	■
Middle	3	10	♥	45
Bottom	19	44	61	54

Two numbers are represented by the symbols ♥ and ■. What is $♥ \times ■$?

30	60	80	120	240
A	B	C	D	E

9 Each of the symbols ⬠, ◆ and ○ represent a non-zero number.
If $⬠ = ◆ + ◆ + ◆$ and $⬠ = ○ + ○$, then which of these equals $⬠ + ◆ + ○$?

A $⬠ + ⬠ - ◆$
B $○ + ○ + ○ + ○$
C $⬠ + ⬠$
D $◆ + ◆ + ◆ + ◆$
E $◆ + ○ + ○ + ○$

10 Lucy squared her age and subtracted 18. This equalled the age of her grandmother who is nine times the age of Lucy's brother Aiden. If Aiden is 7 years old, how much older is Lucy than Aiden?

A 1 year   B 2 years   C 3 years
D 4 years   E 9 years

☞ **Answers and explanations on page 202**

- A recount is a text in which you write about a **series of events that happened in the order that they happened**. You might recount events that happened in one hour, one day, one week, or over a whole lifetime. You might recount events that actually happened or that you have imagined.

- A **diary** is one example of a recount. In a diary you record events that happened in your day, but usually only the **interesting or important events**. You also write **personal comments**—expressing your feelings and opinions about particular events, people or places. This is what makes your diary interesting and lively.

- Recounts vary a little depending on where and how they are written. Many **newspaper reports**, for example, are recounts. A newspaper report begins quite differently from a diary. The first paragraph usually gives the reader the main information (what, who, when, where) and then subsequent paragraphs recount the details. The newspaper report also may include comments from people involved. However, it basically relates what happened at a particular time or place.

- Recounts are **useful types of texts** to practise before your test. You will often be able to write a recount in response to a question that gives you an open choice about what and how to write.

- It is also possible that you will be given a question that particularly **suggests a recount**. For example, you might be given an entry from a diary and asked to write the entry for the day before or after, or you might be given a picture of a scene and asked to write about what happened at the scene.

- If you write a recount in your test, you might be able to choose whether to make your recount **factual or imaginary**. You might also be able to choose the **form** of your recount (e.g. diary, letter, newspaper report, biography or autobiography, or account of how you did or made something).

- One really good thing about recounts is that they are quite **straightforward to structure and write**. So in a test, you don't have to spend much time planning.

- On the next page is an example of a recount written in response to a test question, though not under test conditions. In your test, you **might not have time** to produce a polished piece of writing like this. However, if you are **well prepared**, you will be able to aim for this standard.

Sample

Question

Look at the picture below. Write about what happened before this scene occurred. You might write about any length of time—a whole day, a half hour, an hour, or just a few minutes. You can write in any form.

Response

Structure

Title—adding a title tells the reader the topic and writing form

Orientation to topic tells your reader about what, who, when, where

Series of events are related in the order they happened

Paragraphs help to show different time periods

Personal comments make the recount interesting

Conclusion—usually a comment on events or experiences

Language

Proper nouns to name individual people and places

Pronouns (e.g. we, me, he) when referring to the same people again and again

Interesting detail about events, people or places

Time words and **phrases** to make order of events clear

Usually **past tense verbs**

Thinking and **feeling verbs** to comment on events

Correct **spelling**, **grammar** and **punctuation**

My Camp Diary

Friday 6 March

Well, I'm writing this at Lithgow Hospital—not camp! I'm waiting for Mum and Dad to arrive. I think I'll be in big, big trouble but maybe they'll just be happy to see me alive.

Today was the last day of our camp. I was looking forward to getting home and showing Mum and Dad that they were right to let me go. They had been so scared of all the things that could go wrong—snake bites, spider bites, sunstroke, broken arms and legs, lightning strikes—you name it, they were worried about it.

When we got up this morning, Mr Rosso told us that if we packed up the tents really quickly, we could just fit in a quick swim before we made our way to the pick-up point. So at about ten o'clock we set off down the hillside for one last swim in the crystal-clear pool under the waterfall.

We swam for about a quarter of an hour. The water was cool and green and we all talked about how it was better than a swimming pool any day. The best place was just under the waterfall where it was like being in a shower and a bath at the same time.

Mr Rosso had just told us (for the hundredth time) not to jump off the rocks under the falls, but they were hard to resist and they didn't really look very dangerous. Anyway, I jumped one last time as he looked away.

Disaster! I guess I wasn't concentrating because I fell sideways as I jumped and banged my leg badly on the rocks. I felt a terrible piercing pain as I fell into the water. Mr Rosso saw immediately that I was in trouble and swam over to me. Jaya and Zac helped him to pull me out and lay me by the side of the pool. It was pretty obvious that my leg was broken.

Getting from there to here was not easy, to say the least. But here I am and feeling a lot better. Oh-oh, here they come. Will I ever be allowed to go on a school camp again?

Practice Tasks

50 MIN

These tasks will give you some ideas about how to start writing quickly and complete an interesting recount in the short time you have in the test.

You will have to look back at *My Camp Diary* to answer some questions, and then do some recount writing yourself based on the practice writing question below.

Look at the question now before you start the tasks.

Practice writing question

Today was the best/worst day of my/his/her life. When I/he/she woke up this morning …

Use this sentence as a prompt for writing a recount of some kind. Decide whether to write about the best or worst day and the form your recount will take. You could write, for example, a diary entry, an email or a newspaper report. If you wish, you can change the wording of the sentence above but keep the focus on recounting a series of events.

- The first thing to decide is what you are going to write about—the **main idea** of your recount. The writer of the camp diary decided to write about himself breaking a leg at camp. However, he also jotted down these ideas:
  - ○ snakebite—school camp
  - ○ broken leg—skateboarding competition
  - ○ athletics carnival—winning, then accident.

- Use your own experiences and, of course, your imagination. This writer had not ever broken a leg at camp, but he used his camp experiences. He also made good use of his parents' fears about accidents.

- You will also have to decide how you are going to shape your writing—the **form of your recount**. You can just write it as a plain recount with no real context or purpose (except, of course, to answer the question). The writer of the camp diary could have written something like this:

  > Last week we went on our school camp. It all went really well until …

However, it is much more interesting to write the recount in a 'real' form—as a diary entry, a letter, a newspaper report, or even an official statement (such as you might give to the police). The writer of the camp diary could have written his recount in any of these forms.

- Once you decide on the main idea and form, you can do a very quick plan. Recounts are quite easy to plan. There are basically two parts—the **orientation** and the **series of events**.

Look at the plan for *My Camp Diary*.

Orientation	at hospital—last day of camp—Mum and Dad
Series of events	pack up
	set off to pool for last swim
	waterfall—jump off rocks
	break leg
	go to hospital

- Although a recount is simpler to write than a narrative and is sometimes about quite everyday events, you should still try to add an element that makes it **stand out from the average piece of writing**. You might not always know what this is as you plan—it might come to you as you write—but it is good to think about this **extra element** before you start.

  The writer of the camp diary uses the idea that his mum and dad did not want him to go to the camp to make the recount something special. It also gives a sense of completeness to the piece. Notice how the writer returns to the idea in the last paragraph—cleverly pulling the whole thing together.

Task 1

Think about the question on page 68. There are a million different topics you could write about. Write down three ideas for the best day and three for the worst day. Give yourself no more than two minutes.

Best day	Worst day
1 _____	1 _____
2 _____	2 _____
3 _____	3 _____

Task 2

Now choose one of your ideas to write about and do a rough plan for your recount. Try to think of a way to add something that will make your writing 'special'—but this might only come to you once you start writing. Give yourself about two minutes.

Orientation

_____

_____

_____

Events

_____

_____

_____

_____

_____

The orientation usually answers these basic questions for the reader: **Who? What? Where? When?** You don't usually need to answer all these questions, and you may only say something very general, but in some way you should show your reader what you are going to write about.

The orientation should also clearly suggest the **form and purpose** of the writing. A title can help to do this.

 Tips: A good way to begin a diary is to say where you are as you write (e.g. the writer of the camp diary mentioned Lithgow Hospital). This will get you moving quickly into the main events.

If he had been writing a newspaper article on the same general topic he might have begun differently, perhaps with something like:

Lithgow, 6 March 2021
Late yesterday afternoon a young boy was rescued after a fall at a local waterhole. He was taken to Lithgow Hospital …

If you have chosen a newspaper report for the practice writing task you might begin with, for example,
September 8 was meant to be the best day of young Angie Martin's life. Unfortunately it turned out to be the worst.

Task 3

Circle 'yes' or 'no' to show if the orientation of *My Camp Diary* tells you something about:

who: yes/no   what: yes/no   where: yes/no   when: yes/no

Task 4

Write the orientation for your recount for the question on page 68. Give yourself about five minutes.

_____

_____

_____

_____

_____

_____

_____

_____

_____

☞ **Answers and explanations on page 203**

Practice Tasks

WRITING
Recount response—Recounting the events

- You usually recount what happened **in the order that it happened**, although sometimes you might change the order around for a special effect.

- Use **time words, phrases and clauses** to show the order of events. Look at these from the camp diary: When we got up this morning, at about 10 o'clock, for about a quarter of an hour.

- ⚡ *Tip:* Try using these time words and expressions: next, after, afterwards, before, beforehand, during, immediately, later, later that morning, some time later, meanwhile, at about the same time, simultaneously, previously.

- You should select only the **most important or interesting things** about people or events to tell your reader. You can't tell them everything, or you will be writing for far too long and you just can't do that in a test! Remember: You only have 30 minutes.

- You should also focus mainly on the **events that move the writing on**—those that take the recount to the next time period. The writer of the camp diary had many experiences that day, but only wrote about those that explained how he turned up in a hospital. This is especially important in a short recount.

- **Paragraphing** can help you indicate to your reader that you are moving to a new time period.

- Although you need to concentrate on the main events, you also need to add at least some detail to make your recount come to life and seem real. It would be fairly boring if you just kept to 'this happened, then that happened' or 'then I did this, then he did that'. Look back at *My Camp Diary* and note how much detail the writer gives about the pool. This helps us to appreciate why he jumped in when he was told not to. If it was a newspaper report, he probably would have added comments from those involved in the event.

Task 5

1. Look back at *My Camp Diary*. Underline all the words and phrases that show when things happened, or in which order.

2. Look at paragraphs 5 and 6. Tick the ideas the writer gives details about.
   - ☐ who Mr Rosso is
   - ☐ what Mr Rosso said
   - ☐ why the writer jumped
   - ☐ how the accident happened
   - ☐ what everyone said
   - ☐ who helped him

☞ **Answers and explanations on page 203**

- One main way you can add interest to a recount is to **add your own personal comments** about the events and people you are writing about. For example, the diary writer writes '[the rocks] were hard to resist and they didn't look very dangerous' and 'Oh-oh, here they come'.

- **Thinking and feeling verbs** can sometimes help you introduce these comments—verbs like think, feel, look forward, guess, imagine, reckon, suspect and hope. For example, the writer states:

  'I think I'll be in big, big trouble ...'

  'I was looking forward to getting home ...'

  'I guess I wasn't concentrating ...'

- *Tip:* Look back at the tip on page 39 for more thinking and feeling verbs.

- If you are writing a recount as a newspaper report, you might add the comments of other people involved in the events. You could use direct speech with quotation marks or indirect speech to do so.

Task 6

Now use your plan to write about the series of events for the question on page 68. Remember to keep to the most important or interesting events and to add your personal comments or those of other people involved, if appropriate. Give yourself about 10 minutes.

You don't need a big conclusion for a recount. Usually you just write a comment of some kind—often **evaluating the events and experiences** you have recounted—saying how good/funny/terrible/exciting they were. It is usually the same for a newspaper report.

Our diary writer concludes with a comment on his health (I feel better …), but then he cleverly links it back to the orientation by expressing his fears about his parents' reactions. This makes the ending more interesting.

Task 7

Write a conclusion for your recount for the practice writing question. Give yourself about three minutes.

_____

_____

_____

_____

_____

_____

_____

_____

Note: If you like, you can work on your writing some more, refining what you have written so far and writing it out again on your own paper. Use the checklist below to review your writing.

Checklist for writing a recount
Have you:
1 *oriented your reader to who, what, where, when?*
2 *chosen only important events to write about?*
3 *included at least some interesting detail?*
4 *added personal comments or those of others involved?*
5 *used time words and expressions to help your reader follow the order?*
6 *written a concluding comment?*
7 *checked your grammar, punctuation and spelling?*

Remember: In the test you won't have time to revise thoroughly and make big changes. You may have time to change a few words, but you will really be aiming to do a good piece of writing in one draft.

Real Test

- Choose **one** of the writing tests below to do now. The first test question particularly suggests that you write a personal recount. The second question gives you the opportunity to write in many different ways. If you choose the second question, write a recount to practise all the points you have just revised. You can choose the form—you could keep to a personal recount or diary entry, or you might make it something different; for example, a human interest story for a newspaper.

- Use your own paper. You are encouraged to use two or three sheets of paper. Use the first one for planning and rough work, and do your response on the second and third sheets.

- If you like, you can do both tests. However, it would be better to do them on different days. For extra practice, you could use the tests again, writing in different ways each time.

- Set yourself a time limit of 25 or 30 minutes, depending on the test you are sitting. Use the checklist on page 73 to give it a quick review.

---

1 Write about a task you have completed or about something you have made or created—by yourself or with others. Tell how you made it, what the highs and lows were, and how you felt when you had finished. Here are some ideas to get you going: a birthday cake for a friend or family member, a long bushwalk, a performance, an artistic creation, a toy, a campsite or an experiment of some kind.

OR

2 Use this picture as the basis for a piece of writing of your own choosing.

☞ **Checklist on page 73**

We're halfway there!

Week 3

This is what we cover this week:

Day 1   **Reading:** Factual texts

Day 2   **Thinking Skills:**   ◎   Problem solving—Shapes and patterns

◎   Problem solving—Word problems

◎   Problem solving—Numerical reasoning

Day 3   **Mathematical Reasoning:**   ◎   Length and area

◎   Volume, capacity, mass, speed and time

Day 4   **Writing:** Narrative response

- Factual texts are texts that **focus on information**. This does not mean they only contain facts. They might also include ideas and opinions. Generally, factual texts aim to inform, instruct, discuss ideas or persuade.

- In your test, you might be asked, for example, to answer questions about extracts from informative books or websites, or from travel brochures or newspaper reports. These are all examples of factual texts. These can be the most difficult kinds of texts to understand because they may contain **ideas and information** that are new to you.

- In the NSW Selective Schools Test you will be asked to do a **cloze activity** instead of answering multiple-choice questions. In the Scholarships Tests you will probably still be asked to answer **multiple choice** (as you were with Literary prose and Poetry in this book).

- A cloze activity is where you have to look through a **list of words, phrases or sentences** which have been taken out of a text, and put them back into the blank spaces they come from so that the text makes sense. You are probably familiar with this type of activity. In the Selective Schools Test you will be replacing missing sentences.

> This part of the book will give you practice with this type of question format. But remember: Always check the advice about the test you are going to sit.

- With cloze, the best approach under test conditions is to read the whole text quickly and then quickly skim the missing sentences. Then proceed one by one through the sentences and roughly **work out where they should go.** You might reconsider these as you firm up your ideas. You may easily see where one or two go, so start with these, crossing them off to eliminate them and then keep going. When you are happy with all your answers, write them in.

- In the Selective Schools Test and here in the following Practice Tasks you will be given **one spare sentence** which does not belong in the text.

- As with multiple-choice questions, the cloze activity will ask you to consider **main ideas and detail** and sometimes **ideas not definitely stated** in the text. You will have to read the sentences around the missing sentence and sometimes the whole paragraph and those before and after it to get the answer right. You will have to look at **linking words and phrases** such as 'however', 'as a result', 'then, 'eventually' and 'because'. And you will have to pay attention to little words such as 'the', 'this', 'these' and 'another' which we use often to link up ideas when we write.

- Whichever test you are sitting, the cloze activities which follow will give you good practice with factual texts and help you prepare.

Practice Task 1

READING
Factual texts

15 MIN

Use this first practice task as a guide. It is shorter than the task in the test, as it has fewer missing sentences, but it will give you the idea. Read the text carefully and then read the sentences A–E and work out which one fits each space. IMPORTANT: There is one extra answer which you do not need to use. Then look at the answers to get explanations about why each answer was right. Don't worry if you don't get every answer right. You should be able to keep within the time limit in this first practice task but, if not, try to improve your speed over the next practice tasks.

Extract: 'Bass Strait', adapted from *Night of the Muttonbirds* by Mary Small

Bass Strait separates the huge landmass of Australia from its smaller shield-shaped island of Tasmania. It is well known to sailors as one of the wildest, most wicked stretches of water in the world, for numbers of islands surrounded by fierce rip tides, rocky shoals and shallows crouch in wait for unwary ships. **1** _____ . Their skeletons lie lost, forgotten, shrouded in kelp beneath its sullen depths.

Although Tasmania was first sighted by Abel Tasman, the Dutch explorer, in 1642, the Bass Strait islands remained undiscovered by Europeans until 1773. **2** _____ . The result was his discovery of a group of islands to the east of the strait which now bear his name.

But it was the savage storm that wrecked the unseaworthy *Sydney Cove* on Preservation Island in 1797 that really drew attention to the little-known area. **3** _____ . By the following year, the intrepid explorers Matthew Flinders and George Bass had made haste in the Colonial sloop *Norfolk* to prove their theory that Tasmania was indeed divided from the rest of Australia by a strait. Their reports and the reports on the abundance of seals on the islands brought the first of the white settlers. **4** _____ . It was easy enough for them to steal Aboriginal women from nearby Tasmania and it was these men and women who were to become the ancestors of a unique group of islanders who still live on Cape Barren Island in the Furneaux Group.

Harcourt Brace Jovanovich, Sydney, 1992

A For the ship carried a full cargo of rum from India.

B Many have come to grief in this strait either from storms or from fog.

C Many of these were rough and ruthless men used to hard living.

D Abel Tasman was born in a little village called Lutjegast in the north of the country.

E Then Tobias Furneaux, aboard the *Adventure*, became separated by fog from the *Resolution* and her captain, James Cook.

☞ **Answers and explanations on page 203**

Practice Task 2

READING
Factual texts

15 MIN

Again, read the text right through and then read the missing sentences A–G and choose your answers. Remember: There is one spare sentence which you won't need to use. When you finish, check the answers. If you did not choose the correct answer or if you were unsure about it, read the answer explanation. Again, don't worry if you don't get every question right—the aim is to give you practice. Try to work more quickly and finish in close to 15 minutes. You will have to work very quickly in the real test.

Extract: Whale of an Encounter

Swimming with humpbacks may well be a life-changing experience, writes DEBBIE NEILSON.

Instead of breathing air I was gulping water. In my excitement I had forgotten to put the snorkel in my mouth before jumping in the water.

Lungs refilled, I swam quickly in the direction our guide had pointed.

1 _____. Peering through the sapphire depths I could just make out a large shape moving below me.

The knot in my stomach tightened as the grey and white figure grew bigger. Soon I could see the sucker fish clinging to his barnacled 40-tonne body.

2 _____. Glancing to the right, I saw a mother humpback and her calf swimming in the shallows just a few metres away. The deep folds on the unblemished creamy underbelly of the youngster suggested he or she was just a few weeks old.

For several minutes we studied each other— four brightly coloured, wide-eyed snorkellers and three gentle giants of the sea, eye to eye just metres apart. **3** _____.

Overwhelmed by what I had just seen, I found it difficult to hold back tears as I swam back to the boat. While there were hoots of delight from some and silent reflection from others, we all felt the same—completely moved and transformed by the experience. **4** _____We enjoyed several similar encounters over 10 days in Tonga with Whaleswim Adventures. The velvety warm waters surrounding the Vava'u group of 40 islands, an hour's flight north of the kingdom's capital, Nuku'alofa, are a favourite playground for about 500 humpbacks which journey here every year from the Southern Ocean to breed and raise their young in June and November.

The sunny South Pacific destination is one of only two places in the world where you can legally swim with cetaceans. **5** _____.

While there is opposition to swimming with whales, strict guidelines ensure the impact on the mammals and their environment is minimal. No contact is allowed and no more than four of us (including a guide) could enter the water at any one time. **6** _____. While these guidelines are yet to be legislated, it was heartening to see most operators abiding by the rules.

Extract from *The Sun-Herald*, 9 February 2003
© Debbie Neilson; reproduced with permission

A The memory will live forever.

B Another glimmer of white caught the corner of my eye.

C Only two boats are permitted within 100 metres of the whales.

D The other is the whale sanctuary at Silver Bank Reef off the Dominican Republic.

E Be quick to book your dive with Whaleswim Adventures as their tours are extremely popular in the whale season.

F A flash of white suddenly stopped me mid stroke.

G Eventually growing tired of the attention, the massive escort led his family off into the deeper waters.

☞ **Answers and explanations on pages 203-204**

Practice Task 3

READING
Factual texts

15 MIN

Again, read the text right through and then read the missing sentences A–G and choose your answers. Remember: There is one spare sentence which you won't need to use. Work as quickly as you can and aim to finish in 15 minutes. When you finish, check the answers and read the answer explanation if needed.

Extract: 'Stone Age Art', adapted from *Hunters of the Stone Age* by Karel Sklenar

Modern humans are cushioned from the effects of nature by science and technology. Our Stone Age ancestors, however, lived much closer to nature. To survive, they had to know and recognise its signs and warnings, for nature could have profound effects on their lives. **1** _____ . However, they could not understand everything they saw or heard.

They did not think and wonder about the changing seasons as they were part of life and reasonably predictable. But lightning, thunder, floods and fires had more violent effects on their lives. **2** _____ . In most cases, no one understood how or why they suddenly occurred. Naturally enough, these kinds of events instilled fear into people. This fear and a sense of helplessness gave them a respect for the unknown and uncontrollable forces that determined people's life and death. **3** _____ .

A few of our ancestors with artistic abilities tried to record what they saw and how they felt. It is to these gifted people that we owe some of the earliest works of art in our history.

The most beautiful and dramatic of these were painted on cave walls in south-western France and Spain. These paintings remained hidden from human eyes for thousands of years. **4** _____ . At first it could not be believed that such beautiful art was produced by 'cave men' who were thought to have been little better than brutes and incapable of producing art of such quality. The discoverers of the art were even labelled fools and frauds. **5** _____ . However, we should not think these were the first works of art. It is generally accepted that art developed from quite humble beginnings—probably simple drawings drawn with fingers and twigs in the dust. **6** _____ . No artistic material has survived from the time of the very earliest men.

Hamlyn, London, 1988

A Then in the 1900s they were discovered by accident.

B So it took some time and fierce debate for the paintings to be accepted as Stone Age in origin.

C From earliest childhood, Stone Age people learnt to use nature's gifts and avoid its snares.

D It is from these fears and respect for natural forces that religions began to develop.

E Not only that, but they were unpredictable and largely inexplicable.

F Unfortunately we don't know much about these stages.

G Writing was once thought to have been invented by one civilisation but now we know differently.

☞ **Answers and explanations on page 204**

Real Test

15 MIN

Again, read the text right through and then read the missing sentences A–G and choose your answers. Remember: There is one spare sentence which you won't need to use. Work as quickly as you can and stop at 15 minutes. When you finish, check the answers and read the answer explanation if needed.

Extract: Ernest Shackleton of the Antarctic

Already a celebrated polar explorer, Sir Ernest Shackleton coordinated the British Imperial Trans-Antarctic Expedition with the goal of accomplishing the first crossing of the Antarctic from sea to sea through the South Pole. His earlier trips had each established new records for reaching the Farthest South latitudes. **1** _____ . With such significant achievements under his belt already, Shackleton turned his sights to the new challenge.

In October 1914, despite the outbreak of World War I in August, Shackleton set sail from Buenos Aires with his 27-man crew. Many had responded to a recruitment notice which read: 'Men wanted for hazardous journey. Small wages. Bitter cold. Long months of complete darkness. Constant danger. Safe return doubtful. Honour and recognition in case of success.—Ernest Shackleton.' **2** _____ . Apparently, he sorted the 5000 responses into three piles: 'Mad', 'Hopeless' and 'Possible'!

He ultimately selected a crew of 56 to be split over the two ships. The *Endurance* would take the main party led by Shackleton to the Weddell Sea from where they would begin their ice crossing. **3** _____ .

Ice conditions were unusually harsh for the time of the year, and the *Endurance* became trapped in the pack ice of the Weddell Sea. At the end of February, Shackleton reluctantly had to declare the ship to be their winter quarters—protection of sorts from the horrendous blizzards and temperatures. **4** _____ . With meagre food, clothing and shelter and with no means of communication, Shackleton and his men were stranded on the ice floes, where they camped for another five months.

When they had drifted to the northern edge of the pack, encountering open water, the men sailed the three small lifeboats they'd salvaged to a bleak crag called Elephant Island. **5** _____ . However, it was uninhabited and, due to its distance from shipping lanes, provided no hope for rescue.

Realising the severity of the physical and mental strains on his men, Shackleton and five others immediately set out to take the crew's rescue into their own hands. In a 22-foot lifeboat named the *James Caird*, they accomplished the impossible, surviving a 17-day, 800-mile journey through the world's worst seas to South Georgia Island, where a whaling station was located.

The six men landed on an uninhabited part of the island, however, so their last hope was to cross 26 miles of mountains and glaciers, considered impassable, to reach the whaling station on the other side. **6** _____ . In August 1916, 21 months after the initial departure of the *Endurance*, Shackleton himself returned to rescue the men on Elephant Island. Although they'd withstood the most incredible hardship and privation, not one member of the 28-man crew was lost.

Adapted from web page Sir Ernest Shackleton and the *Endurance* Expedition, WGBH Educational Foundation, http://main.wgbh.org/imax/shackleton/sirernest.html

A He was quoted as saying 'I never learned much geography at school.'

B The *Aurora* would carry the support party to the other side of the continent and lay supply depots to enable Shackleton's men to do the crossing.

C For 10 months, the *Endurance* drifted, locked within the ice, until the pressure crushed the ship.

D In each of these journeys he had travelled closer to the Pole than anyone had done before.

E Starved, frostbitten and wearing rags, Shackleton and two others made the trek.

F Shackleton strongly believed that character and temperament were as important as technical ability.

G They were on land for the first time in 497 days.

☞ **Answers and explanations on page 204**

Shapes and objects

- **Identify** what the question requires.
- Try to **visualise** the shapes or objects as you work through the questions.

Example 1

Garrett used five pieces of card to make a square.

Here are four of the pieces:

Which could be the fifth piece?

Steps to work out the answer

1   Read the question carefully and understand what is required. In this case the pieces need to be fitted together. The whole thing needs to be a square.
2   Work out how the given pieces might be fitted together. Consider different rotations. Begin with the most obvious and try to picture the result of putting the first two pieces together.
3   There is only one possible piece (from those given and the options) that can go on the left side.
4   The remaining piece of the four that were given can only go at the bottom.

A is correct.

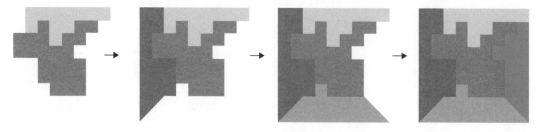

Patterns

- **Identify** what the question requires.
- Work out if a **pattern** is being used and determine the pattern.
- **Apply** the pattern in answering the question.

Example 2

Jacob has a calculator that displays numbers in 'square' shapes, so that 8 should be shown as ⯁.

The display is faulty and the whole top part does not work, meaning that 8 is shown as ⊔.

When the numbers from 0 to 9 are displayed, two of the numbers, in order, are ⌐ and ⼁.

How will the next number appear?

A ⌐ 　　　　　B ⊔ 　　　　　C ⌊ 　　　　　D ⼁

Steps to work out the answer

1 Identify what the question requires. You need to find the next number in a pattern.
2 Determine the pattern. Numbers are to be in order according to the calculator display.
   So, work out what the correct display of the numbers should look like:

　　0 123456789

3 Only the bottom parts of the numbers are displayed by Jacob's calculator. Work out what they will look like. ⊔ ⼁⌊ ⌐ ⼁⌐⊔ ⼁⊔⌐
4 Now look for the parts given in the question and for what comes next.
5 Remember: You may be able to visualise the pattern in your mind's eye, and not need to write out the pattern.

A is correct. The two given numbers ⌐ and ⼁, because they are in order, can only be the bottom of 3 and 4. So the answer must be the bottom part of 5. It is ⌐ .

Checklist

Can you:

1 *identify what is required when working with shapes and objects?*
2 *visualise shapes as they would fit together?*
3 *understand how objects will look when viewed from different directions?*
4 *look for and identify patterns?*
5 *use a pattern to solve a problem?*

Real Test 1

THINKING SKILLS
Problem solving—Shapes and patterns

10 MIN

1 Jade is going to place four pieces of card together to make a rectangle.

Here are three of the pieces:

Which of these could be the fourth piece?

X   Y

A X only   B Y only
C Both X and Y   D Neither X nor Y

2 These five pieces can be placed around the shape in the square below to fill all the spaces. (Each piece might be rotated, but not reflected.)

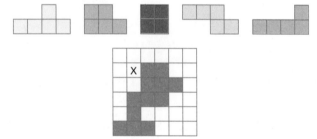

Which piece will cover the square with an X?

A   B   C   D

3 Kylie made a 3D shape using identical cubes. She then drew a top view and a side view.

top view   side view

How many of these could be a front view?

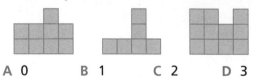

A 0   B 1   C 2   D 3

4 A floor is being tiled in a pattern that uses four different tiles.

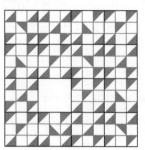

One of the tiles is missing. Which of the tiles is it?

A   B   C   D

5 Maya has some blocks, each made up of five hexagons. She is using the blocks to form a triangle. (The blocks can be rotated or reflected.)

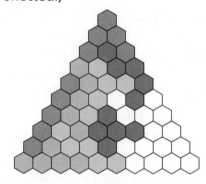

Maya needs three more blocks to complete the triangle.

Which of these blocks will she **not** use?

A   B   C   D

6 Luke made a cross using four pieces, of the same shape and size, like this:

☞ **Answers and explanations on pages 204-206**

Real Test 1

THINKING SKILLS
Problem solving—Shapes and patterns

This is his cross:

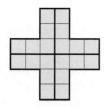

How many other sets of four pieces of the same size and shape could Luke use to make his cross?

A 0   B 1   C 2   D 3

7 Identical tiles have been used to lay a pattern on a floor. Four of the tiles are missing.

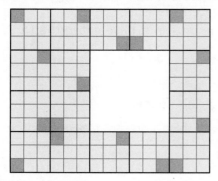

Which of these shows how the missing tiles should appear?

A   B

C   D

8 This is the front view of some books that are standing on a shelf.

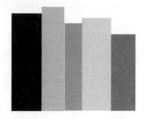

Which of these **cannot** be a view from the right side?

A    B

C    D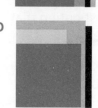

9 Jerry has two of both these shapes.

How many of these can be made using his four shapes?

   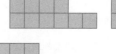   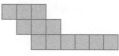

A 4   B 5   C 6   D 7

10 A cube has a face that is blue and another that is white. The other four faces have one of a square, circle, triangle and cross.

Here are two different views of the cube:

Jay made these statements:

X The blue face must be opposite the face with the cross.

Y The white face must be opposite the face with the square.

Which statements are correct?

A X only   B Y only

C Both X and Y   D Neither X nor Y

☞ **Answers and explanations on pages 204-206**

Key Points

THINKING SKILLS
Problem solving—Word problems

10 MIN

- **Read** all problems carefully and **consider** the options.
- Word problems might involve **reasoning** about totally unfamiliar topics. Use common sense and logical thinking.
- **Watch the wording** of questions. For example, if a question asks which option must be true it does not mean that the incorrect options are necessarily false. It just means that we cannot be certain that they are true. Some questions might ask which option is **not** correct. Don't rush and choose the first option that **is** correct.

Example 1

If it is true that 'Whoever ate the fruit will have purple lips and sticky fingers', which statement must also be true?

A If Anne didn't eat the fruit she must not have purple lips.

B If Edwin does not have purple lips he must not have sticky fingers.

C If Craig has sticky fingers and purple lips he must have eaten the fruit.

D If Sara has purple lips but does not have sticky fingers she must not have eaten the fruit.

Steps to work out the answers

1 Read the question carefully.

2 Consider all the options and determine whether they logically follow.

D is correct. If whoever ate the fruit must have sticky fingers and if Sara does not have sticky fingers, then it follows that she did not eat the fruit.

Incorrect answers

A, B and C are incorrect because it does not follow that purple lips and/or sticky fingers can only result from eating the fruit.

Example 2

Ivy read three books one after the other. The books were either novels or biographies. The first book she read was a novel and the last one was a biography. Which must be true?

A Ivy read a novel straight after a biography.

B Ivy read a biography straight after a novel.

C Ivy read one novel and two biographies.

D Ivy read one biography and two novels.

Steps to work out the answers

1 Read the question carefully and take time to think.

2 Consider the different possibilities.

B is correct. The first book Ivy read was a novel. If the second book Ivy read was a biography, then she read that biography straight after a novel. The third book that Ivy read was a biography. If the second book Ivy read was a novel, then she read the third book, a biography, straight after a novel. So, whatever type of book Ivy read second, she must have at some stage read a biography straight after a novel.

Incorrect answers

A is incorrect. Ivy cannot have read a novel after a biography.

The books would have been either two novels and then one biography or one novel and then two biographies. So C and D **might** have been correct but they are not options that must have been correct.

Example 3

At a party, four people are each given a different card: either an ace, king, queen or jack from a deck of cards. They make a statement about their own card and that of one of the others, but none of the statements are true. A prize is given to the first of the other people at the party who is able to work out which card each person has. These are the incorrect statements:

Roger: 'I have the king and Jo has the queen.'   **Tim:** 'I have the queen and Ned has the jack.'

Jo: 'Roger has the ace and I have the jack.'   **Ned:** 'Tim has the jack and I have the king.'

Which must be true?

A   Jo has the ace.   B   Tim has the ace.   C   Ned has the queen.   D   Roger has the queen.

Steps to work out the answers

1   Read the question carefully and note that all the statements are false.
2   Sort through the information and look for the facts that can be worked out.

C is correct. Ned has the queen. All the statements made by Roger, Tim, Jo and Ned are incorrect. So the jack cannot be held by Ned, Jo or Tim. Roger has the jack. So Roger does not have the queen. Neither Jo nor Tim has the queen either. So Ned must have the queen.

Incorrect answers

A and B might or might not be true. Either Jo or Tim has the ace, but there is not enough information to determine which must be true. **D is incorrect**. Roger has the jack.

Checklist

Can you:
1   *read questions carefully and understand what is required?*
2   *consider the options and judge whether they logically follow from the given information?*

Real Test 2

THINKING SKILLS
Problem solving—Word problems

10 min

1 Organisers of a competition insist that all entrants in the competition must be great singers and great dancers.

Which of these statements must be true?

A As Bella is a great singer and great dancer, she must have entered the competition.

B If Josie won the competition, she might not have been a great dancer.

C If Brice is not a great singer, he cannot have won the competition.

D If Stefan did not enter the competition, he cannot be a great singer.

2 In Parker Street, every house that is painted white has a green roof and every house with a green roof also has a green fence.

Which must be true?

A If a house is painted white with a green roof, it must be in Parker Street.

B If a house in Parker Street has a green roof, it must be painted white.

C If a house in Parker Street is painted white, it must have a green fence.

D If a house with a green fence is in Parker Street, it must also have a green roof.

3 Magpies are black and white birds.

Olga made these two statements:

I I saw a bird that was black and white so it must have been a magpie.

II I found a feather. It was black but had no white so it cannot have been from a magpie.

Which statement is correct?

A I but not II   B II but not I

C both I and II   D Neither I nor II

4 At a music college, students study at least one of Music Theory, Voice, Piano or Violin. The following facts are known.

• Music Theory is compulsory for anyone studying Piano.

• Some students study both Piano and Violin.

• All students studying Violin also study Music Theory.

• Some students studying Voice also study Music Theory but do not study either Piano or Violin.

Which must be true?

A More students study Piano than Violin.

B More students study Music Theory than Voice.

C Fewer students study Violin than Voice.

D Fewer students study Piano than Music Theory.

5 A group of people were discussing which of four different types of movies they liked to watch.

Some of the people only liked comedies.

Everyone who liked mysteries also liked comedies.

Everyone who liked sci-fi movies also liked at least one of the other types.

Everyone who liked romance movies also liked mysteries.

Which must be correct?

A Sci-fi movies are the most popular.

B Comedies are the most popular.

C Sci-fi movies are the least popular.

D Romances are the least popular.

☞ **Answers and explanations on pages 206–207**

Real Test 2

6 A person being interviewed made this statement: 'When used correctly, the product always removes chips from paintwork on cars'.

The interviewer produced this table to show that the person's claim was not correct in both cases.

Car owner	Used the product correctly	Chip removed from paintwork
Shannon	Yes	P
Courtney	Q	No

What must have been the values in the table?

A P is Yes and Q is Yes.

B P is Yes and Q is No.

C P is No and Q is Yes.

D P is No and Q is No.

7 Everyone in Class B is older than everyone in Class V. Everyone in Class V is older than everyone in Class P. Everyone in Class P is younger than everyone in Class J.

Based on this information, which must be true?

A If Dave is in Class B, he is older than anyone in Class J.

B If Osman is in Class P, he is younger than anyone in Class V.

C If Hugo is in Class V, he is older than anyone in Class P or Class J.

D If Yvette is in Class J, she is older than anyone in Class V.

8 Georgia, Zac, Fawad, Indi and Millie are playing a game with marbles. The marbles are red, blue, green, yellow and white and each person uses a different colour.

Georgia uses either yellow or blue marbles.

Neither Fawad nor Indi uses red or white marbles.

Neither Millie nor Zac uses green or blue marbles.

Neither Zac nor Fawad uses yellow or green marbles.

Neither Indi nor Millie uses blue or red marbles.

If all of the above statements are true, only one of the sentences below cannot be true. Which one?

A Georgia has the blue marbles.

B Indi has the green marbles.

C Millie has the white marbles.

D Zac has the red marbles.

9 A woman has four children, two boys and two girls, all of different ages. The youngest is a boy.

Which must be true?

A The two girls were born consecutively.

B The oldest is a girl.

C The next child born after at least one of the boys was a girl.

D The next child born after at least one of the girls was a boy.

10 In a sporting competition, five teams, the Diamonds, Rubies, Emeralds, Sapphires and Pearls, played each other once. There were no draws.

The Rubies won all of their matches.

The Pearls lost all of their matches.

The Diamonds won exactly two matches and the Sapphires won exactly one match.

Which cannot be true?

A The Sapphires beat the Emeralds.

B The Diamonds beat the Sapphires.

C The Emeralds beat the Diamonds.

D The Emeralds won exactly three matches.

☞ **Answers and explanations on pages 206-207**

- Problems requiring numerical reasoning usually do not require any special mathematical knowledge. They often involve only **simple addition or subtraction**.
- Read the question **carefully** and make sure you understand exactly what is required.
- Use your **reasoning skills** to solve the problem, working either forwards or backwards through the given information.
- Sometimes you may be able to use the given options to see **which one works**.
- Often it is possible to **check** that your solution is correct.

Example 1

A ferry leaves Packham with passengers and makes two stops, at Westham and Leeville, before reaching its destination, Mayton. At Westham, half the passengers got off the ferry and seven new passengers got on. At Leeville, half of the passengers then on the ferry got off and nine got on. At Mayton, all of the remaining passengers, 20 in total, got off the ferry.

How many passengers were on the ferry when it left Packham?

A 26 　　　　　　　　B 30 　　　　　　　　C 34 　　　　　　　　D 38

Steps to answer the question

1 Read the question carefully and think about what is required.
2 Use the given information and work backwards. (Work forwards as a check.)

B is correct. There were 20 passengers when the ferry reached Mayton. Nine got on at Leeville, so before that there were 11 on the ferry. This was after half got off so half stayed on and half was 11. There were 22 passengers before Leeville. At Westham seven got on, so there were 15 before that. This was half of the original passengers. So 30 passengers were on the ferry when it left Packham.

Example 2

Nelly sells her special cakes for $5 each. She also sells them at slightly lower prices if more than one is bought at the same time. So you can buy 2 for $9, 3 for $13 or 4 for $17.

What is the cheapest price for 11 of Nelly's cakes?

A $50 　　　　　　　　B $48 　　　　　　　　C $47 　　　　　　　　D $45

Steps to answer the question

1 Read the question carefully and think about what is required.
2 To find the cheapest price you need to consider the different ways to buy 11 cakes.
3 Don't assume that the option with the lowest price will be the correct option.

C is correct. You can see that you save $1 when buying 2, $2 when buying 3 and $3 when buying 4. So, if you buy as many 4 packs as you can, followed by 3 packs, you will find the cheapest price. Now 11 = 2 × 4 + 3. So buying two 4-packs and one 3-pack will be the cheapest option. 2 × $17 + $13 = $47. The cheapest price to buy 11 cakes is $47.

Example 3

There were 56 people in a swimming squad. All but 18 won medals in a recent competition. Some won two medals and the others won one medal.

If a total of 65 medals were awarded, how many swimmers won two?

A 11   B 27   C 34   D 38

Steps to answer the question

1   Read the question carefully.
2   Work through the given information.
3   Make sure you give the required answer. In this question it is the number of people who won two medals, not the number who won one medal.

B is the answer. There were 56 people in total and 18 did not win medals. Now 56 – 18 = 38. So 38 people won medals. 65 medals were won altogether. As 65 – 38 = 27, there were 27 more medals won than people who won medals. This means that 27 people must have won two medals.

Checklist

Can you:

1   *read questions carefully and determine what is required?*
2   *work through the given information to find the answer?*
3   *use tables or diagrams if they can be helpful?*
4   *work backwards when required?*
5   *check that your answer is correct?*

Real Test 3

10 MIN

1 A family of seven people—grandfather, mother, father and four children aged 12, 9, 6 and 3—is going to the local show.

Ticket prices

Single: $10

Couple (any 2 people together): $16

Family (any 4 people together): $25

Children (over 4 but under 10): half single price

Children 4 or under: free

What is the cheapest total price the family can pay?

A $30   B $35   C $40   D $41

2 A paddock holds a total of 68 cows and calves. All of the calves, including one pair of twins, belong to cows in the paddock. If there are 30 more cows than calves, how many cows do not have a calf (or two)?

A 19   B 30   C 31   D 38

3 Alexandria sees her doctor on Tuesday 22 July. Her next appointment is for the third Thursday in August.

What is the date of Alexandria's next appointment?

A 20 August   B 21 August   C 22 August   D 23 August

4 There are two classes in Year 6 at Sunnyside School. In Class 6K there are 22 boys and girls altogether and in Class 6P there are 12 boys and 8 girls.

If there are two more boys than girls in Year 6, how many boys are there in 6K?

A 10   B 11   C 12   D 14

5 Maria's car will be out of action for two weeks and she will need to catch a bus to work and back home. The ticket costs are:

One-way	Return	Weekly
$7	$12	$50

Maria works a nine-day fortnight so will go to work on Monday to Friday the first week and Tuesday to Friday of the second week. Each Wednesday Maria will walk from her work to an evening class and get a lift home with a friend.

What is the least amount Maria can pay in fares for the two weeks?

A $90   B $93   C $96   D $100

6 Elsie, Noella and Mary are three sisters. Mary is three times the age of Elsie, who was born 8 years after Mary. The sum of all their ages is three times Noella's age.

How old is Noella?

A 12   B 10   C 9   D 8

☞ **Answers and explanations on pages 207-208**

Real Test 3

7 234 runners entered a race. All those who finished the race were awarded a yellow ribbon. Those who finished within a certain time also received a green ribbon. In total, 287 ribbons were awarded.

If 41 runners did not finish the race, how many received a yellow ribbon but not a green one?

A 53   B 94   C 99   D 193

8 George wants to buy three plants for his garden. Four different nurseries are selling the plants at different prices.

Newman's Nursery sells them for $15 each.

Sergei's Garden Supplies sells them for $20 each, but the third one will be half-price.

Poppy's Plants sells them for $21 each, but Poppy agrees to take $15 off the total.

Hannah's Houseplants sells them for $22 each, but if you buy two you get a third one free.

From which seller will George pay the least?

A Newman   B Sergei   C Poppy   D Hannah

9 A sporting competition will run for two weeks starting on Saturday 8 and finishing on Sunday 23, with different events every day. Tickets cost $10 per day, $15 for two consecutive days and $25 for five consecutive days.

Olly wants to attend on both Saturday and Sunday of the first weekend, then on the following Tuesday, Wednesday and Thursday. He also wants to attend each day beginning Sunday 16 until Wednesday 19 and again on the final Sunday.

What is the least amount that Olly must pay?

A $70   B $75   C $80   D $85

10 There were a total of 47 cars and trucks in the parking lot this morning. Since that time, nine cars and five trucks have left and 12 cars have entered. Now there are eight times as many cars as trucks.

How many cars were there originally?

A 35   B 36   C 37   D 38

☞ **Answers and explanations on pages 207-208**

- **A concept of distance is needed** for some questions, as rulers are not allowed into the examination room. You should know the length of everyday objects. Remember: Most sheets of paper are around 30 cm in length. This is the length of your ruler. Your index finger is around 5 cm in length. These will help you with questions that involve an estimation of length.

  Example: The length of the line •————————————• is close to

  A 2 cm   **B** 7 cm   **C** 15 cm   **D** 22 cm   **E** 26 cm

  The correct answer is **B**. Stretching your finger along the line helps you to estimate.

- **You should know conversions for distance** (10 mm = 1 cm; 100 cm = 1 m; 1000 m = 1 km).

  Example: Which of the following is equal to 3 km plus 16 m plus 2 cm plus 9 mm?

  A 316.209 m   **B** 316.029 m   **C** 3160.029 m   **D** 3016.029 m   **E** 3016.29 m

  The correct answer is **D**. As 3 km = 3000 m, and 3000 + 16 is 3016, the answer could be D or E. 2 cm is 0.02 m and 9 mm is 0.009 m. As 0.02 + 0.009 is 0.029, the length is 3016.029 m.

- **The perimeter of a shape** is the distance around the outside of the shape.

  Example: Find the perimeter of the shape.

  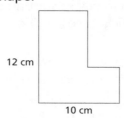

  12 cm

  10 cm

  A 44 cm   **B** 22 cm   **C** 30 cm   **D** 40 cm   **E** 120 cm

  Tip: All the vertical lines add to 12 cm, and all the horizontal sides add to 10 cm.

  The correct answer is **A**, as 2(12 + 10) = 2 × 22 = 44, which means the perimeter is 44 cm.

- **Area is a measure of the space within a plane shape.** The area of a square is side × side, while the area of a rectangle is length × breadth.

  Example: The perimeter of a rectangle is 18 cm. If the length is 5 cm, the area is

  A 20 cm^2 **B** 9 cm^2 **C** 5 cm^2 **D** 15 cm^2 **E** 65 cm^2

  Tip: The sum of the length and width of a rectangle is half the perimeter.

  The correct answer is **A**. As 2 × (5 + width) = 18, then the width is 4 cm. This means the area is 5 × 4 = 20, which is 20 cm^2.

Checklist

Can you:

1 *accurately guess the length of everyday objects?*
2 *convert between units of measurement?*
3 *solve problems involving calculations of perimeter and area?*

Real Test 1

MATHEMATICAL REASONING
Length and area

10 min

1 The distance around the outside of a car tyre (the circumference) is 1.5 m.
How many revolutions does the tyre make on a journey of 30 km?

200	2000	20 000	200 000	20
A	B	C	D	E

2 Robert knows that the perimeter of a rectangle is 24 cm and that its length is three times its width. This means that the width of the rectangle is

8 cm	4 cm	3 cm	6 cm	2 cm
A	B	C	D	E

3 A photograph measures 22 cm by 12 cm and is to be mounted inside a timber frame with a border of 4 cm between the photograph and the frame. What length of timber frame is needed to complete the job?

1 m	88 cm	96 cm	1.2 m	1.04 m
A	B	C	D	E

4 An equilateral triangle and a rectangle with identical perimeters are pictured below. The side length of the triangle is the same as the length of the rectangle.

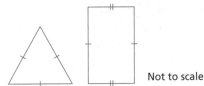

Not to scale

If the perimeter of the triangle is 48 cm, what is the width of the rectangle?

6 cm	8 cm	10 cm	12 cm	16 cm
A	B	C	D	E

5 Two small rectangles are removed from a large rectangle. All measurements are in centimetres.

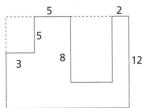

Not to scale

What is the perimeter of the remaining shape?

A 26 cm
B 48 cm
C 52 cm
D 60 cm
E 68 cm

6 A square and a rectangle with the same areas are cut from a large rectangle.

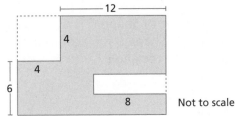

Not to scale

What fraction of the original rectangle remains?

$\frac{5}{8}$	$\frac{3}{4}$	$\frac{2}{3}$	$\frac{7}{8}$	$\frac{4}{5}$
A	B	C	D	E

7 The large square has been cut into smaller squares, and some squares have been shaded. The area of the smallest shaded square is 4 cm^2.

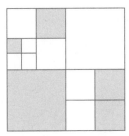

What is the area that remains unshaded?
A 140 cm^2
B 148 cm^2
C 156 cm^2
D 160 cm^2
E 180 cm^2

☞ **Answers and explanations on pages 208–209**

Real
Test 1

MATHEMATICAL REASONING
Length and area

8 Ellie has identical rectangles. She uses two of the rectangles to make Shape *A* and three rectangles to make Shape *B*.

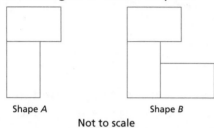

Shape *A*   Shape *B*

Not to scale

The perimeter of Shape *A* is 44 cm and the perimeter of Shape *B* is 60 cm. What is the length of the rectangle?

A 4 cm

B 8 cm

C 12 cm

D 16 cm

E 20 cm

9 Two identical squares *PQRS* and *WXYZ* overlap to form a rectangle *PXYS* of dimensions 12 cm by 8 cm.

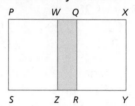

What is the area of the shaded rectangle *WQRZ*?

A 12 cm²

B 16 cm²

C 20 cm²

D 24 cm²

E 32 cm²

10 A rectangle and an equilateral triangle are pictured.

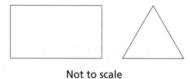

Not to scale

The perimeter of the triangle is 80% the perimeter of the rectangle. The length of the rectangle is twice its width. What is the length of the rectangle if a side of the triangle is 40 cm?

25 cm	32 cm	48 cm	50 cm	64 cm
A	B	C	D	E

☞ **Answers and explanations on pages 208–209**

Real Test 2

MATHEMATICAL REASONING
Length and area

1 A rectangle is 3 cm longer than it is wide. When the width is increased to form a square, the perimeter is 20 cm. What was the original width of the square?

1 cm	2 cm	3 cm	4 cm	5 cm
A	B	C	D	E

2 The perimeter of a regular octagon is 2 m. This means the length of each side is

125 mm	250 mm	25 mm	80 mm	333 mm
A	B	C	D	E

3 A piece of wire 2.4 cm in length is bent to form a square. Find the area of the shape.

A 3600 mm²

B 3.6 mm²

C 360 mm²

D 36 000 mm²

E 36 mm²

4 The two shapes have the same perimeter.

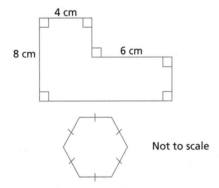

Not to scale

What is the length of each side of the regular hexagon?

3 cm	4 cm	6 cm	8 cm	10 cm
A	B	C	D	E

5 Square P has a perimeter of 24 cm. The area of square Q is nine times the area of square P. What is the perimeter of square Q?

72 cm	96 cm	144 cm	192 cm	216 cm
A	B	C	D	E

6 Four identical squares are removed from a rectangle. The perimeter of the new shape is 44 cm.

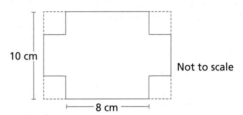

10 cm

8 cm

Not to scale

What is the total area of the removed squares?

4 cm²	8 cm²	16 cm²	24 cm²	32 cm²
A	B	C	D	E

7 Part of a square is shaded. Equal lengths are shown on the diagram.

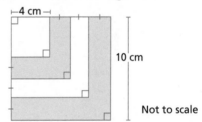

4 cm

10 cm

Not to scale

What is the total area that is shaded?

A 48 cm²

B 56 cm²

C 60 cm²

D 62 cm²

E 64 cm²

8 Pete uses identical rectangles to make two shapes. The perimeter of Shape P is 56 cm and the perimeter of Shape Q is 68 cm.

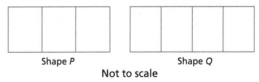

Shape P   Shape Q

Not to scale

What is the area of Shape P?

A 120 cm²   B 144 cm²

C 160 cm²   D 180 cm²

E 240 cm²

☞ **Answers and explanations on page 209**

Real Test 2

MATHEMATICAL REASONING
Length and area

9 The diagram shows a square of side length 6 cm and a rectangle measuring 12 cm by 8 cm. One-quarter of the surface of the rectangle is covered by the square.

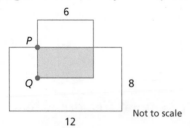

6

P

Q

8

12

Not to scale

What is the length of *PQ*?

A   3 cm

B   4 cm

C   4.25 cm

D   4.5 cm

E   4.8 cm

10 The diagram shows a large square made from a small square and four identical rectangles. The perimeter of one of the rectangles is 24 cm.

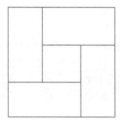

What is the area of the small square?

A   6 cm²

B   9 cm²

C   16 cm²

D   25 cm²

E   36 cm²

☞ **Answers and explanations on page 209**

MATHEMATICAL REASONING
Volume, capacity, mass, speed and time

- **Volume is a measure of the space within a solid.** The volume of a rectangular prism is length × breadth × height.

  Example: The volume of the rectangular prism is 24 cm³.
  What is the area of the shaded face?

  A 8 cm²   B 2 cm²   C 6 cm²   D 12 cm²   E 9 cm²

Tip: Volume of a prism = Area of base × height

  The correct answer is **C**. As 4 × 3 × height = 24, then
  height is 2 cm. This means the area of the shaded face is 2 × 3 = 6. The area is 6 cm².

- **Conversions:** A square with sides 100 m has an area of
  1 hectare (1 ha = 10 000 m²).

  Example: The diagram shows a square paddock of length 2 km.
  Find the area of the paddock in hectares.

  A 4 ha   B 40 ha   C 400 ha   D 4000 ha   E 0.4 ha

  The correct answer is **C**. As 2 km = 2000 m, the area is 2000 × 2000 = 4 000 000. Changing to hectares, 4 000 000 ÷ 10 000 = 400.

- **Capacity:** The basic unit is the litre (L), where 1000 mL = 1 L and 1000 L = 1 kL.

  Example: A truck carries 60 cartons of soft drinks, each containing 24 cans. If each can contains 375 mL, the amount of soft drink in litres on the truck is

  A $\dfrac{60 \times 24}{375 \times 1000}$ B $\dfrac{1000 \times 60 \times 24}{375}$ C $\dfrac{375 \times 1000}{60 \times 24}$ D $\dfrac{375 \times 60 \times 24}{1000}$ E $\dfrac{375 \times 60 \div 1000}{24}$

  The correct answer is **D**, as 375 × 60 × 24 gives the number of millilitres. Divide by 1000 to convert to litres.

- **Mass:** The basic unit is the kilogram (kg), where 1000 kg = 1 t, 1000 g = 1 kg, and so on.

  Example: The mass of an unopened jar of strawberry jam is 500 g. When half the jam is used, the jar is weighed again and its mass is 300 g. The mass of an empty jar would be about

  A 100 g   B 50 g   C 120 g   D 140 g   E 200 g

  The correct answer is **A**, as half the jam has a mass of 200 g. This means the mass of the entire contents is 400 g and the jar weighs 100 g.

- You should be able to find the number of minutes between **different times** on a digital clock.

  Example: The amount of time from 10:57 am to 3:25 pm is

  A 228 minutes   B 2588 minutes   C 268 minutes   D 278 minutes   E 468 minutes

  The correct answer is **C**. From 10:57 to 11:00 is 3 minutes, then 240 minutes (4 hours) to 3 pm, then 25 minutes. This means 3 + 240 + 25 = 268.

MATHEMATICAL REASONING
Volume, capacity, mass, speed and time

- **You should know time differences.**

    Example: The table shows the local times in a number of international cities when it is 10:45 pm in Sydney. Later in the day, when it is 3 pm in New York, what is the local time in Paris?

     Tip: Use the table to find time differences between cities.

City	Local time
Paris	13:45
New York	08:45
Sydney	22:45

    A 10 am   **B** 8 pm   **C** 5 pm   **D** 1:45 pm   **E** 1 pm

    The correct answer is **B**, as Paris is 5 hours ahead of New York. This means 3 pm plus 5 hours is 8 pm.

- **You should be able to calculate distance, speed and time.**

    Example: Gavin travels 320 km in 4 hours. His average speed is

    A 80 km/h   **B** 8 km/h   **C** 64 km/h   **D** 85 km/h   **E** 128 km/h

     Tip: Distance = speed × time, speed = distance ÷ time, time = distance ÷ speed

    The correct answer is **A**. As speed = distance ÷ time, then 320 ÷ 4 = 80. This means Gavin has an average speed of 80 km/h.

Checklist

Can you:

1 *convert between units of measurement?*

2 *solve problems involving calculations of volume, capacity, mass, time and speed?*

Real Test 3

MATHEMATICAL REASONING
Volume, capacity, mass, speed and time

10 MIN

1 Water collected from a roof measuring 20 m by 10 m runs into a tank. On one day 50 mm of rain fell. If 1 L = 1000 cm³, how many litres were collected?

10 L	100 L	1000 L	10 000 L	1 L
A	B	C	D	E

2 A tap drips 8 mL in every drop. If it drips every 4 seconds, how much water, in litres, is lost every week?

A $8 \times 4 \times 60 \times 24 \times 7$

B $\dfrac{8 \times 15 \times 60 \times 24 \times 7}{1000}$

C $\dfrac{8 \times 60 \times 60 \times 24 \times 7}{1000}$

D $\dfrac{8 \times 15 \times 24 \times 7}{1000}$

E $8 \times 15 \times 60 \times 24 \times 7$

3 Costa takes 10 mL of medicine three times a day from a bottle containing 270 mL. How many days will the medicine last?

27 days	10 days	9 days	8 days	25 days
A	B	C	D	E

4 Celia walks for 16 km at 8 km/h, rests for 3 hours, then walks for 24 km at 6 km/h. If she starts her journey at 6 am, what time will she complete her journey?

noon	2 pm	3 pm	5 pm	6 pm
A	B	C	D	E

5 Using the table, if it is 3:20 am on Wednesday in Singapore, what is the local time in Johannesburg?

City	Local time
Sydney	Mon 2:45 pm
Singapore	Mon 11:45 am
Mumbai	Mon 9:15 am
Johannesburg	Mon 5:45 am
London	Mon 3:45 am
New York	Sun 10:45 pm

A 9:20 am on Wednesday

B 9:20 pm on Tuesday

C 9:20 am on Tuesday

D 9:20 pm on Wednesday

E 9:20 am on Thursday

6 A plane leaves Mumbai at 5:20 pm on Friday (local time) and arrives in Sydney at 11:50 am on Saturday (local time). Use the table in question 5 to work out how long the flight was from Mumbai to Sydney.

A 13 h   B 18 h 30 min

C 5 h 30 min   D 11 h

E 6 h 30 min

7 Jacob catches a train at 1440. He is on the train for three-quarters of an hour. What time does he get off the train, in 12-hour format?

A 4:45 am   B 2:25 pm   C 3:05 pm

D 3:15 pm   E 3:25 pm

8 When full, a glass holds 360 mL. It is half full of water. Sophia drinks 40 mL of water from the glass. She then opens a bottle containing 1 L of water and fills her glass to the top. How much water is now in the bottle?

A 600 mL   B 640 mL   C 680 mL

D 780 mL   E 860 mL

9 An empty container is placed on a set of scales. The digital display shows a mass of 80 g. Layla places four identical blocks in the container. The scales now show a mass of 2.5 kg. Three blocks are now removed. What mass will be shown on the display?

A 605 g   B 625 g

C 645 g   D 665 g

E 685 g

10 The time in Chicago is 15 hours behind Sydney. The time in Mumbai is $4\frac{1}{2}$ hours behind Sydney.

Ryilee lives in Chicago and starts a video call to her friend Amaira in Mumbai at 8:20 am Chicago time. The call lasts for 26 minutes. What was the local time in Mumbai when the call ended?

A 6:16 pm   B 6:46 pm   C 7:16 pm

D 7:46 pm   E 11:16 pm

☞ **Answers and explanations on page 210**

Real Test 4

MATHEMATICAL REASONING
Volume, capacity, mass, speed and time

10 MIN

1 The average mass of three boys is 40 kg. When a fourth boy is included, the average mass is increased by 5 kg. The mass of this fourth boy is

45 kg	50 kg	70 kg	60 kg	20 kg
A	B	C	D	E

2 A concrete slab is to be laid for a garden shed. The area of the slab is measured as 5 m by 4 m, and will be concreted to a depth of 20 cm. The amount of concrete required is

4 m^3	2 m^3	6 m^3	8 m^3	0.8 m^3
A	B	C	D	E

The table is used to answer questions 3 and 4.

City	Local time
Auckland	Saturday 12:27
London	Friday 23:27
Boston	Friday 18:27

3 If it is 8:20 pm on Monday in Boston, what is the local time in Auckland?
- A 2:20 pm Monday
- B 2:20 pm Tuesday
- C 2:20 am Monday
- D 2:20 am Tuesday
- E 2:20 pm Sunday

4 Jordan lives in Auckland and when it is 8:50 pm he rings his girlfriend Delta in London. They talk for 12 minutes. What time (in London) does Delta complete the phone call?

8:02 pm	7:02 pm	8:02 am	7:02 am	12:02 pm
A	B	C	D	E

5 Elijah has just finished watching a movie at the cinemas. The film ran for 112 minutes. If it is now 1905, at what time did the movie commence, in 12-hour format?

4:53 pm	4:57 pm	5:13 pm	5:15 pm	5:57 pm
A	B	C	D	E

6 Nupur has a glass and a jug both containing water.

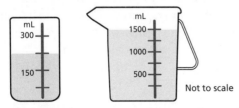

Not to scale

Nupur drinks 100 mL of water from the glass. She then uses the jug to fill the glass to the 300 mL level.

How much water remains in the jug?
- A 1250 mL
- B 1275 mL
- C 1325 mL
- D 1350 mL
- E 1375 mL

7 Bianca measures the mass of an unopened jar of tomato paste. The mass is 670 g. The label on the jar reads that it contains 510 g of tomato paste. Bianca uses half of the tomato paste for lasagna. What will be the mass if the jar is now placed on a set of scales?

415 g	285 g	425 g	435 g	455 g
A	B	C	D	E

8 Eleanor has three objects: a prism, a cylinder and a cone.
- The prism and the cylinder have a combined mass of 16.5 kg.
- The cylinder and the cone have a combined mass of 16.2 kg.
- The prism and the cone have a combined mass of 17.3 kg.

What is the total mass of the three objects?

16.7 kg	50 kg	27 kg	30 kg	25 kg
A	B	C	D	E

9 Willow lives in Paris and she visits her brother Jack who lives in Sydney. Willow leaves Paris on Wednesday at 1930 local time on a 14-hour flight to Singapore. She spends 4 hours in the airport. She then catches an 8-hour flight to Sydney. The time in Paris is 9 hours behind the time in Sydney. What time is it in Sydney when Willow arrives?
- A 1730 on Thursday
- B 1930 on Thursday
- C 0530 on Friday
- D 0630 on Friday
- E 0730 on Friday

10 A digital clock is showing 6:54, where the digits are consecutive and in a descending order. How many minutes will pass until the clock is showing digits that are consecutive, but in an ascending order?
- A 240 minutes
- B 258 minutes
- C 289 minutes
- D 340 minutes
- E 383 minutes

☞ **Answers and explanations on pages 210–211**

- A narrative is a text that **tells a story about events in a way that entertains and interests the audience**. It might be true or imaginary, funny or serious. A narrative should keep the reader interested right to the very end.

- A narrative is different from a recount. A recount simply tells about events in the order that they happened, as in a diary or biography, for example. A narrative **introduces at least one event that is unusual or interesting in some way**, and that then 'drives' the story.

- Narratives are **challenging texts to write in tests**. It can be difficult to think of good ideas and shape them into an interesting short story in half an hour or less.

  ○ So if you **do not** feel confident about writing stories, and you are given a choice about how to write, it would be best to avoid narratives. Sometimes, however, you may not get a choice, so it is worth practising them now.

  ○ If you **do** feel confident about writing stories, then it might be best to choose this kind of writing if you are given a choice. But remember: You will have a lot less time than you usually do to write a good story. So again, practice with a time limit is useful.

- **Your own experiences are extremely useful** for writing narratives—especially in test conditions. You don't have much time to think up imaginary characters and settings (though you might be able to if you are a very good story writer).

  So it is a good idea to think about your life and about things that have happened to you before you go in to the test. You might be able to write a story, for example, about your family, your class, a favourite possession, or a place you go for holidays. You might use an experience of winning or losing a competition, getting or losing a pet, a new baby in the house, or a new friend in the street.

- There are many **different kinds of stimulus** materials used in these tests as story prompts—for example, a picture, a story title, the first or last sentences of a story, a group of words, or even a piece of writing (e.g. a note, a text message, a newspaper advertisement). In all cases, there will be many ways to respond to the prompt. There is no single right or best way.

- On the next page is an example of a narrative written in response to a test question, though not under test conditions. In your test, you **might not have time** to produce a polished piece of writing like this. However, if you are **well prepared**, you will be able to aim for this standard.

Sample

WRITING
Narrative response

10 MIN

Question

Write a story with the title *The Race* or *The Competition*.

Response

Structure

Title—Make one up if none is given—this adds interest to your story.

Orientation tells your reader about who, what, when, where, and grabs the reader's attention

Short paragraphs help build interest and tension

Complication—unusual or interesting event or events

Climax—highest point of excitement or tension

Resolution—complication is resolved (e.g. a problem is solved, a task is done)

Comment on events

The Race

I was being pounded to the ground. My body shrieked with pain. Suddenly I sat bolt upright with a horrified gasp, and opened my eyes. My breathing was harsh and uneven and I was shivering with terror. I'd just had another ghastly nightmare about the school cross-country race!

It wasn't surprising that I was terrified. I was the smallest in the class and the worst runner.

The actual race was a disaster from the beginning. Someone's elbow crashed into my ribs and winded me. Then I was kicked on the shin and shoved onto the muddy ground.

A mixture of pain and determination pulled me to my feet. I didn't care if I died at the end of the race, as long as I finished. My legs felt as though they would collapse and I was breathing like a hoarse old dog.

The race had barely started and the leaders were out of sight. I despaired but concentrated fiercely on one step at a time.

Suddenly there was a crashing sound in front of me. I heard shouting and swearing as my short legs dodged nimbly around an enormous pile of waving arms and legs sliding around in a mud patch! Amazingly, there were now only three runners between me and the finishing line.

Then the miracle happened. The front runner gasped for air and knocked over the second runner. He slipped sideways, and tripped the third. For a brief few seconds I seemed to be the only one in the entire race still running.

I was going to win! The crowd was cheering for me! I felt triumphant, powerful and unbeatable. How envious my taunters would be!

Suddenly I collapsed to the ground. My outstretched hand was just short of the line. I was going to lose! The other competitors thundered up. I lunged under the tape, as the crowd gasped. Then the front runners stampeded over me.

Afterwards I lay collapsed on the ground, heaving for breath, bloody and bruised. An ear-splitting grin cracked the mud covering my face. I had won. Short kids could do big things!

Reproduced with permission of Cameron Little.

Language

Rich, **descriptive language**

First person narration—writer is a character in the story (in some stories the writer is 'outside' the story)

Interesting images

Vivid, precise **action verbs** and **adverbs**

Thinking and **feeling verbs**

Past tense (some stories use present tense throughout)

Correct **spelling, grammar** and **punctuation**

Practice Tasks

WRITING
Narrative response—Getting started

50 MIN

These tasks will give you some ideas about how to start writing quickly and complete an interesting narrative in the short time you have in the test.

You will have to look back at *The Race* to answer some questions, and then do some narrative writing yourself based on the practice writing question below.

Look at the question now before you start the tasks.

Practice writing question

Write a story using this single word as a prompt. You may use the word in your story as a title, beginning or ending, or you may simply make the word the story theme.

FREEDOM

- The first thing to do is to **brainstorm some story ideas**. There are always many different ways to interpret a story theme. *The Race* is about a cross-country race, but it could have been about many other kinds of races or competitions, for example:

  ○ a race between two friends, or brothers or sisters

  ○ a spelling competition

  ○ a race between two countries to reach another planet

  ○ a race against the clock in an exam.

  You also have to decide what kind of story you are going to write—whether it will be funny, happy, sad, mysterious, realistic, fantasy, and so on. **Write the kind of story you are best at**.

 Tip: Don't try anything too complicated or you will not finish in time. Remember: You are only writing about one and a half pages.

- In a test, you do not have time to do a detailed plan of your story before starting writing, but it is important to spend a few minutes working out a **rough plan** of how your story will develop. If you start without any plan at all, you risk writing on and on without knowing where you are going. You might fill up the pages, but you won't write a successful story.

- Many stories follow the basic narrative stages of *The Race*—**orientation, complication and resolution. Some also have a climax, and some have a comment (coda)** at the end. There are other ways to structure stories, but this broad structure can help you get going quickly in a test.

Here is the plan for *The Race*.

Orientation	cross-country race—nightmare—real race—everyone beating me
Complication	everyone falls over, one by one
Climax	I fall over
Resolution	I win

Practice Tasks

💡 *Tip:* Also think about these questions before you start:

● Will I write myself into the story (I watched, we watched) OR will I be 'outside' the story (he watched, they watched)?

● Will I write in the present tense (She stops suddenly) OR the past tense (She stopped suddenly)?

Task 1

Think about the practice writing question on page 105 and jot down two or three story ideas.

_____

_____

_____

_____

Task 2

Choose one of the ideas from Task 1. Now do a brief, rough plan for your idea. Use the headings below, or use your own paper if you have ideas about a different kind of story structure. Give yourself about two minutes.

Orientation _____

_____

_____

Complication _____

_____

_____

_____

_____

Resolution _____

_____

_____

Practice Tasks

- Your orientation should **capture the reader's attention** and make them interested in reading further. It usually also tells the reader **what or who** the story is about, and **where or when** the events are happening. It might also tell something about **why or how**.

- The orientation is often just the first paragraph, but sometimes it is much longer (as in *The Race*).

Task 3

Fill in the blanks to show what you know about *The Race* by the end of the orientation.

The Race is about a school _____, and the main character is very _____

and a _____ runner. He has a _____ about the race, and then the

_____ race starts out just like the nightmare.

Task 4

Now write the orientation for the practice writing question (page 105) using your rough plan. Try to grab the reader's attention at the same time as orienting them to who, what, where and when. Give yourself about five minutes.

_____

_____

_____

_____

_____

_____

_____

_____

_____

_____

_____

_____

_____

_____

_____

☞ **Answers and explanations on page 211**

Practice Tasks

- Your ideas and the way you express them are as important as good structure. Even if your narrative does not work exactly as you want it, you will still get marks for expressing your ideas well—**creating clear and vivid images** of the characters and the action.

- There are many ways to do this. You might use an unusual **simile** to compare two things. For example, in *The Race* the main character 'was breathing like a hoarse old dog'. Or you might simply choose **rich, vivid, interesting words** such as these from the story: 'ghastly', 'triumphant', 'envious', 'taunters'.

- Another way to create vivid images is to choose action verbs that precisely describe what is happening. For example, don't use went or walked or ran if you can use a more precise and expressive verb, such as rushed, slipped, stamped, slid, trudged, slithered or fled.

- Also try to be precise about the **way people speak**. Don't just use 'say' or 'said' the whole way through your story. Instead, use interesting verbs such as wail, shriek, announce, protest, whimper and gasp.

- 💡 *Tip:* In such a short story you would not use much dialogue, but if you do, remember to use quotation (speech) marks if you write exactly what your characters say.

Task 5

The original verbs from these extracts from *The Race* have been replaced with more common, less precise ones. Find the more interesting verbs used by the writer and underline them in the text.

1 I was being <u>pushed</u> to the ground. (paragraph 1)

2 … and <u>pushed</u> onto the muddy ground. (paragraph 3)

3 … my short legs <u>stepped</u> nimbly around … (paragraph 6)

4 The other competitors <u>ran</u> up. (paragraph 9)

5 I <u>moved</u> under the tape … (paragraph 9)

6 Then the front runners <u>ran</u> over me. (paragraph 9)

Task 6

Underline the words or sentences in *The Race* used to express the following ideas.

1 the narrator's pain (paragraph 1)

2 the runners after they fell over (paragraph 6)

3 the narrator's happiness at the end of the race (paragraph 10)

☞ **Answers and explanations on page 211**

Practice Tasks

WRITING
Narrative response—Writing the complication

- The complication is the unusual or interesting event that makes your writing into a narrative rather than just a recount of what happened. Generally the complication will be funny or unusual, or spooky or exciting, or sad.

- *Tip:* Even if you have written about your own experiences, you will usually need to invent something to make your complication.

- **Stick to your rough plan and try to make it work.** In general, you won't have time to change your mind and start going in a different direction. Of course, you might get an absolutely brilliant brainwave that leads you to write something completely different from your plan!

- Some narratives build up to one especially interesting or exciting event (the **climax**). For example, in *The Race* the main character falls over just before the line.

- *Tip:* Many stories have more than one complicating event. However, in the time you have to write for the test, it is probably best to stick to one or maybe two.

Task 7

1 Circle the correct answer. The first complicating event of *The Race* is that
  a   the main character falls over in the mud.
  b   all the runners fall over in the mud.
  c   most of the runners fall over in the mud.

2 Is there a second complicating event and, if so, what is it?

_____

_____

_____

_____

☞ **Answers and explanations on page 211**

Practice Tasks

Task 8

Now write the complication for your story. Try to include words and sentences that create vivid images of the characters and the action. Give yourself about ten minutes.

_____

_____

_____

_____

_____

_____

_____

_____

_____

_____

_____

_____

_____

_____

_____

_____

_____

_____

_____

_____

_____

_____

_____

_____

_____

_____

- You have to end your story somehow. For example, you might have the character solve a problem, reveal a mystery, complete a task, or explain why someone did something. The end—or resolution—can be the most difficult part to write, so think about how you will end your story when you are planning.
- Many stories end with a comment of some kind (e.g. a warning, a lesson or a funny comment). This can be a good way to 'wrap up' a story and bring it to a quick conclusion. In *The Race*, the writer uses his story to make the point that 'Short kids could do big things'.

Tip: Your ending does not have to be 'neat'. You can leave things 'up in the air'.

Task 9

Write a resolution for your story. Add a comment to end it if you think it would improve your story. Give yourself about five minutes.

_____

_____

_____

_____

_____

_____

_____

_____

_____

Note: If you like, you can work on your narrative some more, refining what you have written so far and writing it out again on your own paper. Use the checklist below to review your writing.

Checklist for writing a description
Have you:
1 *written at least one sentence to orient the reader and to capture their attention?*
2 *included an event that gives interest to the story and makes it worth telling?*
3 *resolved the story in some way?*
4 *used vivid, interesting images to describe people, things and activities—for example, through verbs, adjectives, similes?*
5 *checked your grammar, punctuation and spelling?*

Remember: In the test you won't have time to revise thoroughly and make big changes. You may have time to change a few words, but you will really be aiming to do a good piece of writing in one draft.

Real Test

- Choose **one** of the writing tests below to do now. Each test gives you the opportunity to write in many different ways, but you should write a narrative to practise all the points you have just revised.

- Use your own paper. You are encouraged to use two or three sheets of paper. Use the first one for planning and rough work, and do your response on the second and third sheets.

- If you wish, you could do both tests. However, it would be better to do them on different days. For extra practice, you could use the tests again, writing in different ways each time.

- Set yourself a time limit of 25 or 30 minutes, depending on the test you are sitting. Use the checklist on page 111 to give it a quick review.

---

1 Use this picture as the basis for your writing. You might choose to write a story, letter, a poem, or another kind of writing.

OR

2 Write a story or other text that includes the word 'stranger'. You might like to make this the title of your story, but that is not necessary.

☞ **Checklist on page 111**

Only one week to go!

Week 4

This is what we cover this week:

Day 1   **Reading:** Varied short texts

Day 2   **Thinking Skills:**
- ◎ Problem solving—Position and order
- ◎ Problem solving—Logic problems and contradictions
- ◎ Problem solving—Thinking outside the square

Day 3   **Mathematical Reasoning:**
- ◎ Space and geometry
- ◎ Statistics and probability

Day 4   **Writing:** Persuasive text

- In this section of the test you will be asked to match **short text extracts** to questions relating to their content. This question type is used in the Selective Schools Test *only* at present, but practice with it will help you develop your reading skills and benefit you when sitting any test.

> *Remember:* You must check the format of the test you are going to do.

- You will be given a set of **four short texts** to read. Each will be on the **same broad theme** as all the others in the set, but they will vary to some extent in content and style. The texts could be, for example, extracts from novels, personal reflections, information reports, cartoons, advertisements, diaries, newspaper articles, film or book reviews.

- To answer the questions, you will have to think about the main idea, the supporting ideas, the text purpose or the attitude of the writer. Or you might have to look for very specific detail. You will sometimes meet unfamiliar words or phrases and, if so, you will have to **use context and understanding of word parts** to work them out in order to make sense of the text and answer the questions.

- The best way to approach this kind of task is to quickly glance at the questions first to get an idea of what you are being asked to do. Then you should read each text. You must read quickly however. You won't be asked about every single bit of information in the text—you will only have to pick up **two or three ideas from each**.

- As you read, you might start getting some ideas about **which questions relate to which texts**. Make some light marks to show this and keep reading.

- When you have finished the texts, go back and read the questions one by one, and for each question, scan back over each text to see if it matches the question. If you find one that does match the question, **check all the other texts again to make sure they do not also match it**.

- Because each of the texts in the set is on the same general theme, you will sometimes find more than one text which seems right. You will then have to look more closely to **choose the best of those two**.

- Sometimes you will see something in one text that is close to the idea in the question and quickly decide the answer, but **there might be another text which is much closer to the idea**. You will have to be **very careful to check** and recheck your answer all the way through the task.

Practice Task 1

READING
Varied short texts

15 MIN

Use this first practice task as a guide. Read the questions and texts and answer as you think best. Then look at the answers to get explanations of why those answers are correct. The aim is to give you practice with the type of question. It may be a little different from what you are familiar with in reading comprehension tests. Don't worry about time with this first task although you can aim for 15 minutes, but try to improve your speed with the following practice tasks.

For questions 1–10, choose the text which you think best answers the questions.

Which extract …

focuses mainly on the experiences of those who fly the craft?　　**1** _____

describes the important parts of the flying craft?　　**2** _____

describes a psychological response to flying?　　**3** _____

suggests one aspect of the flying experience might surprise some people?　　**4** _____

mentions the usefulness of knowing something about how flying works?　　**5** _____

refers to a physical difficulty of flying?　　**6** _____

refers to the expertise of those who fly the craft?　　**7** _____

explains the mechanisms of flight?　　**8** _____

gives an idea of how many can travel in the flying craft?　　**9** _____

refers to the daily work tasks of the people who work in the flying craft?　　**10** _____

Extract A

What would you ask an astronaut if you got a chance? Here are some examples of questions asked recently of International Space Station astronauts.

Q: What do you do all day?
A: Each morning we get a schedule with tasks to do from morning to night. Then we repair things, we install hardware and we do physical training. Most of the time, however, we do scientific experiments of one kind or another.

Q: What is it like to float around?
A: It's a lot of fun but frustrating too. Here you put something down and then you know where to find it again. Up there you put it down and you might not find it for weeks or even months later.

Q: How long does it take to get used to zero gravity?
A: It takes three or four days the first time you fly and it can make you feel quite sick. The second time, your brain remembers and you adjust pretty quickly.

Q: Why do astronauts get weaker in space?
A: The earth's gravity makes you work when you just stand and walk around. Up in space, there is only a little bit of gravity—microgravity. Your muscles don't have to work as much and so they get weaker.

Q: What's it like to see planet Earth in the window of the spacecraft?
A: It simply takes your breath away.

☞ **Answers and explanations on page 211**

Practice Task 1

Extract B

Many people get anxious when they fly. The minute they step onto the plane they start to feel enclosed by the hard shapes all around them and the tiny space allotted to them for the hours and hours ahead of them. The smiles of the cabin crew might help at the start but many experience an uprush of fear again when the plane leaves the comforting solidity of earth. All of this is normal. Who wouldn't feel a little anxious about being trapped in the air 10 kilometres above ground and travelling at around 800 kilometres an hour? But many people experience something far greater. They avoid getting on a plane at all costs but, if they really must fly, they experience panic attacks and severe anxiety. These people are aerophobic. Luckily such people can get help from therapists who get them firstly to acknowledge their fear and not be embarrassed about it. They may also advise their clients to get educated about planes and safety, for example, to learn how planes stay up in the air. Setting a firm date to travel is also a very good way to get one acting on solving the problem.

Extract C

Our pilots will help to make your hot air balloon trip an exhilarating and safe experience. We have flown several thousand people and they have all ended up having the experience of their lives. Statistically, you are more likely to be injured in your car than in a balloon ride. Balloons are very safe. A main reason is that, unlike fixed wing aircraft, hot air balloons only fly in good weather and slow wind. No steering wheel is used but instead the pilots use the winds to control the balloon's direction. You might expect to feel rocking from side to side when taking off and landing, but while there is some rocking, you won't really feel much movement at all. You also might think you would feel a lot of wind when up in the air, but you don't, because you are travelling with the wind. Occasionally balloons have to land in high wind, but our pilots are expert at understanding the wind and local weather conditions and are able to land your balloon safely. When coming on our balloon adventures you must be sure to listen to the safety briefing before take-off in case a fast wind landing is necessary, and of course you must always follow any pilot instructions.

Extract D

A hot air balloon is a unique flying craft which works because hot air rises. By heating the air inside the balloon it becomes lighter than the cooler air around it and this causes the balloon to float upwards as if it were in water. If the air inside cools, the balloon comes down. A modern hot air balloon has three parts. First there is the balloon itself or the 'envelope'—a bag made of strong light nylon with an opening at one end. This is laid out on the ground before flight and partially filled with cold air from fans before the air is heated. This is attached with very strong metal cable to the envelope. It has reinforced frames and is often clad in woven wicker. These baskets vary in size but can carry up to 24 people. Lastly there is the burner—or the 'engine' of the balloon. It is attached above the basket and under the envelope. The pilot pulls a valve which fires the burner and aims the flame into the balloon to heat the air inside.

☞ **Answers and explanations on page 190**

Practice Task 2

15 MIN

Read the questions and texts and answer as you think best. Then look at the answers to get explanations of why and how those answers are correct. Try to work quickly but, again, don't worry if you can't finish in 15 minutes.

For questions 1–10, choose the text which you think best answers the questions.

Which extract …

mentions the pleasure of caring for animals? **1** _____

explains that animals don't always do what is good for them? **2** _____

refers to the need for humans to use their natural advantages for the good of all? **3** _____

mentions a specific example of humans unintentionally harming wildlife in their gardens? **4** _____

refers to the difficulty of understanding a natural behaviour or event? **5** _____

argues the need to look at early signals of danger to our environment? **6** _____

mentions methods to change the usual behaviour of wildlife? **7** _____

mentions the view that we should not interfere with nature even if a species is in danger? **8** _____

suggests an experience with wildlife has changed someone's life? **9** _____

argues the case for human intervention to protect species in danger? **10** _____

Extract A

According to biologist Dr David Croft, Australian mammals have a 'fatal attraction'. The lush vegetation that is often found at the side of roads appears to be irresistible to native animals such as kangaroos and wombats, placing them at risk of being hit by passing cars. David is leading a team at the University of New South Wales, looking at ways to reduce the number of collisions between animals and cars on Australian roads. 'We will try to develop technologies to discourage animals from being on the side of the road, and inform people about animal behaviour so that they can drive more appropriately to avoid collision,' says David. One way that roadsides could be made less attractive to animals might be to drain nutrient-rich run-off further away from the roadside. Also, the team is investigating if spraying roadside vegetation with synthetic dog urine will trick the animals into believing that the roadside is the territory of predators. By examining the behaviour of animals, David hopes to provide drivers with road safety information for preventing collisions, which can also be dangerous for human travellers. 'We are conducting controlled passes along roads to see how predictable their reactions are,' says David. 'The key thing is they are unpredictable, and that's why people hit them.'

From *The Helix*, Number 93, December 2003 – January 2004 © Janet Bultitude 2003; reproduced with permission

☞ Answers and explanations on page 212

Practice Task 2

Extract B

Endangered species programs are the reason we have such diverse flora and fauna still with us in Australia. Without these programs many of Australia's native plants and animals would have become extinct years, even decades ago. Some people might not think that these species are important but we do need them. We help them for their own survival and for the survival of those that prey on them. By helping one animal we are helping many other animals at the same time. If a plant needs a particular animal to carry pollen to reproduce and another animal relies on that plant to eat, then by saving that animal we are also saving the second animal and the plant. Some people believe that endangered species programs are unnatural and that we should not be 'messing with Nature'. They believe that if a species is going to die out then we should let it. However, because of our higher intelligence, we are the only animal that is able to help other species. By helping other species in need, we are recognising that we are not the most important living thing on the planet and that all living things are worth protecting.

Extract C

Several years ago while driving I saw a kangaroo who had been killed by a car. I decided to take the dead kangaroo off the road to give her a bit of dignity, and I opened her pouch out of curiosity. There was a tiny but very alive joey in there waiting to be rescued. That's how it all began! The purpose of a carer's work is to raise or rehabilitate orphaned or injured native wildlife so that they may be returned to the wild, and live the natural life that was intended for them. By far, the best thing about being a carer is seeing an animal in your care grow healthy and strong and wild. The sight of a kangaroo taking their first hop or a cockatoo fly to freedom is the most satisfying feeling in the world. The opportunity to be so close to these special species is also a huge source of pleasure. Wildlife caring can take over your life. You have to remodel your schedule to put the animals in your care first. A hungry baby possum can't wait until the shopping is done, and a fledgling bird can't feed herself while you clean the house. However it can also be upsetting to see how many native animals are killed or injured unintentionally by humans doing something like using netting in their vegetable gardens.

Adapted from animalsaustralia.org, *Animals Australia for a kinder world*, Louise's story; reproduced with permission

Animals Australia
for a *kinder* world

Practice Task 2

Extract D

All over the world, honeybees have been mysteriously vanishing from their hives. Much of the public attention to this phenomenon came about because of the 2009 documentary film *Vanishing of the Bees*. The film follows two commercial beekeepers who spent three years trying to solve the mystery surrounding the disappearance of these productive and hard-working creatures. Filmed across the US, in Europe, Australia and Asia, the documentary also examines what this means for the relationship between mankind and mother earth. The term 'Colony Collapse Disorder', or CCD, is now used to describe the phenomenon in which the worker bees in a colony disappear leaving behind a queen, plenty of food and a few nurse bees to take care of any remaining young. Because the bees disappear it is difficult to combat the problem or come up with the causes. Conflicting opinions abound, including the increasing use of pesticides which are thought to make the bees disoriented, infections or mites, loss of habitat, or a combination of these factors. Without bees doing what they usually do, numerous foodstuffs will disappear. And even if the problem is solved or goes away, many believe that the world should sit up and take notice about the problem right now. If bees are dying something is wrong.

Practice Task 3

READING
Varied short texts

15 MIN

Read the questions and texts and answer as you think best. Then look at the answers to get explanations of why and how those answers are correct. Try to work quickly and finish in close to 15 minutes.

For questions 1–10, choose the text which you think best answers the question.

Which extract …

refers to the writings of travellers in years gone by?　**1** _____

relates a journey as it is happening?　**2** _____

makes mention of the time before a trip begins?　**3** _____

mentions an unlikely source of enjoyment when arriving in a new place?　**4** _____

refers to the negative thoughts you might have when faced with tourism sites?　**5** _____

refers to a desire to go further and further and see more and more?　**6** _____

mentions three reasons people seek holidays in remote places?　**7** _____

focuses on a particular physical trial of travelling?　**8** _____

suggests a journey was made against someone's wishes?　**9** _____

encourages the reader to take the less well-travelled route?　**10** _____

Extract A

Perhaps you fear being disappointed when you travel. Perhaps you are looking for a reason to travel. Perhaps you're looking for an excuse to stay home. Whichever it is, this thoughtful collection of essays offers something for you. In *The Art of Travel*, modern-day philosopher Alain de Botton shares his own experiences and reflections on travel and also explores the views of various writers and artists who have travelled to foreign lands in times gone by. In so doing, he helps us understand the human urge to be somewhere else and to see something else. Whether you have travelled extensively already, or whether you're just heading abroad for a short beach holiday, *The Art of Travel* will be of interest. De Botton's words will make you feel better when you find yourself still worrying about whether you have left the iron on at home when you are standing before one of the wonders of the world, or when you want to skip another glorious castle so you can sleep in, or when you do go to see it and feel like you'll scream if you hear another fact about how it was built. De Botton's book is the perfect guide to intelligent travel.

☞ Answers and explanations on page 212

Extract B

For two long months now we have been on the *Cairngorm*. The anguish on leaving family and friends is still marked on the faces of the adults on board. The children are the only ones enjoying the experience. They don't seem to notice the noise, the smells and the eternal damp, the stomach-churning heaving of the decks. They still play their games and laugh and squeal. The crew, of course, have no time to feel sick or bored but the passengers do. We have endless hours to endure and it is hard to keep one's thoughts away from the revolt going on in one's body—the sick head, the churning gut. Some days pass easily but for the past few days the swell and surge of the Roaring Forties have tested our group mettle. At least now most of us are beyond the black fear we felt at the start of the voyage but we still wake every day with relief that we have survived another night. They say we will see land later today—the Victorian coast. Despite my despair, I am indeed excited, like all on board. The sight will show us that Australia is real at least and that Sydney, the end of this endless journey, is not too far away.

Extract C

I first laid eyes on the Himalayan mountains from the vantage point of Chail, a hill station in the Indian state of Himachal Pradesh. It wasn't your classic Himalayan view of peaks and glacial lakes; this former Maharaja's retreat is a land of forest and mist. There was just a suggestion, just a hint, of the grander mountains that lie beyond my reach. I found myself besotted with the idea of venturing into those foothills: I needed to see more. I was certainly not alone; people from all over the world have found endless reasons to embark upon a trek in the Himalayas. Travellers are drawn to the highest mountains on the planet seeking adventure, meaningful cultural interaction, and even spiritual enlightenment. However, those visitors considering only the most popular trekking routes may be doing themselves a serious disservice. These well-known routes attract plenty of visitors but heading off the beaten path can yield an even more rewarding adventure. It was on just such a path that I set out at the beginning of the monsoon season.

From Daily Travel Stories website by Mark Smeltz; reproduced with permission

Extract D

Sometimes I think the most enjoyable part of travel is the preparation. By the time I have booked the tickets and researched all the wonderful places I am going to see I am not only thoroughly exhausted but have lost interest in the actual place I am going to. I start to feel as though I have been there and seen it all already. I settle into a strange lull of emotions. I am not totally content with where I am, but I am not too excited about where I am going. Having said that, I usually recover fairly quickly when I arrive at the airport. Suddenly the pulse quickens and the excitement returns. The realisation hits. I am actually going. Nothing can beat that feeling of being about to leave one known and familiar space and enter a completely new and unknown one somewhere else on the planet. Strangely enough, one of the most thrilling parts of travel for me is just emerging from the airport in whatever city I am in and seeing another world before me, filled with people doing much the same as in the place I left but in a slightly different way, on different roads, with different signs and making different noises—even if they are speaking the same language as I do.

Real Test

Read the questions and texts and answer as you think best. Then look at the answers to get explanations of why and how those answers are correct. Finish at 15 minutes.

For questions 1–10, choose the text which best answers the question.

Which extract …

suggests we often remember experiences involving parents' words or actions? **1** _____

compares our memories to a complex puzzle? **2** _____

refers to the earliest age at which we can remember? **3** _____

refers to the need to exercise our memory? **4** _____

mentions the unimportant things we sometimes remember? **5** _____

explains how we might develop memories that are incorrect? **6** _____

suggests we might remember unhappy memories more than happy ones? **7** _____

explains the influence of family and culture on our memories? **8** _____

mentions the importance of learning new things as a way to improve memory? **9** _____

mentions how much we treasure our early memories? **10** _____

Extract A

A recent survey of more than 6000 people showed that nearly 40 per cent reported a memory that was likely to be fictional. Current research indicates that the earliest age at which people remember things is at between three and four. However in this study, over 2500 people claimed to have memories from age two or even younger, and almost 900 people claimed to remember something from when they were aged one or younger. The researchers asked participants to detail their first memory and the age they were at the time. They were told it had to be a memory they were certain they remembered and not be based on a family story or a photograph, for example. They then evaluated the most likely reason that people claimed memories from an age at which research indicates they cannot be formed. The researchers believe that these fictional memories are based on remembered fragments from an early experience after the age of three—for example, the colour of a pram used by a younger sibling—and some later facts about their own infancy which may have come from family or photos. Many participants, when told their memory was false, refused to believe it. We hold onto our memories, false or not, like gold.

Extract B

Our class collected our childhood memories as part of a project about our past. We posted some onto our class page:

* I remember when I was five and I refused to wear any kind of outfit that my friend Amelia had not also worn. And Amelia had some really weird tastes. I remember my mother saying: If Amelia told you to jump into a fire would you do it? And I said yes.

☞ **Answers and explanations on pages 212-213**

Extract B (continued)

- My strongest memory from when I was really little is having to sit at the table with a full plate in front of me when everyone had eaten up and left the table. My mother even turned off the kitchen light!

- I remember that when I was six, my parents woke me up in the morning as they always did. I asked them, 'Can I skip school today?' (I asked almost every day and was always told 'Of course not'.) This time my dad said: 'Of course you can, if you get up now, get dressed and make your bed quickly enough.' I stupidly believed him, and leapt out of bed and did everything as fast and efficiently as I could … And then I learned that it was April Fool's Day. I was so, so, angry with him.

Extract C

Our memory is more like a gigantic jigsaw than a continuing story as you might see played out in a film. Although we experience thousands of events across childhood, as we grow older we recall only a handful. We might remember lots of 'firsts'—our first day at school or the birth of a sibling. But sometimes what we remember is completely trivial—for example, the colour of a dress or the feel of a cushion on the lounge. And not surprisingly, what we remember is shaped by our family and the stories they tell or the photographs they take. One of the most important developments for the onset of memory is language. Interestingly, bilingual adults recall early memories in the language they spoke at the time the memory was formed. The way families reminisce about holidays or funny things that happened also affects the way we remember things. So too does the culture of the family we are born into. One culture, for example, might focus more on emotional experiences, another on the social responsibilities with the family, and this will be reflected in our memories.

Extract D

By the time human beings have reached adulthood, their brains have developed millions of neural pathways that help them process and recall information quickly and perform habitual tasks with little effort. However, if they just stick to these more familiar paths they do not give their brains the stimulation needed to keep growing and developing. Memory, like muscular strength, needs us to 'use it or lose it'. The more you work out your brain, the better you will process and remember information. There are four key elements of a good brain-strengthening activity. Firstly, the activity teaches you something new. No matter how demanding the activity, if it is something you are already good at, it's not a good brain exercise. Secondly, it is challenging. The best activities demand significant mental effort. Thirdly, it is a skill that you can build on further. When a level starts to feel comfortable, it's time to tackle the next level. And lastly, the activity is rewarding. The more you like doing something the more likely you are to continue doing it. Think of anything you have always wanted to try—playing the guitar, juggling, playing chess, or learning a language. Any of these can help you to improve your memory as long as they meet these four criteria.

THINKING SKILLS
Problem solving—Position and order

- Read the question **carefully** and make sure you understand what is required.
- You might need to work through and **place people or objects in order**.
- Use a **diagram** or **table** to help.
- Remember: You only need to answer the question. You don't need to sort out all the information. Be careful to **answer the question that is asked**.

Example 1

These facts are known about five girls.

- Mia is taller than Amy and younger than Bella.
- Ivy is taller than Tilly and older than Amy.
- Amy is older than Tilly but younger than Mia.

Which of the following **cannot** be true?

A   Bella is taller than Mia.   B   Ivy is older than Bella.
C   Tilly is older than Mia.   D   Amy is shorter than Ivy.

Steps to work out the answer

1   Read the question carefully. Take note of what is required. We are looking for the statement that cannot be true.
2   Consider the given information. Is there enough information to immediately see the answer? Is there enough information to place all the people in order?
3   Consider each option and determine whether it might be true or false.

C is correct. Mia is older than Amy and Amy is older than Tilly. So Mia must be older than Tilly. The statement that cannot be true is that Tilly is older than Mia.

Other options

A, B and D are not correct options because the statements might be true. There is no information about the height of Bella or who is older out of Bella and Ivy or who is taller out of Amy and Ivy.

Example 2

Five teams from different towns competed in a netball competition. The following facts are known.

- The team with the white uniform finished fourth.
- Unicomb was the town that competed in yellow.
- Atwood finished ahead of Cleveland.
- The team with the blue uniform finished ahead of the green team but behind the team with the red uniform that didn't finish first.
- Stewart, whose uniform was not red, finished ahead of Cleveland who were ahead of Musgrave.

Which team came third?

A   Atwood   B   Cleveland   C   Stewart   D   Unicomb

Steps to work out the answer

1 First read the question carefully and make sure you know what is required.
2 If the answer is not obvious or easily apparent, work through the information and find what is readily available.
3 Work out which positions can be determined. Use a table if you find it helpful.

C is correct. The team that finished first isn't the white team (it was 4th) or the red, green, or blue teams. So the yellow team finished first and we know that it is Unicomb. The red team must be second, the blue team third and the green team fifth. Now Cleveland finished ahead of Musgrave. Both Atwood and Stewart finished ahead of Cleveland. So, Cleveland must have finished fourth (and had the white uniform) and Musgrave finished fifth (green). Now Stewart did not have the red uniform, so it must have had the blue. We already know that the team with the blue uniform finished third, so Stewart is the team that finished third.

Position	Team	Colour
1	Unicomb	yellow
2	Atwood	red
3	Stewart	blue
4	Cleveland	white
5	Musgrave	green

Checklist

Can you:
1 *read the question carefully and work out what is required?*
2 *sift through the given information and place items or people in order?*
3 *use a table or diagram to help find the solution?*
4 *answer the question that is being asked?*

Real Test 1

1 Kate is taller than Jack and Jill. Alice is taller than Oliver but shorter than Jack.

Which must be true?
A Oliver is the shortest.
B Jack is taller than Jill.
C Alice is shorter than Kate.
D Jill is shorter than Oliver.

2 Ellen, Jenny, Angus, Tim, Paul and Stuart sit at a round table. Stuart sits directly opposite Tim, who is on Ellen's left. Jenny sits on Paul's left.

Who is sitting on Ellen's right?
A Angus   B Jenny   C Paul   D Stuart

3 Five friends—Alison, Julie, Margaret, Robyn and Stephanie—sit in a row at the theatre in seats 1 to 5.
Alison is not in seat 5.
Robyn is somewhere between Julie and Margaret.
Stephanie is in a lower numbered seat than Alison and there is exactly one seat between them.
Margaret's seat number is even.

Who is in seat 3?
A Alison   B Julie
C Robyn   D Stephanie

4 Six babies—Oliver, Louis, James, Isaac, Molly and Thea—were born in the last six months of last year. All were born in different months. Louis and Isaac were born two months apart. Molly was born in September. Thea was born the month before James, who was born some time after Oliver.

Which of the following must be true?
A Louis was born before Molly.
B Isaac was born after Thea.
C James was born in November.
D Oliver was born in July.

5 On one side of High Street, four shops—the chemist, the bank, the newsagency and the post office—are all in a row, although not necessarily in that order.

1	2	3	4

High Street

Three of the shops are the newsagency, the one in position 4, and the one where Ruth works, which is not next to the newsagency.

The bank is not next to the chemist.

Two of the shops are the post office and the one in position 1.

The chemist is somewhere between the post office and the newsagency.

Which shop is in position 2?
A chemist   B bank
C newsagency   D post office

6 A competition between five boys required them to find items in the least possible time. The boys all found at least one item and no two boys found the same number.
Luke was faster than David, but found two fewer items.
Oscar finished first, but found the least number of items.
Patrick found more items than Jonathan, but was not as fast.
David was the only boy who finished in the same position as the number of items he found.

Which must be true?
A Luke finished second.
B Oscar found two items.
C David found four items.
D Patrick finished third.

7 These facts are known about five children.
• Ted is taller than Matilda but younger than Pip.
• Arabella is older than Ted but shorter than Xavier.

☞ **Answers and explanations on pages 213–215**

Real Test 1

- Matilda is older than Xavier but shorter than Arabella.
- Pip is younger than Arabella and shorter than Matilda.
- Xavier is older than Pip and taller than Ted.

Which might **not** be true?

A Pip is the shortest.

B Xavier is the tallest.

C Arabella is the oldest.

D Ted is the youngest.

8 Ten people live in the five houses that are found opposite the park in Pringle Street. All people who live in the same house use the same last name and one is Chang. One first name is Maree.

Pringle Street

Pringle Park

The Dawsons live in the house that is furthest right.

Xavier and Henrietta live in the same house.

There are two houses between that of George and that of Isabel Ford.

The centre house is the only one that has just one occupant.

Alison, whose surname is not Dawson, lives next door to Liz Elliott. Both live with one other person.

Marshall Smith lives with his two children.

Peter lives somewhere between Victor and George.

Who lives with Liz Elliott?

A George B Maree C Peter D Victor

9 Five girls—Alice, Helen, Jennifer, Megan and Selma—and six boys—Benjamin, Dylan, Frank, Oliver, Ross and Thomas—live in the houses along Candy Lane.

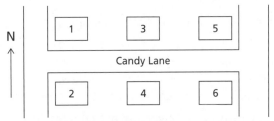

N

Candy Lane

Helen has two brothers but no sisters. They live in a house at the eastern end of the lane.
Alice lives next door to Megan.
Selma lives next door to Frank, who lives opposite Thomas.
Benjamin, who has one sister but no brother, and Dylan who has no siblings live the furthest possible distant apart.
Jennifer and her brother live at No. 1.

Where does Ross live?

A 2   B 4   C 5   D 6

10 Three boys—Henry, John and William—and three girls—Grace, Rosie and Zara—each care for a different type of animal (including a pig) at an agricultural show. The animals have pens in a large shed on either side of a central walkway.

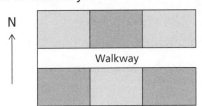

N

Walkway

A girl looks after the chickens.
John has a centre pen, opposite the goats.
Henry and William are next to each other on the same side of the walkway.
Zara looks after the sheep which are directly opposite the horse.
Rosie and her cow are on the northern side of the shed.
Grace's pen is somewhere on the right of John's pen.

What animal is found in the centre pen on the southern side of the shed?

A chickens B goats   C horse   D pig

☞ **Answers and explanations on pages 213-215**

- **Proof by contradiction** is a means of solving logic problems.

- Problems might have two (or more) pieces of information that contradict each other. One statement is the **opposite of the other** and only one can be true. For example, Rusty is a dog and Rusty is not a dog. One of those statements must be true and the other must be false. By finding contradictory statements we can then often determine which other statements must be true.

- Be careful to **answer the actual question**. For example, you may have to work out who did it, not who lied about it.

Example 1

Four boys were playing in a garden. One left the gate open and the dog escaped. When they were asked who had left the gate open, they gave the following replies.

Jake: 'I left it open.'

Sam: 'I didn't leave it open. It was Dane.'

Dane: 'It wasn't Noah or Jake.'

Noah: 'Dane's right. It wasn't me.'

Three of the boys told the truth but one lied. Who left the gate open?

A Jake   B Sam   C Dane   D Noah

Steps to answer the question

1   Read the question carefully. Establish how many of the statements can be true or false. Here, the information from three of the boys is correct.
2   Look for contradictions. Jake says that it was him and Dane says that it wasn't.
3   Use the other information to answer the question.

C is correct. In this question the statements of three boys must be true and one must be false. Now Dane and Jake give contradictory statements. One, and only one, of these statements must be correct. So both Sam and Noah must be telling the truth. Sam says that it was Dane. So Dane is the person who left the gate open.

Take care to answer the question. This question hasn't asked who is telling the lie. In this case Noah's statement is that Dane's right, and as this is true, Dane is also telling the truth. The person who is lying is Jake.

Example 2

Three sisters were talking about a horse that one of them owned. They each made two statements and at least one of the statements each made was correct.

Kylie: 'This is my horse. Her name is Sally.'

Randa: 'This is my horse. Her name is not Sally.'

Maddie: 'This is not my horse. She is Kylie's horse.'

Which must be true about the horse?

A Her name is Sally.

C She is not Kylie's.

B Her name is not Sally.

D She is not Maddie's.

Steps to answer the question

1 Read the question carefully and check what is required. At least one of the two statements each sister made must be true. So one statement might be true and one might be false, or they might both be true.

2 The question asks which option **must** be true. There are two contradictory statements in options A and B, but that doesn't mean that one of those is the answer. It might not be possible to determine which of those two options **must** be true.

3 Consider the statements each girl made.

4 Once you have worked out the answer, it is not necessary to work things through further, but if you have time to spare then that can be a check to your reasoning.

D is correct. Kylie and Randa made contradictory statements. One said that the horse's name is Sally and one said that it is not. One of those statements must be false. Whoever made that false statement has to have also made a true statement and so that must be 'This is my horse.' So either Kylie or Randa owns the horse. This means that Maddie does not own the horse so the correct option is that 'She is not Maddie's'.

Checklist

Can you:

1 *understand what is meant by a contradiction and identify contradictions in given information?*

2 *determine which statements must be true and which false?*

3 *consider different possibilities?*

4 *understand that it is important to answer the question that has been asked?*

Real Test 2

10 MIN

1 Five people witnessed a robbery. All told the police that the thief was wearing a hoodie, but when asked what colour it was their answers were all different, although only one answer was incorrect. They were:

Frances: 'Blue'

Connor: 'Black'

Lui: 'Not red'

Mo: 'Not black'

Kel: 'Not green'

What colour was the hoodie?

A blue   B black

C red   D green

2 Four children were riding their bikes when one accidentally went into a man's garden and knocked over a plant. The man asked the children who did it and their replies were:

Ash: 'I didn't do it.'

Pete: 'No Ash, it was you!'

Sia: 'It wasn't me.'

Polly: 'It wasn't Ash. It was Pete.'

The children all told the truth except for the culprit. Who was it?

A Ash

B Pete

C Sia

D Polly

3 Four sisters were asked how old their little brother was. Here are their replies:

Nadia: 'He is not 6.'

Simone: 'He is 5.'

Wendy: 'He is not 7.'

Jessica: 'He is 6.'

Three of the sisters were correct, but one was not. Who got it wrong?

A Nadia

B Simone

C Wendy

D Jessica

4 A mother received some flowers. They were sent by one of her four children, but she didn't know which one. When asked, they all gave different replies. Only one told the truth. Their replies were:

Penny: 'It was Guy.'

Samuel: 'It wasn't me.'

Guy: 'Daniel did it.'

Daniel: 'Guy was not telling the truth when he said it was me.'

Who sent the flowers?

A Penny   B Samuel

C Guy   D Daniel

5 Four horses, named Pride, Riverflow, Jim's Boy and Sensation, finished in the top four places in a race. A man asked which one had won and three different people replied. Two of the answers were correct but one of them got it wrong.

The answers, in no particular order, were:

'It wasn't Jim's Boy.'

'It was Riverflow.'

'Sensation didn't win.'

What was the name of the horse that won the race?

A Pride   B Riverflow

C Jim's Boy   D Sensation

6 A group of four people were asked what the time was. There were four different answers, but only one person gave a wrong answer.

Bill: 'It is not 9:45.'

Douglas: 'It is 10:45.'

Celia: 'It is a quarter to ten.'

Vance: 'It's not a quarter past ten.'

Who gave the wrong answer?

A Bill   B Douglas

C Celia   D Vance

☞ **Answers and explanations on pages 215-216**

Real
Test 2

THINKING SKILLS
Problem solving—Logic problems and contradictions

7 Four people made these statements to a police officer.

Oscar: 'Nathan isn't lying.'

Nathan: 'Georgia is lying.'

Georgia: 'Eleanor is lying.'

Eleanor: 'Both Oscar and Georgia are lying.'

Knowing that only one person was telling the truth, the police officer was able to work out who was lying. Who was telling the truth?

A Oscar

B Nathan

C Georgia

D Eleanor

8 Jonathan hid a present for Ali in one of three parcels. He wrote two sentences on each of the tags attached to the parcels. One of the sentences was true and one was false.

Parcel 1: This is the present for Ali. It is a book.

Parcel 2: This is the present for Ali. It is not a book.

Parcel 3: This is not the present for Ali. It is a book.

Which must be correct?

A The present is in Parcel 1.

B The present is in Parcel 2.

C The present is in Parcel 3.

D The present is a book.

9 Three sisters—Maisie, Imogen and Ruby— have a large collection of toy cars. The sisters all make two statements. The statements of one sister are both true, those of another are both false and one sister makes one true statement and one false one.

The statements are:

Maisie: 'I am the oldest. I have the most cars and Ruby has more than Imogen.'

Imogen: 'I am the oldest. Ruby has more cars than Maisie.'

Ruby: 'I am the oldest. Maisie has more cars than me.'

Which of the following **must** be true?

A Maisie is the oldest.

B Imogen is the oldest.

C Ruby is the oldest.

D Maisie has more cars than Ruby.

10 When trying to sell a car a man gave two pieces of information, at least one of which was true, to each of three potential buyers.

He told the first that he had owned the car for 5 years and had never had an accident.

He told the second person that he had owned the car for 3 years and drove it every day.

He told the third person that he only drove the car occasionally but had owned it for 3 years.

Which **must** be true?

A He had owned the car for 5 years.

B He had owned the car for 3 years.

C He drove the car every day.

D He only drove the car occasionally.

☞ **Answers and explanations on pages 215-216**

THINKING SKILLS
Problem solving—Thinking outside the square

- Sometimes you will come across questions that are **totally different** to anything you have seen before. Read the question carefully, again and again if necessary.

- All the information required will be given in the question. Don't assume anything else **must** apply.

- There might be extra information that is irrelevant. You need to be able to sift through the given information and **use what is relevant** and ignore the rest.

- Sometimes you might need to consider different **alternatives** to see if they could be correct. In this case you do make assumptions, but investigate whether they could apply.

- There might be **alternative solutions**. Work through the question carefully and be logical.

[The expression 'thinking outside the square' comes from this puzzle. Join all the dots in this square using four straight lines. Don't lift your pen from the paper.]

● ● ●
● ● ●
● ● ●

Example 1

A survey was taken of the types of transport certain workers had used.

The results were:

Transport type	bicycle	bus	car	train	walking
Number	8	16	28	24	12

The information was placed in a bar chart, but unfortunately it wasn't labelled and the result for walking was mistakenly added to one of the other transport types.

To which of the others was walking added?

A bicycle   B bus   C car   D train

Steps to answer the question

1   Read the question carefully.
2   Work out what each division on the bar chart represents.
3   Compare the different parts of the bar chart with the results in the table.

A is correct. There are 22 divisions on the bar chart. The numbers in the table add to 88. Now 88 ÷ 22 = 4, so each division represents 4 people. That means that bicycle should be 2 divisions. As there is no section of 2 divisions, bicycle must have had the 3 for walking added to it.

bus	bicycle + walking	train			car		

Example 2

There are three toy cars in each of four boxes. The cars are in one of four different colours.

Box 1 has two green cars and one red one. Box 2 has two yellow cars and one blue car. Box 3 has two red cars and one blue one. Box 4 has one yellow, one green and one blue.

Key Points

THINKING SKILLS
Problem solving—Thinking outside the square

Mary takes two cars from one of the boxes and one car from each of the others.

She has two red cars and one each of the other colours.

Max made these statements:

X: If Mary took two cars from Box 3, they must be the two red cars.

Y: If Mary took two cars from Box 4, one of them must be green.

Which of the statements are true?

A   X only   B   Y only   C   Both X and Y   D   Neither X nor Y

Steps to answer the question
1   Read the question carefully and be sure you understand what is required.
2   Consider each statement separately and determine whether it can be true or false.

B is correct. If the two cars came from Box 3, they could be a red car and a blue car. The other red car would need to come from Box 1 and the yellow car would need to come from Box 2. This means that the green car would come from Box 4. So, if the two cars came from Box 3, they do not need to be the two red cars. Statement X is not true.

If the two cars came from Box 4 and were a yellow car and a blue car, there would not be a possible choice from Box 2. But if one of the two cars was green the other could either be blue or yellow and the other yellow or blue car would come from Box 2. One red car would come from Box 1 and the other from Box 3. So statement Y is true.

Checklist
Can you:
1 *read questions carefully and identify what is required?*
2 *sift through given information and find what is relevant?*
3 *take time to stop and think and use common sense?*
4 *apply logic to unusual situations?*
5 *understand what it means to think outside the square?*

Real Test 3

THINKING SKILLS
Problem solving—Thinking outside the square

10 MIN

1 Four people take part in a trivia quiz each week. They receive a score between 1 and 5. These are the results for the first 4 weeks.

	Week 1	Week 2	Week 3	Week 4
Lincoln	3	5	2	4
Max	5	4	5	3
Jessica	4	3	4	2
Thomas	2	5	3	5

After 5 weeks the four people all have the same total. What did Thomas score in Week 5?

A 2   B 3   C 4   D 5

2 Three children—Ebony, Sue and Michaela—play a game. Each begins with 20 marbles. At each turn they roll a dice and depending on the number rolled they either win marbles from each of the others, or they must give some to each of the others.

After three rounds, when each child has had three rolls, Ebony has 18 marbles and Sue has 10 more than Michaela.

How many marbles does Michaela have?

A 12   B 14   C 16   D 18

3 A vote was taken of members of a club to see which colour—blue, green, lemon, lilac or grey—to paint the clubhouse. The results were shown in this graph, but it wasn't labelled.

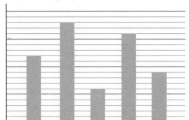

The club president remembered that green received the most votes and the total who voted for green was equal to the sum of those who voted for grey and lilac. The club secretary remembered that more than twice as many voted for blue as lilac.

If that is all correct, which of these statements is **not** correct?

A Twice as many voted for green than for lemon.

B More people voted for blue than for grey.

C The least favourite colour was lilac.

D Together, the numbers who voted for green and grey was the same as those who voted for blue, lemon and lilac combined.

4 Tyler, Joseph and Cooper play a game with cards. They begin with 10 cards each and take it in turns to spin this spinner.

If they spin an odd number, they must give a card to each of the others, but if they spin an even number each of the others must give two cards to them.

After each person has had one spin, Joseph has 7 cards and Tyler has more than Cooper.

How many cards does Tyler have?

A 12   B 14   C 15   D 16

5 Two three-digit numbers were added together, but ink was spilled on the sum so that some of it cannot be seen.

$$\begin{array}{r} 3 \\ +06 \\ \hline 91 \end{array}$$

It is known that the nine digits in the sum were all different.

Which **digit** was not used in the sum?

A 2   B 4   C 5   D 7

6 Four drivers are competing in a rally. The winner of the rally is the driver who takes the least total time over four stages. These are the times taken for the first three stages:

Driver	Stage 1	Stage 2	Stage 3
Nelson	24 min	19 min	35 min
Melissa	35 min	16 min	37 min
David	21 min	18 min	32 min
Shona	29 min	15 min	30 min

One driver is certain to win provided that he or she is not more than a few minutes behind any of the others in Stage 4.

☞ **Answers and explanations on pages 216–218**

Real Test 3

What is the maximum time that this driver can afford to finish behind any other driver?

A 1 min **B** 2 min **C** 3 min **D** 4 min

7 A pictograph was drawn to illustrate the information in this table:

Day	Mon.	Tues.	Wed.	Thurs.	Fri.
Number	24	36	48	32	28

The days were not shown on the graph in any particular order. Unfortunately, the left side and the top of the graph have been torn off. This means the information for one of the days is missing.

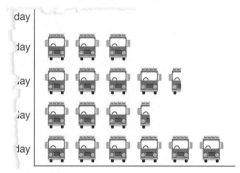

Which day is missing?

A Monday **B** Wednesday
C Thursday **D** Friday

8 Ed, Mick and Morgan are sitting at a table playing a game.

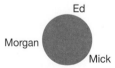

Each begins with 20 counters and they take it in turns to roll a dice. If they roll an odd number, they must give the number of counters equal to the number rolled, to the person sitting on their right. If they roll an even number the person sitting on their left must give them that number of counters.

Ed goes first and rolls a 4. Mick then rolls 3 and Morgan 1. Ed then rolls again and after that roll has 29 counters.

How many counters does Mick then have?

A 12 **B** 16 **C** 17 **D** 21

9 These five clocks have been brought in for repairs as they all lose time.

At the moment, together they are a total of $12\frac{1}{2}$ hours behind the correct time.

Peter's clock is twice as slow as one of the others. Which is Peter's clock?

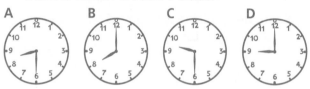

10 Two boys, Alistair and James, and two girls, Sophie and Lily, are sitting in a row. The children are all wearing different coloured shirts and all are different ages from 7 to 10 years old.

left	1	2	3	4	right

The two girls are seated next to each other. James is further to the left than Alistair.

The blue shirt was worn by someone seated immediately to the left of the 9-year-old, but somewhere to the right of the child in the yellow shirt.

Sophie was immediately to the left of the 7-year-old who was somewhere left of the child in the red shirt.

Lily was immediately to the right of the child in the green shirt who was somewhere to the right of the 8-year-old.

What colour shirt did the 10-year-old wear?

A red **B** blue **C** green **D** yellow

☞ **Answers and explanations on pages 216–218**

MATHEMATICAL REASONING
Space and geometry

● A solid is constructed from a **net**.

Example: The diagram shows a piece of cardboard with eight identical strips. Each of the strips is numbered and the net is used to build a hollow octagonal prism. If opposite sides are to add to the same number, what number replaces X?

2	7	X	3	10	5	8	9

A 1   B 12   C 6   D 4   E 1

 Tip: Practise at home making a variety of solids.

The correct answer is **D**. As opposite numbers are (2, 10), (7, 5), (X, 8) and (3, 9), the total is 12 and therefore X equals 4.

● A solid contains faces, edges and vertices. **Polyhedra** are solids with flat surfaces which are bordered by straight lines.

Example: What is the sum of the number of edges, the number of vertices and the number of faces of a pentagonal prism?

A 15   B 18   C 20   D 25   E 32

The correct answer is **E**.

The pentagonal prism has 15 edges, 10 vertices and 7 faces. As 15 + 10 + 7 is 32, the total is 32.

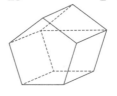

● A **line of symmetry** passes through the middle of a plane shape and divides the shape into identical halves.

Example: In the diagram, which of the following squares should be shaded to make *AC* a line of symmetry of square *ABCD*?

  A *P* and *Q*

  B *P* and *T*

  C *P* and *S*

  D *Q* and *R*

  E *T* and *R*

The correct answer is **B**.

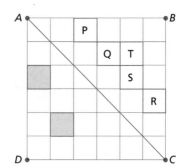

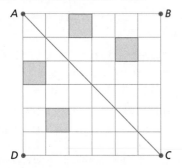

MATHEMATICAL REASONING
Space and geometry

- **Rotational symmetry** occurs when a shape is rotated about a point and fits over its shape again. If a rotation of 180° (half a turn) is needed, the shape has **half turn symmetry,** and the **order of rotational symmetry** is 2 (as 360° ÷ 180° = 2).

  Example: Which of the following has half turn symmetry?

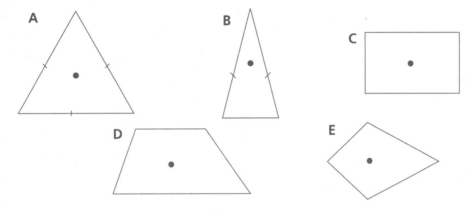

  The correct answer is **C**, as the rectangle can be rotated 180° and the image will fit over the original shape.

- A shape has **quarter turn symmetry** when it has a rotational symmetry of 4 and repeats itself after a rotation of 90°.

  Example: The diagram shows a figure consisting of 36 squares.

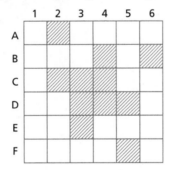

  The figure has quarter turn symmetry if another square is shaded. The square to be shaded is at

  A C2   B B3   C D1   D E1   E B1

  The correct answer is **D**. The square at A2 rotates to B6, then F5 and then E1.

Checklist

Can you:

1 *view solids from different directions?*
2 *count the number of faces, edges and vertices in a polyhedron?*
3 *identify the lines of symmetry on a 2D shape?*
4 *identify shapes with half turn and quarter turn symmetry?*

Real Test 1

MATHEMATICAL REASONING
Space and geometry

10 MIN

1 The diagram shows the net of a solid.

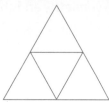

The solid is a

A rectangular pyramid
B triangular prism
C triangular pyramid
D hexagonal prism
E square pyramid

2 How many faces are on an octagonal prism?

10	9	8	12	6
A	B	C	D	E

3 How many axes of symmetry has the shape?

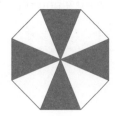

2	4	6	8	16
A	B	C	D	E

4

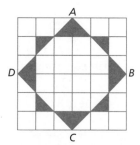

The diagram has

A quarter turn symmetry

B half turn symmetry

C axis of symmetry *AC*

D four axes of symmetry

E all of the above

5 The grid contains shaded squares.

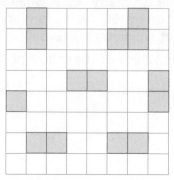

Austin needs the shape to have two lines of symmetry. What is the smallest number of squares he needs to shade?

5	6	7	8	9
A	B	C	D	E

6 The net of a prism consists of hexagons and rectangles. What is the sum of faces, edges and vertices of the prism?

18	24	36	38	40
A	B	C	D	E

7 The shape below consists of an arrow inside a square.

The shape is now rotated in an anticlockwise direction.

Through how many degrees has the shape been rotated?

45°	90°	180°	225°	270°
A	B	C	D	E

☞ **Answers and explanations on pages 218-219**

Real Test 1

8 What percentage of the circle is shaded?

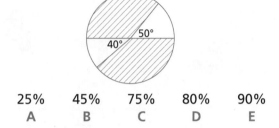

25%	45%	75%	80%	90%
A	B	C	D	E

9 The diagram shows an equilateral triangle *RSV* and a hexagon *PQRSTU* which has rotational symmetry order 6.

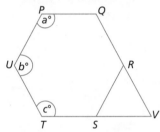

What is the value of *a* + *b* + *c*?

180	240	300	330	360
A	B	C	D	E

10 Here are eight letters.

Z H E S N O I X

Bridgett used letters from the list to make words which have symmetry. Which of these statements is correct?

A Every letter in the word **SHIN** has rotational symmetry.

B Every letter in the word **OXEN** has line symmetry.

C Every letter in the word **ZONES** has line symmetry.

D Every letter in the word **NOISE** has rotational symmetry.

E Every letter in the word **SHINE** has line symmetry.

☞ **Answers and explanations on pages 218-219**

Real Test 2

MATHEMATICAL REASONING
Space and geometry

10 MIN

1

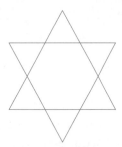

The net is made up to form a solid. The solid formed is

A an octagonal prism
B an octagonal pyramid
C a hexagonal prism
D a hexagonal pyramid
E a pentagonal pyramid

2

The order of rotation is

5	4	3	2	10
A	B	C	D	E

3 The diagram shows a 4 by 4 square with one square shaded at B3. If the large square is rotated 180°, the location of the shaded square will be

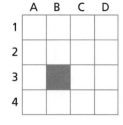

C2	C3	B2	D2	B3
A	B	C	D	E

4 Which of the following has quarter turn symmetry?

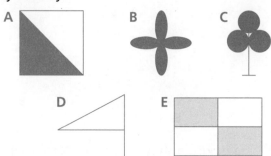

5 When the net is used to build the cube, what is on the missing face?

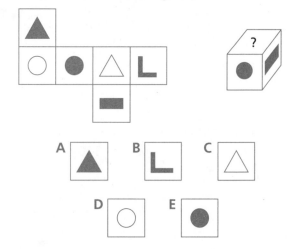

6 Amelia has made a pattern using black and white squares.

She wants to add tiles to the right-hand end so that the finished pattern has a vertical line of symmetry. What is the smallest number of squares she needs to add?

3	4	5	6	7
A	B	C	D	E

☞ **Answers and explanations on page 219**

Real Test 2

MATHEMATICAL REASONING
Space and geometry

7 Mary has drawn a rectangle *ABCD* and *M* and *N* are the midpoints of sides *DC* and *BC* respectively. The size of angle *MNC* is 50°. She completes the diagram, drawing *BM*, *AM* and *PM*, so that the shape has a line of symmetry.

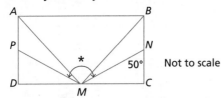

Not to scale

What is the size of the angle represented by *?

90°	100°	110°	120°	130°
A	B	C	D	E

8 Which two squares should be shaded so that this shape has one line of symmetry?

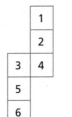

A P and Q
B P and R
C P and S
D Q and R
E Q and S

9 A regular hexagon has been divided into small triangles. Alexis has shaded some triangles.

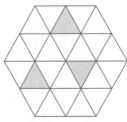

What is the smallest number of extra triangles Alexis must shade for the shape to have rotational symmetry order 3?

1	2	3	4	5
A	B	C	D	E

10 Cameron uses these nets to make three cubes. He places the cubes on a glass table so that the face-up number is a multiple of 5.

What is the product of the face-down numbers?

252	272	288	324	432
A	B	C	D	E

☞ **Answers and explanations on page 219**

Key Points

MATHEMATICAL REASONING
Statistics and probability

10 MIN

- You should be able to read a **timetable**.

  Example: Laura needs to travel by train from Campleton to Hudson. She misses the 11:01 by five minutes. What is the earliest she can get to Hudson?

Train timetable					
Campleton	11:01		11:41		12:48
Mangue	11:23	11:38	11:57	12:30	13:04
Chesterwod	11:56				13:37
Stripeton	12:10	12:19	12:38	13:11	13:51
Hudson	12:14	12:23		13:15	13:55
Brankston	12:22	12:31	12:45	13:23	14:03

 Tip: She can get off one train and wait for another.

  A 12:19   B 12:23   C 13:15   D 13:55   E 14:03

  The correct answer is **C**, as Laura catches the 11:41 and gets off at Mangue (or Stripeton), then catches the following train, which reaches Hudson at 13:15.

- You should be able to read a **graph**. Graphs include the familiar column, line, bar, picture and sector graphs, but there are also lesser-known formats.

  Example: The **radial graph** shows the temperatures at Mulbring on one day.

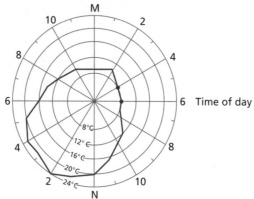

**Temperature graph
06:00 Tuesday to 04:00 Wednesday**

According to the graph, the difference between the highest and lowest temperatures is

A 6 °C   B 8 °C   C 10 °C   D 16 °C   E 18 °C

The correct answer is **D**. The difference between 24 °C and 8 °C is 16 °C.

Key Points

MATHEMATICAL REASONING
Statistics and probability

- The **travel graph** represents the distance from a given location a person/object has travelled over a period of time. The steeper the graph is, the higher the travel speed. A horizontal interval means no travelling.

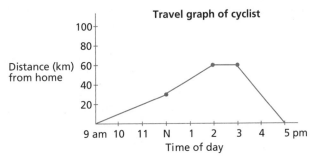

Travel graph of cyclist

Distance (km) from home

Time of day

Example: The graph represents the journey of a cyclist who leaves her home at 9 am and returns at 5 pm.

Here are three statements about the graph.

1. The cyclist travelled fastest between 3 pm and 5 pm
2. The cyclist rode a total of 120 km.
3. The cyclist stopped three times.

Which of these statements are correct?

A   statement 1 only
B   statement 2 only
C   statement 3 only
D   statements 1 and 2 only
E   statements 1 and 3 only

The correct answer is **D**. The line is the steepest between 3 pm and 5 pm which means the cyclist is travelling the fastest. Statement 1 is correct. As 60 + 60 is 120, the cyclist rode a total of 120 km. Statement 2 is correct. The cyclist only stopped once—between 2 pm and 3 pm. Statement 3 is incorrect. Only statements 1 and 2 are correct.

- **Probability** is the study of chance and can be expressed as a fraction, decimal or percentage. Probability ranges from 0 (impossible event) to 1 (certain event).

Example: The probabilities of five events are listed. Which event is most likely to occur?

A   The probability of winning a game is 0.63.
B   The probability of catching the bus is $\frac{3}{5}$.
C   The probability of getting a question correct is 61%.
D   The probability of catching a cold is $\frac{32}{50}$.
E   The probability of selecting a red ball is 0.075.

The correct answer is **D**. Rewrite the probabilities as decimals. 0.63, $\frac{3}{5}$ = 0.6, 61% = 0.61, $\frac{32}{50}$ = 0.64, 0.075. The largest decimal is 0.64. The probability of catching a cold is the highest, and hence is most likely to occur.

Checklist

Can you:

1 *interpret a variety of tables and graphs?*
2 *solve word problems involving probability?*

Real
Test 3

MATHEMATICAL REASONING
Statistics and probability

10 min

Questions **1**, **2** and **3** relate to the graph below, which shows the results of a survey of 120 students detailing their favourite sports.

Students' favourite sports

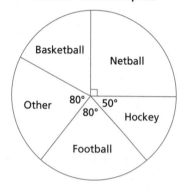

1 How many students nominated basketball?

20	24	48	60	72
A	B	C	D	E

2 Two-thirds of the students who chose netball play each weekend. How many students who chose netball do **not** play each weekend?

20	60	10	30	40
A	B	C	D	E

3 A second survey of a different group of 120 students was taken. In this survey, 35% of the students chose netball. If the two groups are combined, what percentage chose netball?

60%	70%	30%	35%	42%
A	B	C	D	E

Questions **4** and **5** relate to the table.

Bus timetable			
	am	am	am
Averill	08:05	08:18	08:31
Blatchford	08:14	08:27	08:40
Cootha Station	08:27	08:40	08:53

Train timetable			
	am	am	am
Cootha	08:00	08:31	10:12
Drayton		08:43	10:24
Endford	08:14		10:31
Flinders	08:26	08:57	10:43
Gresford	08:37		10:54

4 Bill lives in Blatchford. Each work day he travels by bus and train to Flinders. Bill needs to arrive at Flinders by 9:00 am. What time does he need to catch the bus at Blatchford?

08:14	09:51	09:46	08:29	08:27
A	B	C	D	E

5 Bill's friend, Bruce, lives at Averill. If he catches the 8:05 bus, what time will he get to Gresford?

08:37	08:57	10:12	10:54	8:18
A	B	C	D	E

Questions **6** and **7** relate to the conversion graph, which is used to convert US dollars to Australian dollars to euros.

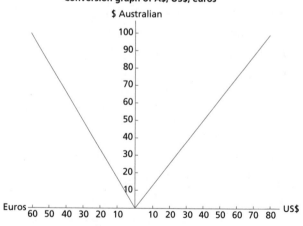

Conversion graph of A$, US$, euros

6 Change A$500 to US dollars.

$740	$300	$400	$600	$800
A	B	C	D	E

☞ **Answers and explanations on pages 219-220**

Real Test 3

MATHEMATICAL REASONING
Statistics and probability

7 Change US$80 to euros.
A 80 euros   B 60 euros   C 75 euros
D 45 euros   E 50 euros

8 Students from 6K were surveyed to find the method they used to travel from school to home last Friday.

Transport home from school

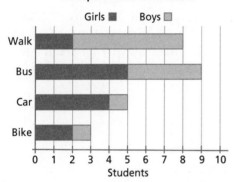

Girls ■   Boys ▨

Here are three statements about the graph.
1. Twenty-five students were surveyed.
2. Two-thirds of the walkers were boys.
3. Half of the boys in the class walked.
Which of these are correct?
A statement 1 only
B statement 2 only
C statements 1 and 2
D statements 2 and 3
E statements 1 and 3

9 A bag contains red balls, blue balls and green balls. There are twice as many red balls as green balls. A ball is chosen at random from the bag. The probability that it is red is 0.6.

What is the probability that the ball is blue?

0.1	0.2	0.3	0.4	0.5
A	B	C	D	E

10 Ivy made this spinner where each number is equally likely to be spun.

The spinner is spun two times and the results multiplied to give a score. Which of these scores are equally likely?
A 4 and 6
B 8 and 12
C 9 and 24
D 18 and 24
E 24 and 36

☞ **Answers and explanations on pages 219-220**

Real Test 4

MATHEMATICAL REASONING
Statistics and probability

10 MIN

Questions **1**, **2** and **3** relate to the graph, which shows the manner in which Samoi spent her weekly $18 allowance.

Allocation of weekly allowance

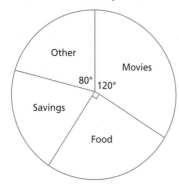

1. The amount allocated to movies was

$12	$18	$6	$14	$9
A	B	C	D	E

2. If the amount saved in the week was repeated for four weeks, Samoi will have

$12	$14	$16	$18	$20
A	B	C	D	E

3. Due to a price rise, Samoi needs to increase the allocation to movies by $2. What will be the new angle for movies?

122°	140°	150°	160°	172°
A	B	C	D	E

Questions **4**, **5**, **6** and **7** relate to the table, which shows the approximate road distances and the air and rail travelling times between major cities.

City	Road (km)	Air (h)	Rail (h)
Salarki–Bullawa	982	1.5	16
Salarki–Makira	872	1.1	10.5
Salarki–Amstrada	1412	1.4	25.3
Salarki–Pantana	2781	3.1	38
Makira–Amstrada	731	1.05	12
Bullawa–Amstrada	2045	2.15	40

4. From Salarki, how much further by road is Pantana than Bullawa?
   - A 1801 km
   - B 1899 km
   - C 1701 km
   - D 1699 km
   - E 1799 km

5. The air travelling time from Salarki to Makira is 1.1 hours, or 1 h 6 min. How long will it take to travel by air from Amstrada to Makira?
   - A 1 h 5 min
   - B 1 h 3 min
   - C 1 h 50 min
   - D 1 h 15 min
   - E 1 h 30 min

6. Travelling by rail, what is the total travel time between Bullawa and Pantana?
   - A 44 h
   - B 38 h
   - C 54 h
   - D 62 h
   - E 40 h

7. Craig uses the table to plan a plane trip, stopping at each of the cities. Starting in Pantana and finishing in Bullawa, what is the total travelling time taken?
   - A 7.4 h
   - B 10.3 h
   - C 5.15 h
   - D 8.2 h
   - E 8.15 h

8. A group of students was surveyed to record the colour and style of their hair.

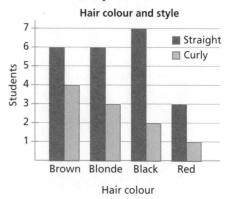

Hair colour and style

☞ **Answers and explanations on page 220**

Real Test 4

MATHEMATICAL REASONING
Statistics and probability

Here are three statements about the graph.

1. Thirty students were involved in the survey.
2. Twice as many blonde-haired students have straight hair than curly hair.
3. Black is the most common hair colour.

Which of these are correct?

A statement 1 only

B statement 2 only

C statements 1 and 2

D statements 2 and 3

E statements 1, 2 and 3

9 A box contains yellow, white and black marbles. A marble is selected at random from the bag. The probability that the marble is white is $\frac{1}{10}$. Selecting a black marble is twice as likely as selecting a yellow marble. What is the probability of selecting a black marble?

$\frac{1}{4}$	$\frac{1}{3}$	$\frac{2}{5}$	$\frac{3}{5}$	$\frac{2}{3}$
A	B	C	D	E

10 Sam has a box containing red balls and blue balls. If he chooses a ball at random, the probability that it will be red is 35%. What is the smallest possible number of blue balls in the box?

3	5	13	20	65
A	B	C	D	E

☞ **Answers and explanations on page 220**

WRITING
Persuasive text

- A persuasive text **gives an opinion on a question or topic** and the **reasons** for the opinion. When you write persuasive texts, you are aiming to convince your reader that you are right.

- For this reason, persuasive texts need to be **well organised and clear**. If they are not, the reader will not follow the ideas and so will not be convinced.

- You may not be given any choice about writing an opinion, so it is important to practise writing persuasive texts before your test. Then you will be ready for this type of question and will be able to attack it quite quickly.

- The stimulus prompt for a persuasive text will usually be a **question**. Some common ways to ask you to give your opinion are:
  Give your opinion on X.
  Do you agree or disagree?
  What do you think is/are …?
  What would you do if …?
  What changes would you like to see …?
  Is X a good or bad idea?
  Who or what do you think is …?
  If … happened, what three things would you …?

- For each of these questions, you would be expected to **give your reasons**. Sometimes the question might actually instruct you to do this (e.g. 'Why do you think this way?' or 'Give your reasons'). Even if it doesn't, it is important that you support your opinion with your reasons.

- One good thing about these kinds of questions is that the **topic will be very general**. It will be something that every student will be able to write about using their own experiences. So don't worry about being asked to write about something you know very little about. And don't think you need to study specific topics before the exam.

- You might sometimes be asked to write a kind of **combination description and opinion**. For example, you might be asked to write about or describe a person you like or admire very much, and then to say why you like or admire them. Even though you will need to write some descriptive text, you will still need to structure your writing as a persuasive text—you are still basically giving your opinion on a topic.

- Sometimes you will be able to write a persuasive text in **response to an open-ended question**. For example, you might be shown a picture of an old, deserted warehouse, and asked to use the picture as a prompt to write in any way you like. You could write a letter to a newspaper editor giving your opinion on why the warehouse should be converted to a youth centre.

- On the next page is an example of a persuasive text written in response to a test question, though not under test conditions. In your test, you **might not have time** to produce a polished piece of writing like this. However, if you are **well prepared**, you will be able to aim for this standard.

Sample

Question

An 'invention' is something that has been developed by human effort and that did not exist before. There have been hundreds of inventions in the history of humankind—for example, the wheel, pen and ink, the steam engine, electricity, the telephone, the aeroplane and the computer, to name just a few.

What do you think has been the most important invention of all time? Give reasons for your choice.
Note: You can choose any invention you like—you don't have to choose one of those above.

Response

Structure

Title—tells the topic of your writing

Introduction to the topic or question, and your opinion

Facts and sensible arguments to support your opinion

Paragraphs separate arguments

Topic sentences state arguments

Other sentences develop arguments

Conclusion— sums up opinion

Language

Thinking, saying verbs

Words like *points, aspects, reasons*

'Signpost words' help the reader follow your ideas

Words to show the **strength of your opinion**

Writing about people and experiences in a **general way**— not just your own personal experiences

Usually **present tense**

The Wheel

In my opinion, the wheel is the most important thing that human beings have ever invented. It might seem strange to say that something so simple-looking and so ordinary could be so important, but if you consider the following points, you will probably agree with me.

Firstly, wheels affect almost every part of our lives. Wheels are used, for example, in clocks, windmills, engines and transport. If you visit just one factory, you will see how important wheels are. You will see a wheel on almost every machine.

Secondly, wheels are especially important in food production. Wheels are used to grind wheat and other grains into flour. They are then used to mix flour and other foods into bread. We would all have to make our own bread, starting with grinding the wheat, if we did not have the wheel. In fact, we would have to grow the wheat because there would be no way to transport it.

Thirdly, our world would be completely different if we did not have the wheel for transport. Before the wheel was invented, people used to have to travel by foot or by riding on an animal. Travellers had to pull their luggage on a branch or roll it on logs of wood. That is what we would be doing now if we did not have the wheel. Everything would take longer to do.

We would be back to living in the Stone Age if some of our brilliant ancestors had not invented the wheel. Our modern world would simply not exist. The wheel is surely the most important invention of all time.

Practice Tasks

These tasks will give you some ideas about how to start writing quickly and complete a strong persuasive text in the short time you have in the test.

You will have to look back at *The Wheel* to answer some questions, and then do some opinion writing yourself based on the practice writing question below.

This time we will use the sample question on inventions as the practice writing question, because there are so many different answers to the question. However, you should choose a different invention to the one in the sample response—in other words, don't choose the wheel! We have given you a few more ideas in the pictures below.

Here is the question again.

Practice writing question

An 'invention' is something that has been developed by human effort and that did not exist before. There have been hundreds of inventions in the history of humankind—for example, the wheel, pen and ink, the steam engine, electricity, the telephone, the aeroplane and the computer, to name just a few.

What do you think has been the most important invention of all time? Give reasons for your choice.
Note: You can choose any invention you like—you don't have to choose one of those above.

- It is important to take a few minutes to plan an opinion response, but the good news is that persuasive texts are quite easy to structure. You are basically saying to the reader: 'I think …', and 'I think this way for these reasons: X, Y and Z'.

- So your first step is to ask yourself: What do I think about this question? If you had plenty of time, you could carefully consider the arguments for and against choosing a particular invention, but you don't have much time at all. So you really have to ask yourself: What is a reasonable answer to this question? What can I choose that I can make an argument for? What do I know something about?

For example, I could probably make a reasonable argument for most of the examples given in the question. I could also come up with a reasonable argument for everyday household items such as sticky tape, a garden spade, Velcro tape, a belt or a sewing needle. I would find it harder to come up with an argument for the steam engine, because I don't know much about it.

Tip: There is no ONE right answer!

● Your next step is to ask yourself: What are two or three good reasons I can use to support my opinion? (you won't have time for more than two or three). Then quickly write down your reasons in a plan. Don't waste time on your conclusion when planning—just think about it when you get to it.

Here is the plan for *The Wheel*.

Introduction (opinion)	the wheel
Arguments	1 affects most parts of our lives—clocks, windmills, machinery
	2 very important in making food
	3 very important in transport

Task 1

Write a brief plan for your response to the practice question (page 150) in the space below. For this practice just think of two arguments. Give yourself about two minutes.

Introduction (opinion) _____

_____

_____

_____

Arguments _____

1 _____

_____

_____

2 _____

_____

_____

_____

Practice Tasks

WRITING
Persuasive text—Writing the introduction

- When **writing the introduction** the important thing is to **make your opinion perfectly clear** at the very start. So in the introduction clearly **state your answer to the question**, as the writer of *The Wheel* did. If you like, you can say something else about your choice—for example, the writer could have said when the wheel was invented.

- You can begin your opinion sentence with phrases such as: I think …, I believe …, In my opinion …, It is my opinion that …

- It can be a good idea to write a **sentence to summarise the arguments** you are going to make. This gives the reader a kind of 'map' to follow as they read.
  For example, the writer of *The Wheel* could have written this sentence: 'The wheel affects almost all parts of our lives, and is very important in food production and in transport.' This sentence would have given a good summary map of the text. However, this map is not absolutely necessary, especially if you are writing a short piece.

Task 2

Write your introduction for the invention question now. Give yourself about five minutes.

Practice Tasks

- The main part of your persuasive text will be the **arguments (or reasons for your opinion)**. Your arguments might be facts or examples, or just sensible reasons for thinking the way you do. Either way, if you don't write any arguments to back up your overall opinion, you won't write a very convincing text.

- You will probably need to break up your arguments into paragraphs—**one argument per paragraph**. This helps the reader follow your ideas. (In a very short piece of writing, you would not need to do this.)

- A common way to write argument paragraphs is to write one sentence that gives the argument. This is called a **topic sentence**. It is a general statement of the argument. For example, in *The Wheel* the student writes (paragraph 2): 'Firstly, wheels affect almost every aspect of our lives'.

- After the topic sentence, you write **one or two sentences to support or develop the argument**. For example, in paragraph 2, the student writes: 'Wheels are used, for example, in clocks ...' This makes the argument more convincing—we now have some proof that 'wheels affect almost every aspect of our lives'.

- You can help the reader follow your arguments by giving them 'signposts'—**words and phrases that show how your ideas are connected**. Examples of signpost words are firstly, first of all, secondly, thirdly, next, one reason, another reason, the most important thing, for example, in fact.

- Your opinion will be more powerful and interesting if you use words that show **how strongly you feel or how certain you are about your opinions**. There are many words that help you do this, for example: very, extremely, so much, so many, every, all, most, almost all, especially, definitely, certainly, simply, surely, completely, totally, absolutely, probably, perhaps, must, might, could.

- *Tip:* These kinds of words are useful when writing an opinion and stating arguments: aspect, part, issue, question, matter, reason, point, result, consider, compare, discuss, believe, imagine, difference.

Task 3

1 a Look back at *The Wheel*. Underline the topic sentence in paragraph 3 and in paragraph 4.

  b Write one word to show what every sentence in paragraph 3 is about. _____

   Write one word to show what every sentence in paragraph 4 is about. _____

2 Underline any of the signpost words above used in *The Wheel*.

3 Look at these extracts from *The Wheel*. Underline the word that shows the strength or certainty (or uncertainty) of the writer's feelings.
  a ... if you consider the following points, you will probably agree with me. (paragraph 1)
  b ... wheels are especially important in food production. (paragraph 3)
  c ... our world would be completely different if we did not have the wheel... (paragraph 4)
  d The wheel is surely the most important invention of all time. (paragraph 5)

☞ **Answers and explanations on page 220**

Task 4

Write your two argument paragraphs now. Give yourself about 10 minutes.

Argument 1

_____

_____

_____

_____

_____

_____

_____

_____

_____

_____

_____

Argument 2

_____

_____

_____

_____

_____

_____

_____

_____

_____

_____

_____

Practice Tasks

- A strong conclusion helps to make your opinion more convincing. It **reminds the reader of your opinion**, and rounds off the whole text.
- You may not have time to write very much, but if you can, try to **restate your overall opinion** (varying your words if possible) and write something interesting or powerful to **'wrap up'** all your ideas.
- Some ways to start your conclusion are:
  In conclusion …, To sum up …, In summary …, Overall …

Task 5

Write a conclusion for your invention text. Give yourself about three minutes only.

_____

_____

_____

_____

_____

_____

_____

_____

_____

_____

Note: If you like, you can work on the invention text some more, refining what you have written so far and writing it out again on your own paper. Use the checklist below to review your writing.

Checklist for writing a persuasive text
Have you:
1 *introduced the topic/question and stated your overall opinion?*
2 *given two or three good arguments to support your opinion?*
3 *developed your arguments—for example, with facts or examples?*
4 *used signpost words to help your reader follow your arguments?*
5 *written a conclusion (summing up your opinion)?*
6 *checked your grammar, punctuation and spelling?*

Remember: In the test you won't have time to revise thoroughly and make big changes. You may have time to change a few words, but you will really be aiming to write well in one draft.

Real Test

- Choose **one** of the writing tests below to do now. Both test questions clearly ask you to write your opinion. The second question includes some description, but you still have to choose what to write about and say why, so it is still an opinion question.

- Use your own paper. You are encouraged to use two or three sheets of paper. Use the first one for planning and rough work, and write your response on the second and third sheets.

- If you wish, you could do both tests. However, it would be better to do them on different days. For extra practice, you could use the test questions again, writing in different ways each time.

- Set yourself a time limit of 25 or 30 minutes, depending on the test you are sitting. Use the checklist on page 155 to give it a quick review.

1 Imagine you are to be left alone on a small deserted island for two weeks. You will be allowed to take three items with you. What do you think would be the three most useful things to take with you, and why? (The island has fresh water.)

OR

2 Write about a place you know well—perhaps a place you love or hate. Briefly describe the place and then say why you feel the way you do about it.

☞ **Checklist on page 155**

How will you go?

Sample Test Paper

Instructions

- There are 30 questions in this sample paper. You have 40 minutes to complete the section. Each of the four parts of this Reading section reflect what you have done in your practice tasks.

- For questions 1 to 14, read each text extract or poem and then choose the best option (A–D) to answer each question.

- For questions 15–20, you must read the text extract and match the answers A–G to six spaces in the text.

- For questions 21–30, you must read the short texts A–D and match the options to the questions about them.

- Either circle or write your answers in the book or on your own piece of paper. In your real examination you will have to write your answers into a special booklet or possibly on the computer screen.

- Do not expect to get every answer correct. Some questions may be difficult for you within the time limit.

Extract A: from 'Miss Faberge's Last Daze' by Jenny Wagner

1 The girls in Miss Faberge's class cried when she left. Even the boys seemed quieter than usual; their clamour as they crowded round to say goodbye was muted and melancholy, and they signed her going-away card with gruff, tough messages to remember them—or else …

2 Miss Faberge was young, sweet-faced and elegant, had Italian shoes with matching hand-bags, and never worried about homework, or why you were late, or whether you talked in class.

3 Her replacement, Miss Blackstone, arrived three days later on a wet Monday morning…

4 'That's her,' said Tracey, watching her get out of the car.

5 It had to be. Only someone called Miss Blackstone could be so gross, so ugly, so badly dressed, so utterly opposite from everything Miss Faberge had stood for. She was tall and heavily built. She wore flat, thick shoes like a man's, with ankle socks instead of stockings, and a checked skirt that looked like a horse blanket. She wore no make-up, and her hair, flattened to her head by the rain, was so thin that her white scalp shone through.

6 'She needs a hat with horns,' said Marianne. She giggled as the woman, covering her head with a newspaper, lumbered towards the verandah. 'And saucepan lids for her chest.'

7 'I think she needs a broomstick,' muttered Tracey.

8 They met officially a few minutes later when the bell went for assembly. The whole school, smelling of wet wool, squeezed into the hall to mumble its way through the oath of allegiance and the national anthem, and to salute the flag, which was hanging in a corner of the hall like damp washing.

9 Miss Blackstone stood on the stage with the rest of the staff, and stared down.

10 If Tracey had needed another reason to dislike Miss Blackstone, that stare was enough. There was something unnerving about it; even at this distance her eyes looked odd; they were pale and round, as if she had found them in a riverbed.

Extract A (continued)

⑪ Tracey suppressed a giggle; she had a sudden image of Miss Blackstone fossicking among the pebbles in a dry river, trying them in her eye-sockets until she found a pair she liked.

⑫ She nudged Marianne, wanting to share the joke with her, and in that moment found herself looking straight into those terrible eyes. A fear as cold as stone struck through her; in panic she fixed her eyes on a portrait of the Queen that hung at the back of the stage, and pretended she had been looking at that all along.

From *Dream Time*, ed. Gascoigne et al., Penguin Group (Australia), Melbourne, 1990; reproduced with permission

Extract B: adapted from *Jane Eyre* by Charlotte Bronte

① A quarter of an hour passed before lessons again began, during which the schoolroom was in a glorious tumult; for that space of time it seemed to be permitted to talk loud and more freely, and they used their privilege.

② A clock in the schoolroom struck nine; Miss Miller standing in the middle of the room, cried—

③ 'Silence! To your seats!'

④ Discipline prevailed: in five minutes the confused throng was resolved into order. All seemed to wait. Ranged on benches down the sides of the room, the eighty girls sat motionless and erect; a quaint assemblage they appeared, all with plain locks combed from their faces, not a curl visible; in brown dresses, made high and surrounded by a narrow tucker about the throat; all, too, wearing woollen stockings and country-made shoes, fastened with brass buckles.

⑤ I was still looking at them, and also at intervals examining the teachers—none of whom precisely pleased me; for the stout one was a little coarse, the dark one not a little fierce, the foreigner harsh and grotesque, and Miss Miller, poor thing! looked purple, weather-beaten, and over-worked—when, as my eye wandered from face to face, the whole school rose simultaneously, as if moved by a common spring.

⑥ What was the matter? I had heard no order given: I was puzzled. Ere I had gathered my wits, the classes were again seated: but as all eyes were now turned to one point, mine followed the general direction, and encountered the personage who had received me last night. She stood at the bottom of the long room, on the hearth; she surveyed the two rows of girls silently and gravely. Miss Miller approaching, seemed to ask her a question, and having received her answer, went back to her place, and said aloud—

⑦ 'Monitor of the first class, fetch the globes!'

⑧ While the direction was being executed, the lady consulted moved slowly up the room. I retain yet the sense of admiring awe with which my eyes traced her steps. Seen now, in broad daylight, she looked tall, fair, and shapely; brown eyes and a fine pencilling of long lashes round, relieved the whiteness of her large front; on each of her temples her hair, of a very dark brown, was clustered in round curls, according to the fashion of those times; her dress, also in the mode of the day, was of purple cloth, relieved by a sort of Spanish trimming of black velvet; a gold watch (watches were not so common then as now) shone at her girdle. Let the reader add, to complete the picture, refined features; a complexion, if pale, clear; and a stately air and carriage, and he will have, at least, as clearly as words can give it, a correct idea of the exterior of Miss Temple.

First published in 1847

1 Both extracts describe the physical appearance of
A   a teacher arriving in the school or classroom.
B   the students at the school.
C   all the teachers at the school.
D   the school or classroom itself.

2 What is the main reason that the girls in Extract A don't like Miss Blackstone?
A   because her eyes look like pebbles
B   because she constantly stares at them
C   because she is so different from Miss Faberge
D   because she is ugly and dresses badly

3 The word 'clamour' is used in paragraph 1 of Extract A. Which word in Extract B in either paragraph 1 or 2 means something very similar?
A   throng   B   tumult   C   assemblage   D   all of the above

4 What does Miss Blackstone remind Marianne of?
A   a witch
B   a warrior
C   an evil queen
D   a wild animal

5 The atmosphere of the school assembly in Extract A could best be described as
A   excited and energetic.
B   bad-tempered and sullen.
C   sour and angry.
D   flat and unenthusiastic.

6 The atmosphere in the classroom in Extract B could best be described as
A   obedient and respectful.
B   silent and terrifying.
C   warm and loving.
D   active and industrious.

7 In Extract A, how would you describe Tracey's feelings about Miss Blackstone's stare?
A   She is terrified by it the first time Miss Blackstone looks at her.
B   She is terrified by it at first but then realises she is being silly.
C   She is unsettled by it at first but terrified by it the second time.
D   She thinks it funny because it makes her think of Miss Blackstone hunting for eyeballs.

8 In Extract B the dominant feeling of the storyteller (the student) is one of
A   envy.   B fear.   C   admiration.   D   astonishment.

☞ **Answers and explanations on pages 221-223**

Old Man Platypus

Far from the trouble and toil of town
    Where the reed beds sweep and shiver,
Look at a fragment of velvet brown—
Old Man Platypus drifting down,
5 Drifting along the river.

And he plays and dives in the river bends
    In a style that is most elusive;
With few relations and fewer friends,
For Old Man Platypus descends
10 From a family most exclusive.

He shares his burrow beneath the bank
    With his wife and his son and daughter
At the roots of the reeds and the grasses rank;
And the bubbles show where our hero sank
15 To its entrance under water.

Safe in their burrow below the falls
    They live in a world of wonder,
Where no one visits and no one calls,

They sleep like little brown billiard balls
20 With their beaks tucked neatly under.

And he talks in a deep unfriendly growl
    As he goes on his journey lonely;
For he's no relation to fish nor fowl,
Nor to bird nor beast, nor to horned owl;
25 In fact, he's the one and only.

AB Paterson

9 The phrase 'fragment of velvet brown' (line 3) captures the fact that platypuses are
  A small, dark and soft.   B fast, dark and soft.
  C plump, fuzzy and soft.   D fast, slippery and soft.

10 Stanza 2 is mostly about the platypus's
  A loneliness.   B friends and family. C playfulness.   D unusualness.

11 In Stanza 3 (line 13), what does the word 'rank' mean?
  A beautiful   B smelly   C green   D order

12 Which statement is true, based on the description in the poem?
  A The platypus is friendly towards other river animals.
  B The platypus is related to other river animals.
  C The platypus is not friendly towards other river animals.
  D The platypus likes to play with other river animals.

13 Overall, the poem focuses on
  A the beauty of the platypus.   B the uniqueness of the platypus.
  C the contentment of the platypus.   D the freedom of the platypus.

14 How would you describe the poet's feeling towards the platypus?
  A respect and wonderment   B envy and jealousy
  C amusement and joy   D love and caring

☞ **Answers and explanations on pages 221-223**

Six sentences have been removed from the text below. Choose from the sentences A–G the one which best fits the spaces 15–20. There is one spare sentence you will not need.

Jenolan Caves

① The Jenolan Caves are located within the Blue Mountains and are a major system of limestone caves. They are a popular tourist destination in New South Wales with around 250 000 visitors per year. **15** _____ . They are one of the most important areas of natural and cultural history in Australia and a significant site of geological interest.

② As you would expect, the caves were known to the local population for many years and the First Nations name for the area was Binoomea, which means a dark place. **16** _____ . The First Nations Australian people knew of the caves but probably did not enter them since the caves were cold, wet and unsuited for habitation. The First Nations word 'jenolan' means a high mountain. The first recorded discovery by Europeans was in 1838, by pastoralist James Whalan, although there are reports that an escaped convict, James McKeown, was the first settler in the area.

③ The cave network follows the course of a subterranean section of the Jenolan River and has more than 40 kilometres of passages at multiple levels and over 300 entrances and archways. **17** _____ . It is 24 metres high, 55 metres wide and 127 metres long. There are 22 caves to visit in the Jenolan system.

④ The Lucas Cave has the highest and widest chambers. The Cathedral in the Lucas Cave is just over 50 metres high. Because of its size and acoustics, this cave has sometimes been used for wedding ceremonies and musical recitals. The cave was found in 1860 by George Whiting and Nicholas Irwin. It is named after the politician John Lucas, who worked hard to protect the caves and to have them declared as a reserve. You may also see a blue–green underground river in this cave. **18** _____ . Another cave of interest is the Imperial which contains some of the best fossil deposits and even some Tasmanian devil bones.

⑤ The clay in the Jenolan Caves has been found to be approximately 340 million years old, making it one of the oldest cave systems in the world. The caves are made of limestone or calcium carbonate—the cemented remains of marine organisms including corals and brachiopods. When rainwater enters the cave, it is a little acidic and dissolves the limestone. **19** _____ . Also, the formations in the caves are formed by drops of water that form crystals. The crystals are made of calcium carbonate, called calcite. **20** _____ .

⑥ In the caves there are two well-known formations, called stalactites and stalagmites. Stalactites come down from the roof of the cave. Stalagmites reach up from the floor. Columns are a third formation. A column is a continuous pillar that is formed when a stalactite joins a stalagmite. Other formations are flowstone, or a large sheet of crystal; shawls, which are like sheets of upright crystal; and curly forms called helictites.

A Over time, this enlarges any breaks or openings in the rock.

B The caves are about 200 kilometres west of Sydney near Oberon, and about a 2–3 hour drive.

C There is some mention of the caves in accounts of the Gundugarra people.

D Caves can be scary places.

E It takes around an hour and a half to inspect this cave.

F Some more recent scientific views of how the caves were formed include water also bubbling up from below.

G Visitors to the caves pass through the Grand Arch, which is the largest open cave in Australia.

☞ **Answers and explanations on pages 221-223**

For questions 21–30, choose the text which best answers the question.

Which extract …

suggests some people could have damaged their careers with their technology predictions?　**21**　____

compares the life of a child today with the life of someone in times gone by?　**22**　____

mentions someone who wrote about something like the internet long before it existed?　**23**　____

suggests it is good to be stimulated to think of life in the future?　**24**　____

describes a scene from a book, a film or a TV show?　**25**　____

mentions the possibility of people living forever?　**26**　____

describes someone who can travel through time?　**27**　____

focuses primarily on a book about future possibilities?　**28**　____

does not ask you a question related to the future?　**29**　____

suggests science fiction can highlight problems with our modern way of living?　**30**　____

Extract A

Every year for years gone by, scientists, engineers and leaders of industry have made predictions about future technology. Some have been accurate. Others have got it horribly wrong. We can laugh now at how terribly they did, but we can also see how easily we might make the same mistakes. My personal favourites are:

'This telephone has too many shortcomings to be seriously considered as a means of communication.' 1876, the President of the Western Union in the USA.

'The horse is here to stay, but the automobile is only a novelty, a fad.' 1902, a leading banker giving advice not to invest in the Ford Motor Company.

'The cinema is little more than a fad. It's canned drama. What audiences really want to see is flesh and blood on the stage.' 1916, famous actor Charlie Chaplin.

'Television won't last because people soon get tired of staring at a plywood box every night.' 1946, Darryl Zanuck, movie producer

'A rocket will never be able to leave the Earth's atmosphere.' 1936, *The New York Times.*

'There is no reason for any individual to have a computer in his home.' 1977, the founder of a large digital equipment corporation.

Over to you. What do you predict will take off in the next 20 years?

☞ **Answers and explanations on pages 221-223**

Extract B

Science fiction (or sci-fi) is a type of literature that deals with imaginative and futuristic ideas such as space exploration, time travel, and extra-terrestrial life. Besides providing entertainment, it can also criticise present-day society. It may surprise you but science fiction had its beginnings in ancient times when the line between myth and fact was often blurred. Even ancient tales such as *The Arabian Nights* with its magic flying carpets and fantastic creatures contain themes and characteristics of modern-day science fiction such as travel to other worlds and extra-terrestrial lifeforms.

Many people consider HG Wells one of science fiction's most important authors. Writing in the late 1800s, his works imagined alien invasion, biological invisibility, space travel and even something resembling the World Wide Web. Today there are many, many science fiction novels, and of course a number of popular and sometimes disturbing science fiction films. Think *ET*, *Avatar*, *Blade Runner*, *The Matrix* and of course *Star Wars*. And in television series we have, amongst others, *Star Trek*, *The X-files* and *Dr Who*.

Extract C

Some people hate *Dr Who* but I love it. *Dr Who* is a British science fiction television programme which began in 1963 and is now seen all over the world. It tells of the adventures of a Time Lord called Dr Who, an extra-terrestrial being who appears to be human. Dr Who explores the universe in a time-travelling spaceship called the TARDIS which from the outside looks like a blue British police box. With various trusty companions the Doctor fights off extremely nasty enemies and works to save civilisations from the past, present and future. I love the show because it really makes you think about future possibilities. One episode included a scene where the Doctor and his companion are driving a car in the skies above a busy city of the future. They are using clearly marked sky roads and expressways. These roads have lanes and signs and traffic lights just like any roads here on Earth. The Doctor and his companion are chatting about the heavy traffic and trying to change lanes and cursing the driver in front—just as happens with drivers on every road now. I remember thinking: I wonder if that will happen? Will we one day travel *over* our cities rather than *through* them. I don't think it will be long actually. Do you?

Extract D

We're living in a rapidly changing world—are you ready for it? Around the year 1900, human knowledge doubled every 100 years. It now doubles almost every year. Many things that you use in your day-to-day life would be unrecognisable by your great-grandparents. Just imagine what the world of your great-grandchildren would look like to you! Just 30 years ago, making a phone call meant sitting in one place inside the house, talking into a telephone wired via a plug to the outside world. The thought of making a call from the beach, the top of a mountain or a car was crazy. Other inventions common today that seemed like science fiction just decades ago include instant electronic communication, a space station visited by reusable spacecraft and 3D colour television. Our new book *Imagining the Future: Invisibility, Immortality and 40 Other Incredible Ideas* shows young Australians the world they may well find themselves in, all based on current scientific advances. Printed food, designer babies, weather control and immortality: some concepts are more likely than others, some are already happening, but all have science behind them. However, we need to get more young people hooked on science and maths. We'd like to see the next generation dream big, believe in their ability, and turn science fiction into science fact.

From Simon Torok and Paul Holper, *Imagining the Future: Invisibility, Immortality and 40 Other Incredible Ideas* seen on www.kids-bookreview.com. Reproduced with permission.

Instructions

1 There are 35 questions in this sample test. You have 40 minutes to complete the test.
2 There are five possible answers to each question (A, B, C, D, or E). For each question, you are to choose the ONE answer you think is best. To show your answer, circle one letter (A, B, C, D, or E).
3 If you decide to change an answer, rub it out completely and mark your new answer clearly. Remember that the answer sheet in the real test is computer marked, so rub it out completely before marking your new answer.
4 You may write on these pages (or on the question booklet in the real test).
5 Calculators, rulers and geometrical instruments are not allowed.
6 Ask your parent, teacher or an adult if you need any special help.
7 Do not attempt this test if you are tired or ill—wait until another day.
8 Do not expect to get every answer correct—some questions may be difficult for you.

1 Brendan leaves home at 1545 to walk to soccer training.

Training starts at 1600 and lasts for an hour and a half.

His dad picks him up and he arrives home five minutes later.

How many minutes has Brendan been away from home?

A 105 minutes
B 110 minutes
C 115 minutes
D 120 minutes
E 150 minutes

2 A rectangle is divided into identical squares.

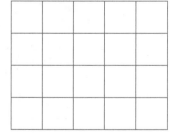

Scarlett shades $\frac{2}{5}$ of the squares and Bianca shades $\frac{3}{4}$ of the remaining squares.

Ben now shades 2 squares.

How many squares remain unshaded?

1	2	3	4	5
A	B	C	D	E

3 What is the product of the first four multiples of 10 greater than 75?

A 504 000
B 750 000
C 7 920 000
D 50 400 000
E 79 200 000

4 Jack places a container half filled with water on a set of scales. The scales show a mass of 8.5 kg.

When Jack completely fills the container with water the scales show a mass of 14.3 kg.

What is the mass of the empty container?

2 kg	2.7 kg	2.9 kg	3.2 kg	5.8 kg
A	B	C	D	E

5 Barsha wrote the letters of the alphabet.

She wrote these three statements:

1. S and Z do not have a line of symmetry.
2. There are more letters with one line of symmetry than letters with two lines of symmetry.
3. All the vowels have at least one line of symmetry.

Which of the following is/are correct?

A statement 1 only
B statement 3 only
C statements 1 and 2 only
D statements 1 and 3 only
E statements 1, 2 and 3

☞ **Answers and explanations on pages 223–226**

6 Ben and his daughter Jen compared their ages.

Ben's age is a multiple of 8 and the digits add to 10.

Jen's age is 3 more than a factor of 50 and is also 2 less than a multiple of 6.

If Jen is more than 5 years old, how old was Ben when she was born?

28	32	34	36	64
A	B	C	D	E

7 Terry has two rectangular paddocks with the same area.

Not to scale

Paddock *A* has dimensions 120 metres by 40 metres.

The length of Paddock *B* is 40 metres shorter than the length of Paddock *A*.

How much wider is Paddock *B* than Paddock *A*?

5 m	10 m	16 m	20 m	24 m
A	B	C	D	E

8 The petrol tank in Albert's car has a capacity of 60 L.

The diagram shows the petrol gauge when he left home this morning.

Throughout the day, Albert drove a distance of 200 km. His car used petrol at the rate of 8.5 L/100 km.

In the afternoon, Albert filled the petrol tank at a service centre.

How much petrol did Albert buy?

15 L	17 L	25 L	28 L	32 L
A	B	C	D	E

9 The shapes ■, ▲ and ● represent numbers.

7 × ■ = 63

■ + ▲ = 21

▲ − 8 = ●

What is the value of ● ?

4	6	7	9	12
A	B	C	D	E

10 Joshua is making a pattern of isosceles triangles. The triangles are white, grey or black.

Joshua wants the pattern to have a line of symmetry.

He adds more triangles to the right of the existing triangles.

How many more black triangles will be added?

0	1	2	3	4
A	B	C	D	E

11 Two normal dice are rolled and the numbers on the uppermost faces are multiplied together. When this number is 10 or more, only the unit is recorded. For example, 4 × 6 = 24, so 4 is recorded. A table summarises the results.

	1	2	3	4	5	6
1	1	2	3	4	5	6
2	2	4	6	8	0	2
3						
4						
5						
6						

The complete pattern for row four is

A 4 8 2 6 0 4   B 4 6 8 0 2 4

C 4 8 2 8 4 0   D 4 0 6 2 4 0

E 4 8 2 6 8 2

☞ **Answers and explanations on pages 223-226**

12 Part of a train timetable is detailed below.

Mirannie	07:10	07:25	07:40	07:55	08:20	08:55	09:30	10:05	10:50
Reedy Creek	07:14	07:29	07:44	07:59	08:24	08:59	09:34	10:09	10:54
Highmead	07:20	07:35	07:50	08:05	08:30	09:05	09:40	10:15	11:00
Glendon Brook	07:29		07:59	08:14		09:14		10:24	
Mitchells Flat	07:37		08:07	08:22		09:22		10:32	
Roughit	07:50	08:00	08:20	08:35	08:55	09:35	10:05	10:45	11:25
Elderslie	07:58	08:08	08:28	08:43	09:03	09:43	10:13	10:53	11:33
Cranky Corner	08:05				09:10			11:00	
Stanhope	08:10		08:38		09:15		10:23	11:05	
Branxton	08:20	08:23	08:48	08:58	09:25	09:58	10:33	11:15	11:48

Here are three statements about the timetable.

1. From 7:40 to 10:30 there are four trains that stop at Mitchells Flat.

2. The fastest trip between Highmead and Stanhope takes 43 minutes.

3. Mercia arrives at Glendon Brook station at 7:30. One hour 40 minutes later she can arrive in Cranky Corner.

Which of these statements is/are correct?

A   statement 2 only

B   statement 3 only

C   statements 1 and 2 only

D   statements 2 and 3 only

E   statements 1, 2 and 3

13 Leah, Colton and Prue each have a sum of money to spend at the Black Friday sales.

After Leah has spent $\frac{1}{2}$ of her money, Colton $\frac{1}{3}$ of his money and Prue $\frac{1}{4}$ of her money, they all have an equal amount of money remaining. If they have a total of $180 remaining, what was the total amount spent?

$90	$110	$120	$165	$195
A	B	C	D	E

14 William draws a regular hexagon. Line *L* is a line of symmetry of the hexagon. William uses a protractor to measure one of the interior angles of the hexagon.

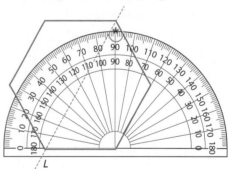

What will be the size of the angle shown as * ?

45°	50°	60°	65°	70°
A	B	C	D	E

15 When 39 oranges and 42 mandarins are shared between six people, each person receives 13 pieces of fruit and there are three pieces left over.

Which number sentence shows this information?

A   13 × 6 − 3 = 39 + 42

B   13 × 6 + 3 = 39 + 42

C   (39 + 42) ÷ 13 + 3 = 6

D   (39 + 42) ÷ 6 − 3 = 7

E   39 + 42 ÷ 6 − 3 = 7

☞ **Answers and explanations on pages 223-226**

16 The diagram shows a rectangle that has a length 4 cm longer than its width.

If the width is then increased to make the shape into a square, the perimeter will be 36 cm. What was the original area of the rectangle?

14 cm²	20 cm²	45 cm²	36 cm²	8 cm²
A	B	C	D	E

17 Iris, Demi and Catriona shared the driving on a road trip from Sydney to Adelaide.

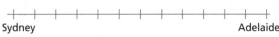

Sydney   Adelaide

Iris drove $\frac{1}{3}$ of the distance, Demi drove $\frac{1}{4}$ the distance and Catriona drove the rest.

Which of the following statements is/are correct?

1. Iris drove further than Catriona.
2. Catriona drove less than half the distance.
3. Demi and Catriona drove less than $\frac{3}{4}$ of the distance altogether.

A   statement 1 only
B   statement 2 only
C   statement 3 only
D   statements 1 and 2 only
E   statements 2 and 3 only

18 In a magic square, when you add up all the numbers in a row, a column or a diagonal, you always get the same result.

The magic square below has some numbers missing.

9		*	7
	3	13	12
15			1
		11	14

What is the missing number at *?

2	4	5	6	8
A	B	C	D	E

19 Pia has a spinner that is split into six sections.

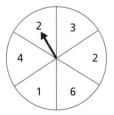

She spins the arrow and it lands on 2.

Her friend Shaun is going to spin the arrow once.

Which of these statements is/are correct?

1. The probability of Shaun spinning an even number is $\frac{2}{3}$.
2. The probability that Shaun's number is 4 more than Pia's is $\frac{1}{6}$.
3. The probability that Pia and Shaun's numbers add to more than 5 is $\frac{1}{3}$.

A   none of them
B   statements 1 and 2 only
C   statements 1 and 3 only
D   statements 2 and 3 only
E   statements 1, 2 and 3

20 The population of a city is 5 679 852.

Gabriela rounds the population to the nearest hundred thousand.

Enrico rounds the population to the nearest hundred.

What is the difference between their numbers?

A   11 100
B   20 100
C   20 200
D   31 100
E   79 800

☞ **Answers and explanations on pages 223–226**

21 A graph shows the travel patterns of two brothers, Goran and Seth, who both live at home.

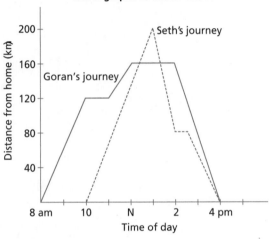

Travel graphs of Goran and Seth

Which of these statements is/are correct?

1. In total, Seth travelled 40 km further than Goran.

2. Seth was away from home 2 hours fewer than Goran.

3. During the morning Goran stopped for 30 minutes.

A statement 1 only
B statement 2 only
C statement 3 only
D statements 1 and 2 only
E statements 2 and 3 only

22 Sally has two tanks.

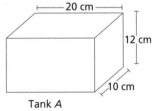

Tank *A*

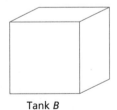

Tank *B*

Not to scale

Tank *A* measures 20 cm by 10 cm by 12 cm.

It is $\frac{2}{3}$ filled with water.

Tank *B* is already $\frac{1}{5}$ filled with water.

Half the water in Tank *A* is poured into Tank *B*.

Tank *B* is now full.

What is the capacity of Tank *B*?

A 600 mL
B 800 mL
C 1 L
D 1200 mL
E 1500 mL

23 A group of friends were comparing the cost of three cereals.

Stefania paid $10.40 for a box of *P* and two boxes of *Q*.

Oliver paid $13.30 for a box of *Q* and two boxes of *R*.

Marlon bought two boxes of *P* and a box of *R* and paid $14.40.

Johannes bought a box of each cereal.

How much did Johannes spend?

$12.70	$12.90	$13.00	$13.10	$13.25
A	B	C	D	E

24 The diagram shows a cube with each of the faces having an area of 16 cm².

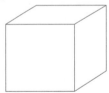

The sum of the lengths of all the edges on the cube is

24 cm	36 cm	12 cm	6 cm	48 cm
A	B	C	D	E

25 In the number 41 280 how many times larger is the value represented by the digit 4 than the value represented by the digit 8?

A 5000 times
B 50 times
C 1000 times
D 2000 times
E 500 times

☞ **Answers and explanations on pages 223-226**

26 The table shows the local times in a number of cities and is useful for identifying the time differences between each city.

City	Local time
San Francisco	Thursday 10:40 am
London	Thursday 6:40 pm
Berlin	Thursday 7:40 pm
Tokyo	Friday 2:40 am
Brisbane	Friday 3:40 am

Lee flies out of Berlin at 9:05 pm Wednesday for Tokyo. If the flight takes 14 hours, what is the local time in Tokyo when the plane arrives?

A   12:05 am Thursday
B   11:05 am Thursday
C   4:05 pm Thursday
D   6:05 pm Thursday
E   8:05 am Thursday

27 The shape consists of rectangles.

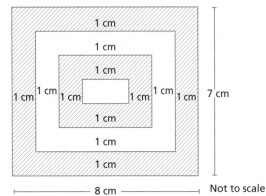

What is the total shaded area?
A   28 cm²   B   30 cm²   C   32 cm²
D   36 cm²   E   40 cm²

28 Leon mixes oil and petrol in a container to use as fuel for his lawnmower. He pours 250 mL of oil into an empty container. He then adds 50 times as much petrol.

How many litres of fuel does Leon have in the container?

2.75 L	12.5 L	12.75 L	15 L	15.5 L
A	B	C	D	E

29 The diagram shows a six by six square with some squares shaded. The diagram will have quarter turn symmetry if more squares are shaded.

What is the smallest number of squares that need to be shaded?

3	4	5	6	7
A	B	C	D	E

30 A cube has all its faces painted red. The cube is then cut into 64 smaller cubes of equal size.

How many of the small cubes have no painted faces?

0	1	4	8	27
A	B	C	D	E

31 The diagram shows a paddock. Pete needs 640 metres of fencing to enclose the paddock.

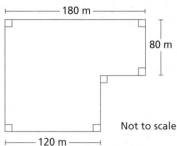

What is the area of the paddock, in hectares?
A   2.08 ha
B   2.16 ha
C   2.365 ha
D   2.64 ha
E   3.2 ha

☞ **Answers and explanations on pages 223-226**

32 At her parent's twenty-fifth anniversary party Laura watched people introducing themselves by shaking each other's hands. She drew up the following table:

Number of people	Sketch	Number of handshakes
2		1
3		3
4		6
5		10

How many people would be standing in a group where everyone shook everyone else's hand when 36 handshakes occurred?

8	9	10	12	11
A	B	C	D	E

33 Ms Dann uses a series of stickers to reward students in her class. Each sticker is worth a certain number of points.

Student	Stickers	Points
Adalyne	☺☺★☺★★☺☺★	44
Jace	★☺☺★☺☺★	34
Clementine	★☺★☺	?

When a student achieves 50 points they receive a Principal's award. How many more points does Clementine need to earn a Principal's award?

20	28	30	32	36
A	B	C	D	E

34 A quilt is to be made by sewing small triangular patches together. Part of the quilt is shown below.

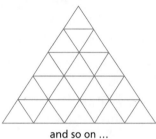

and so on ...

Each patch is an equilateral triangle with sides measuring 6 cm each. The first row has one patch, the second row has three patches, the third row has five patches, and so on. It takes Megan one minute to sew one side of a new triangular patch onto another patch. How long will it take her to sew a quilt with six rows of triangular patches?

A 18 minutes B 30 minutes
C 35 minutes D 45 minutes
E 48 minutes

35 A water tank has a capacity of 12 kL.

Currently the tank is $\frac{2}{3}$ full. Water is pouring into the tank at the rate of 10 L per 15 seconds.

The tank has a tap at its base and water is pouring out of the tank at the rate of 15 L per 10 seconds.

10L/15s

15L/10s

If the rates are maintained, when will there be no water remaining in the tank?

A 2 h B 2 h 20 min
C 2 h 40 min D 3 h
E 3 h 15 min

☞ **Answers and explanations on pages 223-226**

Instructions

1 There are 40 questions in this sample test. You have 40 minutes to complete them.

2 With each question, there are four possible answers: **A**, **B**, **C** or **D**. For each question, you are to choose ONE answer you think is best. To show your answer, circle one letter (**A**, **B**, **C** or **D**).

3 If you decide to change an answer, rub it out completely and mark your new answer clearly. Remember that the answer sheet in the real test is computer marked, so rub it out completely before marking your new answer.

4 You may write on these pages (or on the question booklet in the real test).

5 Ask your parent, teacher or an adult if you need any special help.

6 Do not attempt this test if you are tired or ill—wait until another day.

7 Do not expect to get every answer correct—some questions may be difficult for you.

---

1 482 tickets were sold to an event. A total of 294 people bought tickets. 10 people bought six tickets each but all the others bought either one or two tickets each. How many bought one ticket?

A 128　　B 136　　C 138　　D 146

2 **Isla:** 'We're having pizza for dinner tonight.'
Ben: 'We're having fish again.'
Isla: 'You eat a lot of fish. You must love it.'
Ben: 'No, I hate it. But my uncle owns a fish shop.'

Which assumption has Isla made in order to draw her conclusion?

A Ben loves eating fish.

B Ben does not like pizza.

C Ben's uncle gives Ben's family free fish.

D Anyone who eats a lot of fish must love fish.

3 'Whoever drove the car must have known where to find the key and how to drive a manual vehicle.'

If that statement is correct, which one of these statements must also be correct?

A If Jack did not drive the car, he must not be able to drive a manual vehicle.

B If Jack knew where to find the key and how to drive a manual vehicle he must have driven the car.

C If Jack did not know how to drive a manual vehicle he must not have known where to find the key.

D If Jack did not know where to find the key he cannot have driven the car.

4 Six children—Ben, Ethan, George, Jeannie, Penny and Samara—each rolled a dice while playing a game. Ethan and Penny both rolled the same number, but all the others rolled different numbers. Samara's number was two higher than Ben's. George rolled a number that was higher than that of Jeannie, but two lower than that of Penny. Ethan rolled a 4.

Which is correct?

A Samara rolled 3.　　B Ben rolled 2.

C George rolled 5.　　D No-one rolled 6.

☞ **Answers and explanations on pages 226–230**

5 One of the healthiest things you can do for yourself is go for a walk. A good walk exercises the body and stimulates the heart. It also relaxes the mind as you leave your worries behind and notice the simple things in the world around you. You'll return refreshed, energised and clear-headed.

Which of the following best expresses the main idea of the text?

A Walking is a healthy activity.

B Walking is better than running.

C People have too many worries.

D Walking is good for a healthy heart.

6 Four identical tiles made this pattern on a bathroom wall, but the bottom part of the pattern has been covered by a towel.

What does the missing part of the pattern look like?

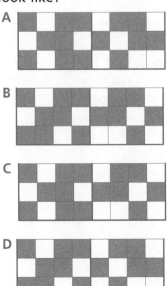

7 Mel raises calves for a dairy farmer. The calves are in three groups that Mel calls babies, teens and springers. New calves go into the baby group and as they get older, they move to the teens and then to the springers before they return to the dairy farmer. There were 32 calves in the baby group, 24 in the teens and 37 in the springers. Mel then received 8 new calves and 5 went back to the dairy.

If 10 were then moved from the babies to the teens and there are now 28 teens, how many springers are there now?

A 33   B 37   C 38   D 43

8 **Dora:** 'The Sunshine Bay Wildlife Clinic is in desperate need of a mobile van. Local vets are being flooded with injured and orphaned wildlife. Many of these vets do not have the time or resources to understand the different wildlife species. A mobile clinic in a van would be able to move around to different areas so more wildlife could benefit from the service. It would also be deployed during emergencies such as bushfires to assist impacted native animals.'

Which statement most strengthens Dora's argument?

A The Wildlife Clinic already has a mobile van.

B Local vets need advice about the best way to start treatment before sending cases on to the Wildlife Clinic.

C Wildlife carers in some areas do not have access to a vet.

D The Wildlife Clinic recently treated a lace monitor that had been hit by a car.

9 Whoever found the needle in the haystack must have had both perseverance and keen eyesight.

Based on the information above, which conclusion must be true?

☞ **Answers and explanations on pages 226-230**

A If Dermot did not find the needle in the haystack, he cannot have keen eyesight.

B If Dermot did not have perseverance, he cannot have found the needle in the haystack.

C If Dermot did not find the needle in the haystack, he cannot have perseverance.

D If Dermot has both perseverance and keen eyesight, he must have found the needle in the haystack.

10 Five pieces of a puzzle form a square. Here are four of the pieces:

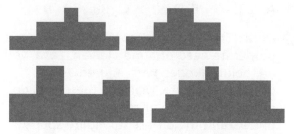

Which of these pieces will complete the square?

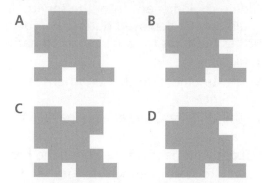

11

Fang: 'My mother is an author.'

Sam: 'It must be fun to just daydream all day.'

Fang: 'Don't say that to her! She says being an author is hard work! She has to keep writing even when she has no ideas at all.'

Which assumption has Sam made in order to draw his conclusion?

A All authors daydream all day.

B Daydreaming is fun.

C Anyone who daydreams all day must be an author.

D Authors sometimes have no ideas.

12 Twelve competitors take part in a competition where the winner will be the person who loses the least points over four rounds.

The points lost in the first three rounds are shown below.

Competitor	Round 1	Round 2	Round 3
Walter	9	1	6
Paige	4	7	5
Anne	8	6	7
Cooper	2	13	4
Olivia	7	4	6
Kirby	3	5	2
Osman	12	3	1
Shae	5	4	8
Matt	1	2	15
Sylvia	6	8	3

One person can be sure of winning if he or she loses fewer than a certain number of points in the fourth round.

What is the maximum number of points that person can afford to lose and be sure of winning outright?

A 3   B 4   C 5   D 6

☞ **Answers and explanations on pages 226-230**

13 Five boys grow vegetables in five plots all in a row. Each boy grows a different vegetable (one is broccoli) and each plot has a fence painted in a different colour.

It is known that:

- Lloyd grows carrots and his plot is next to Barney's which has a blue fence and is on the left end of the row.
- The corn is in a plot with an orange fence.
- Stefan has the plot with the yellow fence and he is not the boy who grows peas.
- Jock grows beans, but not in an end plot.
- The plot with the red fence is somewhere to the right of the one with the green fence and two away from Rafael's.

What is grown in the plot in the middle of the row?

A beans   B broccoli   C corn   D peas

14

> Whenever the light on the cordless drill is flashing on and off, it means that the drill's battery is starting to run low.

Olivia: 'The light is on continuously. The battery might be about to run out. Maybe we should plug it in to recharge.'

Locky: 'No, the light isn't flashing, so the battery must be fine. We should keep working.'

If the information in the box is true, whose reasoning is correct?

A   Olivia
B   Locky
C   Both Olivia and Locky
D   Neither Olivia nor Locky

15 Norbit's mother does not want the new local weekend farmers' market to continue. She claims that the new market takes business away from already established local shops, which have always served the community well.

Which statement most weakens Norbit's mother's argument?

A   The market sells fresh produce and flowers as well as food such as cakes and jams.
B   Prices at the market are more expensive overall than in the local shops.
C   The market supports many local farmers and creates a sense of community.
D   The local shops have ample parking and are open seven days a week.

16 I have an old digital clock that keeps the correct time. To form the numbers that show the time there are seven parts that might or might not light up. Both of the numbers that show the minutes have one part that is faulty and does not light up at all.

One morning, I looked at the clock and it showed:

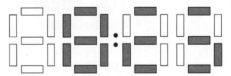

Nine minutes later it showed:

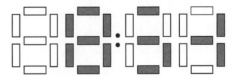

How would the clock look six minutes later?

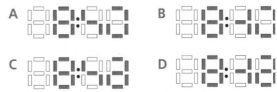

☞ **Answers and explanations on pages 226-230**

17 **Livvy:** 'There's nothing wrong with skipping class to go to the mall. Other students do it all the time.'

Which assumption has Livvy made in order to draw her conclusion?

A   If other students go to the mall they will get caught.

B   There is nothing wrong with doing something if other students do it.

C   It is more fun to go to the mall than to go to class.

D   Other students skip class and go to the mall all the time.

18

> To be successful in the competitive field of hair styling, you need to be artistic, a good listener and have good time management skills.

Travis: 'I am artistic and a good listener. I love talking to people and helping them to look the best they can but I really am terrible at time management. I could probably learn those skills with a bit of effort and practice, so I think I have a good chance of being a successful hair stylist.'

Sybilla: 'I'm artistic and I definitely have a flair for hair styling and I have good time management skills. I'm not a great listener. People are always telling me I need to learn to listen better. I like talking too much. I'm sure that if I tried hard and improved my listening skills I might become a successful hair stylist.'

If the information in the box is true, whose reasoning is correct?

A   Travis only

B   Sybilla only

C   Both Travis and Sybilla

D   Neither Travis nor Sybilla

19 Train tickets between Tia's home and work (and return) cost $7 per day. There is also a weekly ticket (for 5 days from Monday to Friday) for $25 and a fortnightly ticket for $40. Tia works from home some of the time, but in the next month will have to travel to work on Monday 3 and also on the 6, 11, 12, 13, 14, 17, 19, 20, 24, 25 and 28 of the month.

What is the minimum amount that Tia could pay for the train tickets to travel on those days?

A $75   B $77   C $79   D $80

20 Hermione wants to attend the school excursion to Canberra next term. Her parents have agreed that she can go provided she pays half the cost. Her teacher has said that to be allowed to participate in the excursion, students must have achieved an excellent result in either or both the end-of-term test or the major assignment.

Based on the information above, which of the following cannot be true?

A   Hermione will not be allowed to participate because she did not do well in her end-of-term test.

B   Hermione will be allowed to participate because she saved enough money and she did well in her end-of-term test even though she did not do well in the assignment.

C   Hermione will not attend the excursion because she did not do well in the test even though she saved enough money and she achieved an excellent result in the assignment.

D   Hermione will not be allowed to participate because she did not save enough money and she did not do well in her end-of-term test.

☞ **Answers and explanations on pages 226–230**

 21 The lights at the end of the street allow 10 cars through heading east–west/west–east and only four cars through heading north–south/south–north between 7 am and 9 am and between 2 pm and 4 pm. At other times of the day the lights allow the same numbers of cars each way.

Quentin: 'Those times coincide with school traffic hours. The lights must have adjustments to allow for when children go to or from the public school on Hamilton Street that's north of the lights.'

Ariana: 'The lights would be adjusted so that the side with more traffic gets more green time. That can vary at different times of the day, such as school hours in any direction.'

If the information in the box is true, whose reasoning is correct?

A Quentin only
B Ariana only
C Both Quentin and Ariana
D Neither Quentin nor Ariana

22 This is the top view of an object.

Tim said a side view could be X. Tom said a side view could be Y.

X

Y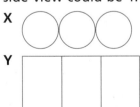

Who is correct?
A Tim only
B Tom only
C Both Tim and Tom
D Neither Tim nor Tom

23 **Lucie** (brand spokesperson for the Love Your Skin range of skin care products): 'Your skin is the largest organ in your body. It has three main layers: the epidermis, dermis and subcutaneous tissue. Your skin functions to protect you from bacteria, chemicals and temperature. It is waterproof and has pores for sweat to help you cool down. You need to look after your skin and the best way to do that is through our range of protective and nourishing Love Your Skin products.'

Which statement most strengthens Lucie's argument?

A Our products for the daytime include all-important sun protection ingredients.
B Skin is flexible to allow for movement but strong enough to hold you together.
C Common skin problems include sun damage, acne, dermatitis and fungal infections.
D All our products are made from natural ingredients such as coconut oil, wild peach, macadamia nut oil, weeping tea tree and mango.

24 The local theatre company is putting on a play in April. The play will be performed every Wednesday, Thursday, Friday and Saturday nights beginning on Wednesday, 2 April, although there will not be a performance on Anzac Day, 25 April. On two Sundays there will be an afternoon performance and the last show will be on 30 April.

How many times will the play be performed?

A 17   B 18   C 19   D 20

☞ **Answers and explanations on pages 226–230**

25 There was at least one bird, either a wren, finch or parrot, in every shrub in the garden. Every shrub that was in flower had a wren. Every shrub with a wren also had a finch, but no shrub with a wren also had a parrot.

Which statement must be correct about the shrubs in that garden?

A   If a shrub has a finch it must also have a wren.

B   If a shrub does not have a parrot it must not have a wren.

C   If a shrub has a parrot it must not have a finch.

D   If a shrub is in flower it must not have a parrot.

26 Gymnastics trials are being held in NSW this week to select gymnasts to compete in the national competition. NSW will have either five or six women competing.

The top two women at trials will earn a spot in the team competition at the national event. Three more spots will be selected by the committee—two of whom will be added to the four-member team competition and one who will only compete in individual events.

A further gymnast, Claire, has already been approved to compete in the individual events at the nationals because of how well she has performed internationally over the past three years. Claire will still compete in the state trials. If she finishes in the top two at the trials, she will automatically enter into the team competition. But that would mean the individual spot she already earned would be forfeited and the state will send just five women.

Based on the information above, which of the following cannot be true?

A   Two gymnasts will earn places in the team competition and two will be selected by the committee.

B   If Claire does not make it into the team competition then she can't compete individually.

C   One woman will be named as an individual competitor by the committee.

D   Claire will compete as an individual competitor based on her own body of work.

27 A gardening book states: Cucumbers will grow successfully in full sun. They need plenty of water in summer.

Noah said: 'My cucumbers have not grown very well. I must have not given them enough water.'

Jeb replied: 'No, you gave them plenty of water. They must not have had enough sun.'

Who has correctly interpreted the gardening book in their statements?

A   Noah only

B   Jeb only

C   Both Noah and Jeb

D   Neither Noah nor Jeb.

28 Yesterday I counted 12 children riding bicycles and tricycles as I walked along a path. Each bicycle had two wheels and each tricycle had three wheels and there was exactly one child on each. I counted 29 wheels altogether.

How many bicycles were there?

A 5   B 6   C 7   D 8

☞ **Answers and explanations on pages 226-230**

29 A hole has been torn in this cloth.

Which of these pieces could be used to fix the cloth, keeping the pattern correct?

A   B

C 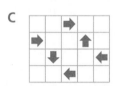   D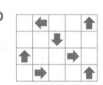

30 Toby, Keith, Sally, Joel and Jenny rode their horses in a jumping event. The time the riders took to complete the course was important and also the number of rails that the horses knocked down.
Toby took the least time but his horse knocked down 6 rails.
Keith's horse only knocked down 1 rail, but he took the longest time.
Sally's horse knocked down 4 rails.
Joel's horse knocked down fewer rails than Sally's but took more time than her.
Jenny took longer than Joel but knocked down fewer rails.

Which cannot be true?

A   Joel had the third fastest time.
B   Sally did not have the second fastest time.
C   Jenny's horse knocked down two rails.
D   Keith's horse knocked down the fewest rails.

31 The effectiveness of a vaccine was being tested. A table was drawn up to show some results.

Patient	Vaccinated	Caught the disease
April	No	P
Jai	Q	No
Zara	R	Yes
Mikey	Yes	S

Which needs to be known to determine whether the vaccine is working?

A   P and Q   B   Q and R
C   P and S   D   R and S

32 **Huw:** 'The best way to get all the nutrition you need is to eat a healthy diet with lots of different kinds of fruit and vegetables, whole grains and healthy protein choices. By eating whole foods you get the additional benefits of phytochemicals and other compounds packaged by nature in balanced ways in real food. Scientists haven't yet learned all there is to know about the way compounds work together in the human body and it's too easy for people to overdo it with supplements.'

Which statement most strengthens Huw's argument?

A   Vitamin and mineral tablets can supplement a healthy diet to provide an increased level of nutrition.
B   Some supplements can cause an imbalance of minerals in the body that can be detrimental to good health.
C   If your diet is inadequate a vitamin and mineral supplement can help you.
D   It's important to consult your doctor before taking any vitamin or mineral supplements.

☞ **Answers and explanations on pages 226–230**

33 Candy wants to buy a dozen cakes at a market. Four stallholders sell the cakes she wants, but at different prices.

Stallholder	Price
Helen	$2.10 each or 2 for $4.00
Louise	$2.50 each or 3 for $5.00
Neil	$2.40 each or 4 for $7.00
Gaynor	$2.20 each or 5 for $8.00

From which stallholder can Candy buy the 12 cakes at the cheapest price?

A Helen
B Louise
C Neil
D Gaynor

34 Not only did Joe forget to label anything on this graph, but he also changed the order and left out one of the columns.

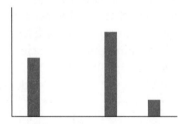

This was the information that Joe was supposed to graph.

Colour	Red	Blue	Green	Yellow
Number	50	35	25	10

Which column did Joe leave out?

A red B blue C green D yellow

35 Online supermarket grocery shopping is becoming increasingly popular. It means that you can order your items from the comfort of your home or office and have them delivered to your door. The ease of online shopping is what makes it so popular and the convenience outweighs any negative consequences such as being delivered bananas that are either too ripe or unripe.

Which of the following statements weakens the argument?

A Online supermarket grocery shopping means no more having to search for a parking space.
B Online supermarket grocery shopping means no more having to lift and lug the items to and from your vehicle or public transport.
C Online supermarket grocery shopping means not being able to choose your own fresh fruit and vegetable items and sometimes that means items are not exactly what you would have liked.
D Online supermarket grocery shopping means the inconvenience of you having to be available to receive your order so choose your time slot carefully and allow some time for drivers to be a bit early or a bit late.

36 Three people each made two statements about an incident involving a car that was caused by one of the three. Each person made one true statement and one false statement.

Max: 'Susan didn't cause it. The car was blue.'
Susan: 'Julie didn't cause it. The car was blue.'
Julie: 'Max didn't cause it. The car was not blue.'

Which statement must be false?

A Susan didn't cause it.
B Julie didn't cause it.
C Max didn't cause it.
D The car was not blue.

☞ **Answers and explanations on pages 226–230**

37 A survey was conducted to see how many people had read each of four books: *Purple Fields*, *Grace*, *Road to Rio* and *Meanderings*. It was found that:

- Some people had read all four books.
- Everyone who had read *Meanderings* had also read *Purple Fields*.
- Some people had read only one book, but more people had read only *Purple Fields* than had read only *Road to Rio*.
- All those who read *Grace* had also read *Meanderings*.

Which book had the most people read?

A *Purple Fields*
B *Grace*
C *Road to Rio*
D *Meanderings*

38 *Alice's Adventures in Wonderland* is a classic children's story written by Lewis Carroll and first published in 1865. It's the story of Alice who follows a talking white rabbit into a rabbit hole and lands in a fantasy world filled with imaginary characters and bizarre situations. The language is rich with humour and full of nonsensical word play and riddles that appeal to adults as well as children. The book has been published in 97 languages, has never been out of print, and it's as entertaining today as it was back in the 1800s. Every child should read this timeless tale.

Which of the following best expresses the main idea of the text?

A *Alice's Adventures in Wonderland* is a classic children's story written by Lewis Carroll and first published in 1865.
B The book has been published in 97 languages and never been out of print.
C The language is rich with humour and full of nonsensical word play and riddles that appeal to adults as well as children.
D Every child should read this timeless tale of *Alice's Adventures in Wonderland*.

39 **Shaun:** 'I'm going to ask the school to allow students to play table tennis as a school sport. It's an alternative to the more common or traditional school sports and so it might appeal to students who are not so keen on team sports. It develops fitness, agility and coordination and it's a good spectator sport too. The school will just need to purchase equipment and work out where to store the tables.'

Which of the following statements weakens Shaun's argument?

A There's nowhere currently to store the equipment.
B A fundraising event could be held to offset the cost of the equipment.
C Equipment needed includes a table, net and post set, four bats and balls.
D Table tennis is also called ping pong.

40 Isabel has these four pieces.

She chooses two of the four pieces and uses them to make each of these three shapes.

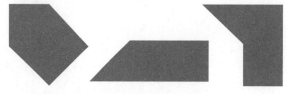

Which two pieces did Isabel choose?

A I and II
B II and IV
C I and III
D II and III

☞ **Answers and explanations on pages 226-230**

Instructions

1   There are two writing tasks in this sample test. Do only ONE of the tasks. (However, you might want to do the other task on another day as extra practice.)
2   You have 30 minutes to do this test. (The real test may give you more or less time than this.)
3   Write your answer on the following pages.
4   Remember: The amount you write is not as important as the quality of what you write.
5   If you finish writing before the time is up, use the rest of the time to go over your work and to make changes you think might improve it.

Writing Task 1

Your school is putting together a time capsule for its centenary celebrations. The time capsule will be put away somewhere safe with a message for future teachers and students to open in 100 years time.

Every student in your school is being asked to write about three items that they think should go in the time capsule, and to give their reasons.

What would you write?

OR

Writing Task 2

Use this picture as the basis for a piece of writing. You may write in any form you like—for example, a description, a story, a recount, a newspaper article, a diary or a poem.

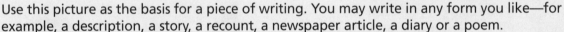

☞ **Checklist page 231**

Your writing will be judged on:

- what you have to say
- how well you organise the way you say it
- how clearly and effectively you express yourself.

Parents and teachers might like to use the checklists in the Answer section on pages 231–232 to give you some feedback.

Remember: This is just practice, so don't worry too much if they suggest you need to improve in some way. You can use this page for planning and rough work.

START YOUR RESPONSE ON THE NEXT PAGE.

WEEK 1

READING
Literary prose texts   Pages 3–12

Practice Task 1

1 D 2 C 3 B 4 C 5 D 6 A 7 C 8 A

EXPLANATIONS

1 The first sentence tells you the answer, but you need to take in the whole sentence not just one or two words. If you read this sentence very quickly you could get this wrong because all the answers seen reasonable and all include words from the first sentence.

2 You have to read and understand the whole text. You have to work out the link between checking the watch and what Mr Pemberley does afterward—you are not directly told this link. The words 'as he did every night at exactly this time' and the repetition of this idea in Paragraphs 3 and 5 are the most obvious signs that the writer is describing a man preparing for a regular routine, and that being on time was an important part of this preparation.

3 All the answers sound quite sensible but there is no evidence for A or D, and Mr Pemberley is unlikely to live in a bank (D). We know he is very rich so C is a possibility. However, you have to think about what 'sound' a bank might make and relate that to the closing of the big strong door. The most logical explanation is that the writer is imagining the sound of the door of a large bank vault or safe closing and is using that as a symbol of security.

4 Paragraph 5 shows this clearly. Mr Pemberley thinks he owns the skies and stars— 'Pemberley heavens, Pemberley lights'. Paragraph 3 also refers to what he thinks he owns but in this case it is to do with his actual property—his land and gardens—so not B. Paragraph 1 is more about his

preparation for his nightly routine and doesn't refer to what he owns, so not A. And Paragraph 8 is the writer's comment on Mr Pemberley's wealth so not D.

5 The contrast between a 'clear night sky' and 'fumes of industry or traffic' should lead you to this answer. The 'un' prefix also helps you work it out.

6 The repetition of 'mine, all mine' in paragraphs 3 and 5, and his satisfied 'Ah!' in paragraphs 4 and 6 shows there is no change in his attitude, and paragraph 7 contains nothing which suggests this attitude has changed as he starts to walk to the gates.

7 The four single-line paragraphs—2, 4, 6 and 8—are very effective in the extract. They mark the different parts of Mr Pemberley's nightly walk as he stops outside his door, looks at his gardens, then looks upwards at the skies above and then walks on, so A. And in doing so, they add to the drama of the tale as Mr Pemberley makes his way to the gates. If you look at the title of the extract you see it is from a story called 'Mr Pemberley Checks the Gates'. By describing the walk in this way and breaking up the stages of the walk he highlights the drama and captures our interest, so also B. This means the answer is C.

8 You have to pick your way through the many clues. Even though the answer might seem obvious, you have to check that you have not presumed too much or missed some information. There is a lot of evidence that Mr Pemberley cares about his possessions, for example 'mine, all mine' so not C. There is no evidence that he is kind, so not B. And on the basis of what we read, it seems likely that he would know exactly how much money he had, so not D.

Practice Task 2

1 D 2 B 3 C 4 C 5 D 6 C 7 B 8 A

EXPLANATIONS

1 The best way to approach this is by eliminating the wrong answers. It is not answer A as Extract A does not tell us how familiar the character is with the city streets, and Extract B's character moves from unfamiliar to familiar. Answer B could be true—Extract B character is definitely struggling to understand, but we are not told for sure that the Extract A character is, so not B. We know that the Extract A character is hiding but clearly Extract B character is not—he is running and walking in the bush and streets. So that leaves D. Both characters are fleeing an unseen enemy—the Carnies in Extract A and the Martians in Extract B.

2 Paragraph 4 in Extract B tells you explicitly about the character's change from terror to disbelief ('I asked myself had these latter things indeed happened?'). There is no evidence that there is any change in Extract A character's feelings.

3 Things are not stated clearly in this text. You have to build up your own image of what is going on from the information given. You have to search for evidence. Try to find more than one indication of the answer to be sure. There are many clues: 'crumbling', 'sagging doorway', 'debris', 'cracked', 'scrapers fell', 'ruins'.

4 The first paragraph tells you the boy is 'framed in a sagging doorway' so it seems he is on the street, so C. But paragraph 8 could lead you to choose B if you don't read this whole sentence: 'The Carnies living in that part of the city had passed by that morning as he watched unseen from his high window'. It seems that he was in a tall building that morning but is now in the street.

5 It helps to know the meaning of the word, but the context should lead you to the right answer. Answer A does not make sense, and B or C do not seem right for the slight noises mentioned.

6 Any of these answers could be true but the focus on the regular behaviour of the workman saying 'good night' and carrying a basket (presumably lunch or dinner) suggests Answer C—the man is going about his daily business and is totally unaware of what is going on elsewhere in the area (which the main character is aware of). The boy too is behaving quite normally, running along with his father (presumably).

7 This is difficult because there is no explicit evidence. You have to imagine why a person might go out in such a scene and take such a risk—hunger seems a likely reason. And we know he is on his own in a deserted city. There is one clear clue: the boy knows that 'anything exposed would be ruined'—this suggests he is thinking of food. There is no suggestion he is about to fight the Carnies—they seem too frightening—so not C, and there is no mention of going home although that may be part of this eventual plan—so not D.

8 Again there is no explicit evidence. However, we know the character is struggling with whether or not he may have imagined these things (paragraphs 4 and 6), and it is likely therefore that he might think they will also think he is imagining things. There is no evidence that they don't want to hear about his experiences (so not B), or that he is being selfish (so not D). He probably does hope they will not have similar experiences but this is not the main reason he would not share what he knows with them (so not C).

Practice Task 3

1 D 2 A 3 D 4 A 5 B 6 C 7 A 8 C

EXPLANATIONS

1 You need to have an understanding of the whole of Extracts A and B to answer this correctly. All answers are reasonable but only D is correct. Not A, as although both extracts mention human beings, Extract A only mentions them keeping inside their houses. Not B—while Extract A does mention the severe storm quietening down, in Extract B the freezing weather is a constant. Answer C is incorrect as only Extract B mentions animals serving men—the tamed dogs who are pulling the sled. Only D refers to both men and animals feeling the impact of nature—to the extent that it has taken the lives of birds in Extract A and men in Extract B.

2 You must look for solid evidence for the statement in both texts. The last line of the fourth paragraph of Extract A confirms this is the correct answer. Paragraph 3 also suggests this with mention of their 'summer breeding grounds' and the 'urgency' with which they flew. The dogs in Extract B may be following a route they have travelled before but this is not stated.

3 You need to look at the sentence the words appear in, but also at other parts of the text to be sure the other choices are wrong. The words 'curtained the rising moon' give you the answer. It is not winter (though cold)—the birds are coming to their summer breeding ground—so the answer is not A. It has been stormy but the weather clears in the scene so not B. It is the sunset (the sun 'dipped') so not C.

4 It helps to have a wide vocabulary and to know the meanings of words like 'undulation', but you should be able to work the answer out from other clues e.g., 'rising then falling' and 'making full use of the up-draughts and currents to bank,

then glide'. Thinking of the way birds fly will help you if you can't get the answer from the text, in other words using your experience of the world.

5 You have to look very carefully at the text to get this answer correct, searching for words that suggest an action or feeling of a living creature (human or animal). Both extracts refer to nature/landscape acting on the animals and humans within it, but only Extract B presents it as having the qualities of a living creature. The first line of Extract A refers to the forest 'frown[ing]' (as in a face frowning). It also says in the second paragraph that 'it is not the way of the Wild to like movement' (only living beings 'like'). The final sentence of the third paragraph also suggests the actions of a living creature— 'does the Wild harry and crush into submission'.

6 The writer refers to the box in exactly the same way at the end of paragraph 2 and in so doing focuses our minds on what could be in it, and leads us to think that he is probably describing a coffin. The box is referred to again in paragraph 3 and we discover that it is indeed a coffin. Answers A, B and D all make sense but do not justify the writer's use of the term 'long and narrow oblong box' twice.

7 In these kinds of questions it helps to be familiar with the word. If you are not, you have to look at the context and to think about what the sentence or sentences nearby are telling you. Here all answers are quite reasonable but the text tells you their faces were 'so coated' with crystals and their faces were like 'ghostly masques'—even if you don't know the word 'masque' you can probably guess it is something like a mask. So their faces could not be seen—so invisible. Also the suffix 'ible' helps you. It points to either answer A or C.

8 To answer this question correctly you have to pick up on clues all over the extract. The writer might feel any one of these things so A, B, C or D could be correct. However the evidence for C comes through in the description of the savage nature of the land, and the fact that the men (and the dogs) are doing their job—the word 'toil' or 'toiled'. The writer uses many words to describe the men which point to the correct answer—'defiant', 'unawed', and ' indomitable'—and their appearance. We know they are suffering great hardship and still they go on. He shows he respects them and wants us to do so too.

Real Test

1 C 2 A 3 A 4 C 5 D 6 B 7 B 8 D

EXPLANATIONS

1 You need to think about the meaning of the whole first paragraph to get this right. You might be tricked by answer A, but 'facts' is not a proper noun. Paragraph 5 also confirms how important facts are to the speaker.

2 The speaker wants the children to learn facts only. He does not mention feelings (so not B) or interests (so not C). You can feel sure he would also want the children to be well-behaved but he does not say this.

3 The first line of the second paragraph gives you the answer—'plain, bare, monotonous vault'. 'Monotonous' means 'all the same/ boring' and 'vault' suggests a large space (think bank vault). There is no evidence for other answers.

4 This is a difficult question. The most useful clues are the 'cellar' part of the word 'cellarage' and the words 'two dark caves'. A cellar is a room underneath a building—a basement. So the writer is using this image to show the speaker's eyes are deep within the two eye spaces

(the 'caves'). The caves are 'overshadowed by the wall'—that is the forehead.

5 You don't need to understand every part of the paragraph to get this. It should be clear that the writer is not praising the man (so not B or C). 'Abusing' is too strong, so not A. All the words and expressions used to describe the man's face, hair, voice and appearance suggest the writer is mocking—making fun of— the speaker.

6 The speaker may be speaking loudly and he may be long-winded (going on for too long) but the overriding impression given is that his speaking style was emphatic. The word 'emphasis' is used six times in the second paragraph to describe how each aspect of the speaker's words and movement and expressions reinforced the emphatic way he delivered the words. He is certainly not hesitant so not D.

7 You need to read the whole sentence that contains the word 'vessels'— it shows that the meaning is that the children are like empty containers which need filling up with knowledge. The imagery is reinforced in paragraph 6 with the word 'pitchers'— another word for jugs or vessels—which are to be 'filled so full of facts'.

8 You need to check each paragraph for mention of military things. In paragraph 7 you will see his speech style was compared to a cannon loaded and preparing to blow the children out of childhood (and into the learning of multiple facts).

THINKING SKILLS
Critical thinking—Identifying the main idea   Pages 14–16

Real Test 1

1 A 2 C 3 D 4 C 5 B 6 D 7 C 8 D 9 D 10 B

EXPLANATIONS

1 The text wants you to accept that all gardens need some hens and A is the

statement in the list that best expresses this. The rest of the text gives you reasons to believe the main idea. It gives supporting information about all the benefits of having hens in the garden and the work they will do there, with the final sentence being a call to action to get some hens.

2 The letter wants you to accept that it is time to stop wasting money on space exploration. C best expresses this and the rest of the text gives you reasons to believe it, with supporting details about where the writer thinks money should be spent on Earth instead.

3 The text wants you to accept that watching a movie is better than reading the book it is based on and D is the statement in the list that best expresses this. The rest of the text gives you reasons to believe this main idea, giving supporting details about different ways the movie is better than the book.

4 The text wants you to accept that zoos play an important role in animal conservation and C best expresses this main idea. The rest of the text gives you reasons to believe the main idea, with supporting information about different things zoos do that help animal conservation.

5 The text wants you to accept that trees talk to help each other out and B is the statement in the list that best expresses this. The rest of the text gives you reasons to believe the main idea. It gives supporting information explaining how acacia trees in Africa communicate with each other to defend themselves from giraffes.

6 The text defines the term idiom and gives examples of idioms and their meaning. The text wants you to accept that idioms make English more colourful and interesting but they can also make it more difficult to understand (especially for people whose first language is not English). The text gives you reasons to agree with statement D.

7 The text wants you to accept that whistleblowers do a great public service. The rest of the text gives you reasons to believe this is true by pointing out what a whistleblower is and does and how they may be protected by law.

8 The text wants you to accept that in the future scientists might be able to work out a way that humans can create wormholes and travel through them in space-time and D is the statement in the list that best expresses this.

9 The main idea in the text is that the Great Barrier Reef is under threat. Every sentence after the introductory sentence mentions this threat.

10 The text wants you to accept that eating fruit is good for your health. Each sentence supports this claim.

> **THINKING SKILLS**
> *Critical thinking—Assessing the impact of further evidence to strengthen an argument*   Pages 18–20

Real Test 2

1 A 2 D 3 B 4 B 5 A 6 B 7 A 8 D 9 C 10 C

EXPLANATIONS

1 The argument is that people generally eat too much salt and should modify their salt consumption. The statement which strengthens the argument is that 'Processed and takeaway foods contain more salt than most of us realise'. This statement adds additional evidence to follow from Isaac's call to action: 'Australians should think about how much hidden salt they are eating'.

2 This argument text is an advertisement for the sale of a home unit. Reasons are offered to support the argument. It ends with a call to action. Note that advertisements

generally make exaggerated claims because their goal is to sell a product or persuade people to a course of action. The exclamation 'Don't miss out!' strengthens the argument by reinforcing the call to action and appealing to the reader's emotions, i.e. their fear of missing out.

3 The argument is that Australia should end homelessness. All the options are true but the statement which most strengthens the argument and underpins any argument to end homelessness is that 'Safe housing is a basic human right'.

4 The argument is that people should definitely not revere Cook with the title 'Founder of Australia' because his voyage led to the claim of *terra nullius* and therefore the dispossession of First Nations Australians. The statement which most strengthens the argument is that Australia was not *terra nullius* when Cook visited.

5 The argument expresses a concern about AI. It lists situations where AI could be detrimental to humans—'banking and finance, traffic, power grids and communications'. The statement that 'The use of AI in military applications is also a concern' strengthens the argument by adding an additional reason for concern.

6 Anh's argument is that cats can jump so high that they would win gold in a high jump competition with other pets. The statement that cats have powerful hind legs to propel themselves up explains how they jump so high. So that statement most strengthens Anh's argument.

7 The argument is that we should not celebrate Valentine's Day because it has become over-commercialised and an excuse for companies to make money. The statement that Valentine's Day is a $14 billion industry is further evidence of this and is the only statement that strengthens the argument.

8 The Student Council wants students to be able to evaluate teachers because this will give an opportunity for students' voices to be heard which will make students happier and more successful in the classroom. The statement that there is a correlation between a student's happiness in class and their academic success most strengthens this argument.

9 The argument is that sitting for too long is dangerous because physical inactivity increases the risk of chronic health problems. The statement that six per cent of all deaths can be attributed to physical inactivity is further evidence of the risks and so most strengthens this argument.

10 Luca's argument is that the City Council should not chop down the trees because they cool the city and produce oxygen. The fact that one large tree produces enough oxygen for 20 people to breathe adds additional evidence to back up this argument, so it is the statement that most strengthens it.

> **THINKING SKILLS**
> *Critical thinking—Assessing the impact of further evidence to weaken an argument* Pages 22–23

Real Test 3

1 D 2 C 3 B 4 B 5 A 6 B 7 D 8 C 9 C 10 A

EXPLANATIONS

1 The argument is that the team needs to find ways to turn around a losing streak. Strategies are listed to support turning around a losing streak. The fact that 'Players have lost so often they now expect to lose' weakens the argument because this is not a way to improve the team's chances of winning.

2 The argument attempts to convince people that Fiji is a perfect holiday destination. It provides evidence or reasons to support this claim. The statement that cyclones can occur

between November and April undermines or weakens the evidence that Fiji has glorious weather all year round.

3 Ahmed says he likes living in Mudgee better than living in the Blue Mountains because he can hike in the Wollemi National Park however the Wollemi National Park is part of the Greater Blue Mountains wilderness area so he could have hiked at his previous address. B undermines his argument as the reason for preferring to live in Mudgee.

4 Alyssa's argument is that you don't need to buy the most expensive running shoes. She says that it's not true that the more you pay the better the shoe will be. She also supports her claims by referencing a market research study which found that the cheaper running shoes were better. Her argument is weakened by the statement that 'Lighter running shoes are better regardless of price'. This statement undermines her argument because the lightest running shoes could be the most expensive.

5 Jessica's argument is that a shark would lose a fight with a dolphin. Her reasons are that dolphins are smarter and support each other in pods. The statement that weakens Jessica's argument is 'If a great white shark managed to capture a dolphin its jaws would kill the dolphin', meaning the shark would win the fight.

6 The town planner's argument is that the new development will beautify the area. The statement that most undermines this claim is that the development will replace existing beautiful native rainforest. If the rainforest is already beautiful, the area does not need beautifying. By calling the claim into question, it weakens the argument.

7 The mining company's argument is that they should commence exploration and mining in Antarctica because resources are drying up elsewhere while Antarctica has valuable resources and the impacts of mining there will be minor. The statement that most undermines this claim is that any changes in Antarctica will have a disastrous global impact. By calling into question the claim that the impact of mining will be minor, it weakens the argument.

8 Ella's father is arguing that dogs should be allowed to run off-leash at the local beach. His supporting evidence that the sand dune vegetation can act as a natural fence is undermined by the statement that the dunes are a habitat for endangered shore birds. This weakens his argument.

9 The argument attempts to convince people to replace a meal a day with a DILL tablet to make sure they get all the vitamins and minerals they need to be healthy. The statement that research shows that vitamins in fresh food are more effective undermines or weakens this argument.

10 The argument is that consumers need products that are built to last because too many break and can't be repaired or updated. The statement that consumers want to have the latest model and prefer to buy new products undermines or weakens this argument.

MATHEMATICAL REASONING
Whole numbers and place value　　Pages 26–27

Real Test 1

1 B　2 A　3 C　4 D　5 B　6 A　7 E　8 B　9 E　10 A
EXPLANATIONS

1 The numbers to be multiplied are 9999 and 100. This means the answer is 999900 which is written as 999 900.

2 Emily's number is 45 and Chloe's number is 18. As 45 − 18 = 27, the difference between the numbers is 27.

3 24 508 329 = 25 000 000 (to the nearest million) and 24 510 000 (to the nearest ten thousand).

$$\begin{array}{r} 25\ 000\ 000 \\ -24\ 510\ 000 \\ \hline 490\ 000 \end{array}$$

4 The numbers are 8 and 6 as 8 − 6 = 2 and 8 × 6 is 48. Also $8^2 + 6^2 = 64 + 36$, which is 100.

5 The four numbers are 1, 3, 6 and 10. The sum is 1 + 3 + 6 + 10 which is 20.

6 As 14 × 7 is 98, there are 14 multiples of 7 less than 100. Ignoring the 7, there are 13 multiples that are two-digit numbers. As there are 90 two-digit numbers (10 to 99), and 90 − 13 is 77, there are 77 two-digit numbers that are not multiples of 7.

7 As we need Q x 6 to end in a Q, then 4 × 6 = 24 is the starting point. We find 74 × 6 = 444. This means PQ is 74.

8 By adding the numbers on the diagonal, we get a total of 21. By filling in the missing numbers, we have X equal to 2.

9 Use the completed puzzle:
6 × 5 − 4 × 2 = 30 − 8 = 22. This means 7 × 4 − 3 × 3 = 28 − 9 = 19.

10 As 4 + 6 + 11 + 13 = 34, fill missing squares to find X is 7.

Real Test 2

1 E **2** B **3** C **4** B **5** A **6** E **7** A **8** D **9** A **10** D
EXPLANATIONS

1 The 8 has a place value of 8 000 000. The 4 has a place value of 400.
As 400 × 20 000 = 8 000 000, then it is 20 000 times bigger.

2 The remainders will be 0, 1, 2, 3 and 4. As 0 + 1 + 2 + 3 + 4 = 10, the total is 10.

3

13	8	15
14	12	10
9	16	**11**

4 Each number can only be used once. So the largest even number is 876 and the smallest even number is 354.

$$\begin{array}{r} 876 \\ -\ 354 \\ \hline 522 \end{array}$$

5 As 14 × 4 is 56 and 14 − 4 is 10, then the numbers are 14 and 4. As 14 + 4 = 18, the sum is 18.

6 Consider the options. If there were 50 students at the start, then 40 were girls and 10 boys. Once 5 girls and 5 boys left there were 35 girls and 5 boys. As 7 × 5 is 35, there were 7 times as many girls as boys.

7 X must be 1 to be placed on the left of the answer number. We then determine the sum is 9999 + 1 = 10 000 so that Z is 0.

8 By adding the numbers 11, 4 and 6, we find the straight lines add to 21. By completing other squares, we have X as 13.

9 Using the complete puzzle
24 ÷ 6 + 6 ÷ 2 = 4 + 3 = 7, then
25 ÷ 5 + 8 ÷ 2 = 5 + 4 = 9.

10 As 13 + 11 + 9 = 33, then X is 16.

MATHEMATICAL REASONING
Fractions   Pages 30–31

Real Test 3

1 D **2** C **3** D **4** C **5** A **6** D **7** E **8** A **9** C **10** B
EXPLANATIONS

1 Distance = 24 (down) + 12 (up) + 12 (down) + 6 (up) + 6 (down) = 60.

2 There are 8 squares. Amrit shades 4 squares, which means there are still 4 unshaded squares. As $\frac{1}{4}$ of 4 is 1, Annona shades 1 square. This leaves 3 squares unshaded.

3 As 4, 10, 5 and 20 are factors of 20, rewrite each fraction with a denominator of 20. $\frac{3}{4} = \frac{15}{20}$, $\frac{7}{10} = \frac{14}{20}$, $\frac{4}{5} = \frac{16}{20}$, $\frac{13}{20}$. The order from smallest to largest is $\frac{13}{20}$, $\frac{7}{10}$, $\frac{3}{4}$, $\frac{4}{5}$. This means the smallest fraction is $\frac{13}{20}$ and $\frac{3}{4}$ is between $\frac{7}{10}$ and $\frac{4}{5}$. Statements 1 and 3 are correct.

4 $\frac{3}{4}$ of 24 is 24 ÷ 4 × 3 which is 18. Now $\frac{2}{3}$ of 18 is 18 ÷ 3 × 2 which is 12. This means Elijah ate 12 biscuits.

5 Asha had 6 lengths of string, which formed 12 pieces. He used 4 pieces, which means 8 remained. This means he did not use $\frac{8}{12}$, or $\frac{2}{3}$, of the original length.

6 If $\frac{2}{3}$ of the audience = 120 then $\frac{1}{3}$ is 120 ÷ 2 = 60. This means there are 60 adults watching the movie. As $1 - \frac{1}{4} = \frac{3}{4}$, and 60 ÷ 4 × 3 is 45, there are 45 women in the audience.

7 The cost of a pencil is less than the cost of a pen, so Charles will be able to buy more pencils than pens. As 15 ÷ 3 × 5 is 25, Charlie can buy 25 pencils.

8 Half of $\frac{2}{3}$ is $\frac{1}{3}$. Colton now has $\frac{1}{3}$ as many as Nolan originally had and Nolan has $1\frac{1}{3}$ times as many as he originally had. This means Nolan now has 4 times as many stickers as Colton. Now, 60 ÷ 4 is 15. Colton now has 15 stickers.

9 As $1 - \frac{2}{5} = \frac{3}{5}$, then $\frac{3}{5}$ of Delilah's spoons is 36. Now, 36 ÷ 3 × 5 is 60, so Delilah originally had 60 spoons. As 60 ÷ 4 is 15, Madeline originally had 15 spoons.

10 As $1 - \frac{4}{7}$ is $\frac{3}{7}$, then $\frac{3}{7}$ of the students are boys. Now, 28 ÷ 7 × 3 is 12, so there are 12 boys in the class. As $1 - \frac{1}{3} = \frac{2}{3}$, and 12 ÷ 3 × 2 is 8, then 8 boys in the class were born in Australia.

Real Test 4

1 C 2 D 3 B 4 D 5 D 6 B 7 D 8 E 9 A 10 A

EXPLANATIONS

1 Let sides be 2 cm and 1 cm. This means the volumes are 8 cm³ and 1 cm³, and so the fraction of the larger cube filled is $\frac{1}{8}$.

2 $\frac{3}{8}$ full = 24, $\frac{1}{8}$ full = 8, $\frac{8}{8}$ full = 64. This means it contains 32 L when half full.

3 As $\frac{1}{4} = \frac{2}{8}$ and $\frac{1}{2} = \frac{4}{8}$ the middle is $\frac{3}{8}$.

4 Jacob shades 4 squares. There are 8 squares not shaded. Henry shades 6 squares. As 4 + 6 is 10, there are 10 shaded squares.

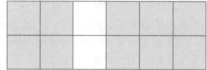

5 As 8, 3, 4 and 12 are factors of 24, rewrite each fraction with a denominator of 24. $\frac{5}{8} = \frac{15}{24}$, $\frac{2}{3} = \frac{16}{24}$, $\frac{3}{4} = \frac{18}{24}$, $\frac{7}{12} = \frac{14}{24}$. The order from largest to smallest is $\frac{3}{4}$, $\frac{2}{3}$, $\frac{5}{8}$, $\frac{7}{12}$. The girls in order are Riley, Lilley, Grace and Leah. This means Lilley is ahead of Leah and Grace is behind Riley. The correct statements are 1 and 2 only.

6 $3 - 1 - \frac{1}{2} - \frac{3}{4}$ is $2 - \frac{2}{4} - \frac{3}{4}$, which is $\frac{8}{4} - \frac{5}{4} = \frac{3}{4}$. This means Savannah ate $\frac{3}{4}$ of a pizza. Now, $\frac{3}{4} - \frac{1}{2}$ is $\frac{3}{4} - \frac{2}{4}$, which is $\frac{1}{4}$. Savannah ate $\frac{1}{4}$ of a pizza more than Naomi.

7 P: $\frac{1}{5}$ of 40 is 40 ÷ 5 = 8. Q: $\frac{3}{4}$ of 20 is

20 ÷ 4 × 3 = 15.

R: $\frac{2}{3}$ of 36 is 36 ÷ 3 × 2 = 24.

As 8 + 15 + 24 is 47, then P + Q + R = 47.

8 There are 2 halves in 1 and 3 halves in $1\frac{1}{2}$.

As 2 out of 3 is written as $\frac{2}{3}$, Josiah only

needs $\frac{2}{3}$ of the flour. Now, 6 ÷ 3 × 2 is 4,

so Josiah requires 4 cups of flour.

9 As $1 - \frac{2}{5}$ is $\frac{3}{5}$, and 60 ÷ 5 × 3 is 36, there

were 36 apples in the box before the Thong

family took their apples. As $1 - \frac{2}{3}$ is $\frac{1}{3}$, and

36 ÷ 3 is 12, the Aldrich family received 12

apples.

10 $1 - \frac{3}{8} = \frac{5}{8}$ and $\frac{5}{8}$ of 160 is 160 ÷ 8 × 5 = 100.

After she gave 60 beads to Layla, Emma

kept 100 beads. Now, 100 − 40 = 60 which

means that Emma had 60 beads left after

she gave beads to Grace. As $1 - \frac{2}{3} = \frac{1}{3}$ and

$\frac{1}{3}$ of 60 is 60 ÷ 3 = 20, in the end Emma

had 20 beads remaining.

WRITING
Descriptive response   Pages 36–39

Task 2

1 The most likely answer is: a child who is in
hiding for some reason and unable to enter
the house. The orientation suggests this,
and the rest of the description confirms it.

2 a a diary entry
    b a newspaper report

Task 4

1 a One of the following adjectives: warm,
       welcoming, blue coloured, small, square
    b One of the following adjectives: old,
       rusty
    c narrow
    d wide

2 a rage outside
    b creaking

---

3 a partly covered by brightly coloured
       creepers
    b paint peeling off them and hanging
       rather crookedly across the grass
    c covered with colourful cushions and
       rugs

Task 5

1 the swing chair creaking; music

2 smoke puffing up from the small
    back chimney

Task 7

Paragraph 1: I imagine sleeping in one of the
brightly lit rooms while the winds rage
outside.

Paragraph 4: How lucky that child is, I think.
Even though the house does not look
especially well cared for, it looks comfortable
and cosy and full of love.

Paragraph 6: Oh, how I want to be inside that
house instead of out here in the cold.

WEEK 2

READING
Poetry   Pages 43–48

Practice Task 1

1 D 2 A 3 A 4 D 5 B 6 D

EXPLANATIONS

1 The poem does not give you this answer
in any definite way. The image of the dog
is suggested more than described. However,
there is evidence that the poet is suggesting
a large, stray dog: 'giant and grey' in line
2 clearly suggests a large dog, as do 'clashing
teeth and shaggy jaws', 'bounds to his
feet' and 'howls and hollos' (little dogs
usually bark and yap). The fact he is 'a
hungry dog' who 'moans' with satisfaction
when he gets a bone to eat, and that he is
howling outside on his own, not inside a
nice warm house, suggests he is an
uncared for, stray dog, rather than a pet.

2 Several phrases—'all day', 'hour upon hour', 'rumbling, tumbling'—suggest the rhythmic crashing of waves on the shoreline. Although the sea (and a dog) can be dangerous and threatening, this is not mentioned (the dog is only interested in getting at the bones). The stanza emphasises regular action, so not C. Although the size of the sea is mentioned—'giant and grey'—its size and depth are not the main focus, so the answer is not D.

3 'May or June' tell you the poet is thinking of a longer period than a day. May and June are in summer in the Northern Hemisphere, so presumably the poem was written there. The impression is of quietness, not noisiness, so not C. Tides are not mentioned, so not D.

4 The dog has his bones—'hour upon hour he gnaws' and 'licking his greasy paws'—so he is not still hungry (so not B). There is nothing to suggest he is in pain or that he is angry.

5 If you read the second line of the stanza, it is clear the poet is definitely referring to the noise of the grasses, so not A or D. Also, the dog makes no sound—'so quiet, so quiet, he scarcely snores'—so definitely not D. When the poet describes summer (May or June), he refers to sounds not there now ('play no more'), so when he describes the sound he is referring to winter.

6 The poet writes that the dog makes the noise 'long and loud'—a continual sound —so this suggests it is not B (yaps) or C (barks), which are short, sharp sounds. There is no suggestion the dog would feel like growling, so not A. The poet has no doubt used 'hollos' because it has a similar sound to 'howls' (alliteration), but the meaning seems something like 'call out loudly'.

Practice Task 2

1 B 2 A 3 A 4 B 5 C 6 D

EXPLANATIONS

1 You need to re-read the first snake poem to get this right. Don't rely on your memory. Be sure both poems mention your chosen answer.

2 You need to draw your own conclusions about this question. The answer is not clearly there, but the frequent mention suggests it takes a long time for the snake to get into the hole. Therefore it is a very long snake.

3 Again, there is no absolute indication of why the poet writes these words, but it seems likely that the words are meant as an image of the snake's power. C and D are true statements about snakes and humans but that does not relate to shaking of the mountain. And dreaming does not necessarily mean a light sleep, so not B.

4 You need to think about the whole poem, not just the first stanza. It also helps to understand that 'relatively' means seeing things from a particular perspective or in a particular way.

5 The words 'in terror' indicate the answer. The stanza talks of other things about the snake but these words clearly indicate the snake is terrified of humans.

6 It should be clear that answer A is correct, but if you think about the phrase carefully, you will see that this is the way we exaggerate how big a snake is, or a caught fish, or anything else seen in the wildlife when we report on this to others (so also answer B).

Practice Task 3

1 B 2 C 3 C 4 A 5 B

EXPLANATIONS

1 This is a difficult poem and a difficult question. You need to imagine looking at a lake in a mountain area, and think

Check Your Answers

about what you see both above and below the water.

2 Same as for Question 1. Getting this answer right will help you get Question 1 right if you have trouble the first time.

3 This is the only line that really gives a human characteristic to the lake (it's thinking).

4 Look carefully at the wording for this question. All could be true, but only A answers why it looks like the fisherman is holding the lake. Also use your own experience of watching someone fishing.

5 There is no negative feeling shown towards the fisherman, but the poet would clearly like to do what the fisherman has done: hold the lake. In other words, he is envious of the fisherman.

Real Test

1 A 2 D 3 B 4 C 5 B 6 A

EXPLANATIONS

1 There are many clues to this answer—in particular, 'wild dog and lone'. You could be tricked into answering D if you don't read carefully, because line 2 mentions hunting. However, the dog does not belong to anyone, so is not a 'hunter's dog'.

2 The dog's attitude to humans is clearly negative, so it could be A or D. However, 'fat souls' suggests quite a strong negative attitude—more than 'annoyance'—so D is best.

3 You need to understand the whole poem to answer this correctly. It shows he is definitely not seeking a master, a mate or other dogs, so the answer is clearly B.

4 You have to read and understand the words 'cringing for my meat' to work this out if you don't know the word 'meek'. These words show that a meek dog has to ask for his food, not hunt it himself, so answer C is closest in meaning.

5 Line 8 gives you this answer clearly. If you don't understand this, you can probably work out the most likely answer.

6 Stanza 2 shows the answer quite clearly. The words 'licking dirty feet', 'meek' and 'cringing' all show his attitude is very strongly negative.

> **THINKING SKILLS**
> *Critical thinking—Drawing a conclusion*
> Pages 50–52

Real Test 1

1 C 2 A 3 C 4 D 5 B 6 D 7 C 8 B 9 A 10 D

EXPLANATIONS

1 It cannot be concluded that deeper purple shades were more calming than shades of blue because you are told that all shades of green were more calming than some of the deeper shades of purple and that all the shades of blue were more calming than all the shades of greens. C cannot be true.

2 You can draw the conclusion the survey results show that horror rated first, historical fiction rated second, non-fiction rated third, comics rated fourth and mystery novels rated last. The librarian needs to order more horror and historical fiction because these are the two most popular categories.

3 The information tells you that Alok prefers pita bread wrap-style sandwiches, and he likes to add cheese and avocado.

4 The text is about the health issues due to extreme heat (heat stroke, mental health issues and death). Because the text also says that extreme heat costs more and more lives globally every year the correct conclusion is 'Extreme heat is a growing health issue'.

5 If you needed both an opportunity and a reason to take the fruit salad then anyone who does not have both an opportunity and a reason cannot be the one who took it.

6 Since Oliver has two leadership positions in the school, the result of the debating challenge was not relevant in his case. He only had to pass the community service challenge in order to be selected to attend the convention. Since he was not selected to attend, he must have failed the community service challenge.

7 This conclusion is not possible. From the information, you can draw the conclusion that if Lily does not do well in the audition, there is no way she will get the solo in the concert.

8 The information tells us that Joe read fewer books than Jim who in turn read fewer than Alex, Grace and Lucia. So it follows that Joe read the fewest books.

9 The information tells us that everyone who would definitely go to Pluto also liked the idea of a holiday on Mars, and (since they liked the idea of Mars) they also didn't want to go to Jupiter. So it is reasonable to draw the conclusion that if Louise would definitely go to Pluto, she does not want to go to Jupiter.

10 If anyone who won the art prize must have been a paid-up member of the art society when they entered the competition and also must have attended the opening night, then it follows that anyone who did not satisfy both requirements cannot have won the art prize. So, if Wei did not attend the opening night, he cannot have won the art prize. B and C are incorrect because you cannot say either with certainty—each *might* be the case, but not definitely. So you cannot say that they *must* be true.

THINKING SKILLS
Critical thinking— Identifying an assumption Pages 54–55

Real Test 2

1 C 2 D 3 A 4 B 5 D 6 C 7 A 8 B 9 D 10 C

EXPLANATIONS

1 Joe's conclusion is that Gemma does not like parties. The evidence this is based on is that she has received an invitation to Tom's party, but she is not going. So, for Joe's conclusion to hold, it must be assumed that anyone who says no to a party invitation must not like parties. (Gemma said no to a party invitation + anyone who says no to a party invitation must not like parties = Gemma does not like parties.)

2 Santi's conclusion is that birds should not be kept in cages. Her evidence is that keeping birds in cages is exploitation for the purposes of entertaining people. So, for Santi's conclusion to hold, it must be assumed that exploitation is wrong. (Keeping birds in cages is exploitation + exploitation is wrong = birds should not be kept in cages.)

3 Aviana's conclusion is that Conner is allergic to peanuts. The evidence this is based on is that he never has peanut butter in his sandwich. So, for Aviana's conclusion to hold, it must be assumed that anyone who doesn't eat peanut butter sandwiches is allergic to peanuts. (Conner never has peanut butter in his sandwich + anyone who doesn't eat peanut butter sandwiches is allergic to peanuts = Conner is allergic to peanuts.)

4 Ramesh's conclusion is that he had better not lose his soccer ball. The evidence this is based on is that they must not do anything to upset Mum. So, for Ramesh's conclusion to hold, it must be assumed that losing the soccer ball will upset Mum.

(We must not do anything to upset Mum + losing the soccer ball will upset Mum = I'd better not lose the soccer ball.)

5 Mari's conclusion is that David loves baking. Her evidence is that he is baking a cake. So, for Mari's conclusion to hold, it must be assumed that everyone who bakes cake loves baking. (David is baking a cake + everyone who bakes cake loves baking = David loves baking.)

6 Sven's conclusion that Colin must be in very good health is based on the evidence that Colin cycles at least 50 kilometres a day. Sven's assumption is that only a person in good health could cycle 50 kilometres a day.

7 Hannah's conclusion is that Antoine must be excited. The evidence for this conclusion is that Antoine has said her completed manuscript is due to be submitted to the publisher in three weeks. Hannah has assumed that because the manuscript is due in three weeks Antoine must be nearly finished writing her book.

8 Yutaka's employer has concluded that Yutaka needs to borrow the mower. The evidence he/she has used to draw this conclusion is that Yutaka has asked to take the mower home from work on Friday when he clearly knows it's not company policy to allow staff to borrow equipment. Yutaka's employer must have assumed that Yutaka's own mower must be broken.

9 Stavros has concluded that it was lucky Ingrid noticed the grasshopper on the path in time to avoid stepping on it. He has drawn this conclusion based on Ingrid stating that she nearly stepped on a grasshopper while out walking. Stavros has assumed that Ingrid would not want to kill a grasshopper.

10 Kiera has drawn the conclusion that Courtney's cooking must be improving. She has drawn this conclusion based on the evidence that Courtney has requested another cookbook from the library, the implication being that she regularly requests cookbooks from her library. Kiera has assumed that because Courtney borrows cookbooks from the library, she uses them to learn.

THINKING SKILLS
Critical thinking—Checking reasoning to detect errors   Pages 57–59

Real Test 3
1 D 2 B 3 B 4 A 5 C 6 D 7 A 8 B 9 C 10 B
EXPLANATIONS

1 Neither Uma nor Noah's reasoning is correct. Uma is correct when she reasons that it must be a garden geodome, however the tour guide does not say that the garden geodomes **only** grow food for the resort. Noah's reasoning is flawed because the tour guide does not say that **all** garden geodomes have tri-layered panels.

2 We know that Muttley barks whenever a parcel is delivered to the neighbour. However, there might be other things that make Muttley bark. So Aanya is correct when she reasons that **maybe** the neighbour received a parcel.

3 We know that any student who does not return their library books in time will not be allowed to go to the party. However, this does not mean that there are no other reasons why a student is not allowed to go to the party. So Arlo's reasoning, that he **definitely** will be allowed to go since he has returned his books, is flawed.

4 Since Jun did not get a chance to audition last term, he will be offered a chance to audition this term. However, just because Jun is offered a chance to audition, it does not mean that he will audition. Something might happen to prevent him auditioning. Nor does it mean that if he does audition, he will get the solo. So, Jun's reasoning is correct when he **hopes** to get a solo this term. Also, just because students who didn't audition last term would definitely be able to audition this term doesn't mean that students who auditioned last term wouldn't also be able to audition. So Melia's reasoning is incorrect.

5 Since Paul has asked for the upgrade offer with the gnome, he is entitled to two extra packets of seeds plus the packet of seeds of his own choice that came with the basic offer. So he needs to choose three packets of seeds. The fact that he has not chosen enough packets of seeds shows the flaw in his reasoning.

6 Neither Mia's nor Hamish's reasoning is correct. Hamish cannot reasonably assert that Greta will win the competition because Greta embellishes on recipes and improves them while the competition expects competitors to follow a recipe exactly so that they produce a replica of the original item. Mia cannot reasonably assert that Jesper is sure to win the competition because Jesper won't cook meat. The information does not state that the competition is vegetarian only so it's possible meat will be in the recipe. If this is the case Jesper won't cook and therefore can't win. Also, she says he is sure to win. She cannot assert that he will win.

7 Jed's argument is that learning conversational French will allow him to order dinner from a menu that is written in French. Brianna is correct when she reasons that reading French menu items will require different knowledge from the conversational French that Jed is learning. She **thinks** Jed will struggle with reading the menu. She does not say he **will** struggle so she leaves open the opportunity for him not to struggle. Her reasoning is correct. Karolina uses incorrect reasoning in stating that conversational French will be useless to Jed in the restaurant. Jed might not be able to read the menu well enough to order dinner but he will be able to say hello and thank you in French and therefore his conversational French will not be useless. Karolina is also too definite in her statement that Jed's conversational French will be useless. She could have correctly reasoned that Jed's conversational French might be useless.

8 Amanda uses correct reasoning to point out that in spite of all the safety checks and inspections and any assurances from operators, accidents can still happen. The ride will be as safe as possible but Ollie cannot be sure that the ride is perfectly safe.

9 The message Peyton receives on her phone is that she is almost out of storage space. Her reasoning is incorrect to think that just because she has not received a message she has plenty of space still available.

10 Aria has decided that the patches on the giraffe are orange-brown and so her reasoning is correct when she says that it's more likely a Rothschild's giraffe (than any of the other subspecies of giraffe). Hiromichi uses incorrect reasoning to declare that the giraffe can't be a Rothschild's giraffe based on the single identifying feature—whether the colour is brown or orange-brown. His declaration is too certain and he hasn't allowed for any error of judgement.

MATHEMATICAL REASONING
Decimals, percentages and money   Pages 61–62

Real Test 1

1 C 2 B 3 C 4 D 5 E 6 D 7 E 8 D 9 C 10 A

EXPLANATIONS

1 As there are 360° in the circle, the birds = 360 − (15 + 120 + 135) = 360 − 270 = 90. This means $90/360 = \frac{1}{4} = 25\%$.

2 Total distance is 80 km and he has already travelled 60 km. This means $\frac{60}{80} = \frac{3}{4} = 75\%$.

3 Melena scores $84\% = \frac{84}{100} = \frac{42}{50} = \frac{21}{25}$. This means she got 4 questions incorrect.

4 10% of the iceberg is above water. This means 10% is 5 m, and so 100% is 50 m. The iceberg is 50 metres in height.

5 2 marks out of $20 = \frac{2}{20} = \frac{1}{10} = 10\%$.

6 Six students out of $20 = \frac{6}{20} = \frac{3}{10} = 30\%$.

7 Elizabeth $300, Austin $300, Cyrus $600. As 300 + 300 + 600 = 1200, and 2000 − 1200 = 800, Sarah gave $800 to Liana.

8 As (41 − 5) ÷ 3 = 36 ÷ 3 = 12, the hourly board rate is $12. As 5 + 12 × 5 = 5 + 60 = 65, the cost will be $65.

9 As $25\% = \frac{1}{4}$, then Claire charges $\frac{3}{4}$ of the previous hourly charge. The hourly charges are $16, $12, $9, $6.75. This gives a total of $43.75.

10 As $1 - \frac{7}{10} = \frac{3}{10}$, then $\frac{3}{10}$ of the cost of the jeans is $45. As 45 ÷ 3 × 10 = 150, the pair of jeans costs $150. As 150 − 45 = 105, and 150 + 105 is 255, the cost of the jeans and the dress is $255.

Real Test 2

1 E 2 C 3 B 4 B 5 E 6 B 7 D 8 A 9 E 10 D

EXPLANATION

1 Distance travelled = 80 × 8 = 640. This means 640 km out of 1000 km are completed, and so there are 360 km to travel, or $\frac{360}{1000} = 36\%$.

2 The area was 8 cm² and is now 16 cm². The increase in area is 8 cm². This means $\frac{8}{8} = 1 = 100\%$ increase.

3 Check each alternative: 0.088, 0.700, 0.720, $\frac{3}{4} = 0.750$.

4 Volume = 50 × 10 × 20 = 10 000 cm³. This means a capacity of 10 L. If 4 L is poured in, it must be 40% full.

5 After one week, $\frac{1}{10}$ of 100 = 10, which means it is 110 cm. After two weeks, $\frac{1}{10}$ of 110 = 11, which means it is 121 cm.

6 As 320 + 130 = 450, then $\frac{450}{600} = \frac{3}{4} = 75\%$.

7 If 1 adult + 1 child = $280, then 2 adult + 2 child = $560. As 2 adult + 3 child = $670, and 670 − 560 = 110, the cost of a child ticket is $110. As 280 − 110 is 170, the cost of an adult ticket is $170.

8 Sebastian: $\frac{1}{4}$ of $800 = $200. Theodore: $\frac{1}{2}$ of $200 = $100. The total of the 2 boys' money was $300. $\frac{2}{5}$ of $300 = $120.

As 800 − 300 − 120 is 380, Isaac received $380. As 380 − 200 = 180, Isaac received $180 more than Sebastian.

9 20% is $\frac{1}{5}$, and 20 ÷ 5 is 4. 50% is $\frac{1}{2}$, and 50 ÷ 2 is 25. Also, 4 × 25 is 100.

10 As 20 ÷ 5 is 4, James paid 40 cents for each of 4 pencils. As $0.40 × 4 is $1.60, and $14.40 − $1.60 = $12.80, James paid $12.80 for the other 16 pencils. As 1280 ÷ 16 is 320 ÷ 4 = 80, the regular price is $0.80 for each pencil.

MATHEMATICAL REASONING
Patterns and algebra   Pages 64–65

Real Test 3

1 E 2 C 3 D 4 A 5 C 6 C 7 B 8 B 9 D 10 E

EXPLANATIONS

1 3 shelves of 16 books is 16 × 3. The correct number sentence is 24 + 16 × 3 + 13 = 85.

Check
Your
Answers

2 8 lots of 5 plus 6 lots of 4 added to 3 will equal 67.
This is written as 8 × 5 + 4 × 6 + 3 = 67.

3 If ■ = 42 – 26 then ■ = 16. As 16 ÷ ▲ = 2, then ▲ = 16 ÷ 2, which means ▲ = 8.

4 If ★ + ★ + 3 = 13, then ★ + ★ = 10 and ★ = 5. Now, 14 – (▲ + 5) = 8 means ▲ + 5 = 6. This means ▲ is 1.

5 The numbers are increasing by 5. As the sixth number is 31 and using 31 + 4 × 5 = 51 and 51 + 10 = 61, the two numbers are 51 and 61. This means the sum is 112.

6 Look for a number that is 5 more than a multiple of 7. Of the options, 68 is 5 more than 63 (which is a multiple of 7).

7 As 8 + 9 is 17, then the sixth number is 9. As 9 + 4 is 13, the tenth number is 13.

8 You need to find consecutive numbers less than 60 where the smaller is a multiple of 6 and the larger is a multiple of 7. The numbers are 48 and 49. As 60 – 48 is 12, Zoe will be 60 in 12 years.

9 There are 12 multiples of 4 less than 50. There are 10 multiples of 5, but 2 have already been crossed out leaving 8 new numbers. There are 8 multiples of 6, but the multiples of 4 and 5 have already been crossed out, which leaves 3 new numbers. As 50 – (12 + 8 + 3) = 27, there are 27 numbers not crossed out.

10 Suppose ● = 1.
This means ■ = 2 and ▲ = 3. Now,
▲■●■ is 3 + 2 + 1 + 2 which is 8.
Looking through the options, ▲▲■ = 8.

Real Test 4

1 B **2** E **3** C **4** E **5** B **6** E **7** E **8** D **9** E **10** B

EXPLANATIONS

1 As there are 7 days in a week, the number of pieces is 34 – 4 × 7 + 5 × 10. As he uses 4 pieces each night, this expression needs to be divided by 4. The number sentence is (34 – 4 × 7 + 5 × 10) ÷ 4.

2 As 26 – 12 – 9 is 5, there are 5 students who will receive 6 stickers. 12 × 3 + 9 × 4 + 5 × 6 will be the number of stickers she gives out. Subtracting this number from 150 gives the number of remaining stickers.

3 As 4 + 6 × 6 = 40, then ■ = 6. Also, as (3 + 6) × ⬬ = 63, and 63 ÷ 9 is 7, then ⬬ = 7.

4 As ▲ × ▲ = 16, then ▲ = 4.
Also, 4 + ⏢ = 7 means ⏢ = 3.
Now, 4 + 3 × ● = 28 means 3 × ● = 24, and so ● = 8.

5 The numbers are decreasing by 4. As the fifth number is 37 then 37 – 5 × 4 is 17 and 17 – 3 × 4 is 5, which means the two numbers are 17 and 5. The product is 17 × 5, which is 85.

6 There are positive and negative numbers in the sequence. The numbers are decreasing by six so the sequence is 27, 21, 15, 9, 3, –3, –9, –15, –21, –27. This means the total is 0.

7 ⊘ = 3 and ▲ = 27. As 27 ÷ 3 is 9, then ▲ ÷ ⊘ = 9.

8 First, 9^2 – (♥ + ♥) = 61.
This means ♥ + ♥ = 81 – 61, which gives ♥ = 10.

Also, ■² – 2 × 45 = 54. This means ■² = 54 + 90, which gives ■ = 12.

Finally, ♥ × ■ = 10 × 12 which is 120.

9 Let ◆ = 2. This means ⬟ = 6 and so ○ = 3.
Now, ⬟ + ◆ + ○ is 6 + 2 + 3 which is 11.
Looking through the options,
◆ + ○ + ○ + ○ = 11.

10 If Aiden is 7, his grandmother is 63 years old. As 9^2 – 18 is 63, then Lucy is 9 years old. This means Lucy is 2 years older than Aiden.

WRITING
Recount response   Pages 70–71

Task 3
who: yes (a school student)
what: yes (a school camp experience that has gone wrong)
where: yes (Lithgow Hospital)
when: yes (Friday 6 March)

Task 5

1 Friday 6 March

   Paragraph 2: Today was the last day of our camp.

   Paragraph 3: When we got up this morning; at about ten o'clock

   Paragraph 4: about a quarter of an hour

   Paragraph 5: just; one last time

   Paragraph 6: immediately

2 You should have put ticks next to:
   - ☑ what Mr Rosso said
   - ☑ why the writer jumped
   - ☑ how the accident happened
   - ☑ who helped him

WEEK 3

READING
Factual texts   Pages 77–81

Practice Task 1

1 B   2 E   3 A   4 C

EXPLANATIONS

1 This sentence clearly continues the paragraph theme relating to the dangers of the rocky coast. The words 'this strait' refer you back to 'Bass Strait' in sentence one of the paragraph and 'It' in sentence two. Always look for words like 'this', 'that', 'these', 'those', 'it' and so on. These refer to ideas in other parts of the text—usually the sentence before or after.

2 The linking word 'Then' coming after two dates relating to ships arriving is the clue. Linking words are another important way we connect ideas in texts. This one is a time linking word.

3 Again a linking word is the clue 'for', meaning 'because', relating back to the reason the savage storm of 1797 finally drew attention to the area.

4 The phrase 'Many of these' is the clue. This refers back to the 'white settlers' in the sentence before. This is the same kind of linking device as in Question 1.

   The unneeded sentence is sentence D. This sentence might be used in a text about Abel Tasman but this text is about Bass Strait and Abel Tasman is mentioned in passing. The name of the town he was born in is not relevant here.

Practice Task 2

1 F   2 B   3 G   4 A   5 D   6 C

EXPLANATIONS

1 The clue words are 'mid stroke'. This links back to 'I swam quickly' in the previous sentence. It is always important to put in a sentence that keeps the sense of the sentences before and after.

2 The word 'Another' at the start of the sentence is the key. This relates back to the first sight of the whale referred to in Question 1/sentence F above.

3 The time word 'Eventually' is the key here. The sentence before mentions 'For several minutes' referring to the time the whales stared at the humans in the water.

4 The whole paragraph is about the high emotion of the experience of meeting the whales in their own environment. This sentence sums that up. The small word 'The' at the start of the sentence is the clue—'The memory' refers back to everything just described.

5 'The other' is the clue. It links back to the words 'one of only two places'.

6 This sentence keeps the theme of the paragraph—the strict guidelines about swimming with the whales. This sentence is one example of those guidelines.

The unneeded sentence is E. You might think this sentence might fit in the last paragraph, but the newspaper report is not really advertising the adventure company. The theme of the report is the excitement and exhilaration of the experience.

Practice Task 3

1 C   2 E   3 D   4 A   5 B   6 F

EXPLANATIONS

1 This sentence is clearly on the theme of the paragraph—the way Stone Age people lived and survived. 'Stone Age' is in contrast to 'Modern humans'.

2 'Not only that' links to the idea in the previous sentence. One challenge is mentioned in that previous sentence and this sentence adds yet another.

3 '[T]hese fears' relates back to the fear mentioned in the previous sentences and is the clue.

4 The time focus is a clue—'thousands of years' in the previous sentence links with 'Then' at the start of this sentence.

5 The linking word 'So' at the start of the sentence shows the focus is on the consequence of something, in this case that it took time for the art to be taken seriously.

6 The clue is in the theme of the sentences around this one and the words 'these stages' linking this sentence to the previous sentence. The sentence which follows sentence F explains why we don't know much about these stages. Always check that your sentence fits the following one.

The unneeded sentence is G. The topic of this sentence is early writing and while this is close to the historic theme of the text it is not about cave art.

Real Test

1 D   2 F   3 B   4 C   5 G   6 E

EXPLANATIONS

1 The clue here is the words 'each of these journeys' referring back to his 'earlier trips' in the previous sentence.

2 This sentence clearly belongs in the paragraph about selecting crew.

3 The clue is the mention of the ship's name *Aurora* in this sentence following the mention of another ship the *Endurance* in the previous sentence and following the mention of 'two ships' in the first sentence of the paragraph.

4 The theme of this paragraph tells you this is the missing sentence. The sentences before and after are all about the difficulties they experienced.

5 The theme of the paragraph again tells you this is the missing sentence. The linking word 'However' in the following sentence is a clue.

6 The word 'trek' refers back to 'cross 26 miles of mountains and glaciers' in the previous sentence.

The unneeded sentence is A. There is no reference to Shackleton's school education or what he thought about it.

> **THINKING SKILLS**
> *Problem solving—Shapes and patterns*
> Pages 84–85

Real Test 1

1 A   2 D   3 D   4 A   5 C   6 C   7 A   8 B   9 B   10 C

EXPLANATIONS

1 Only piece X can be placed with the other 3 pieces to make a rectangle.

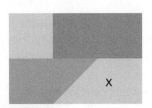

7 The tile is being rotated a quarter of a turn (90°) in a clockwise direction each time it moves through the pattern.

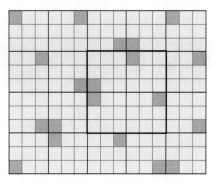

3 All 3 could be a front view.

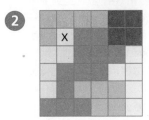

8 The black book on the far left will not be seen in front of the grey book.

4 Every row and every column has one of each tile. The tile in option A must be rotated through a half-turn (180°).

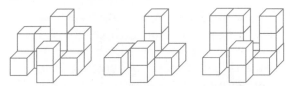

9

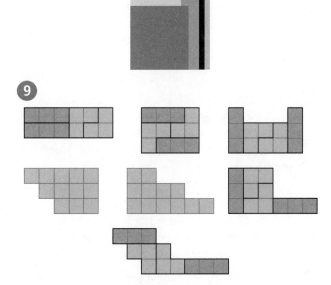

5 The block that Maya will not use is

6

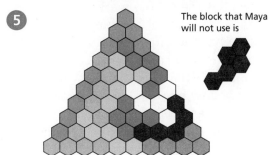

10 In neither view can we see the face opposite the blue face. The only face we cannot see is the one with the cross. So the blue face must be opposite the face with the cross. Statement X is correct.

In the first view, the face with the cross must be at the back. The face at the bottom and the left side must have the square and circle in some order. From the second view, we can see that if that is the

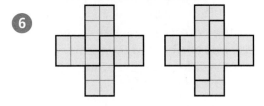

case the circle must be on the bottom and the square on the left side. So the white face must be opposite the face with the square. Statement Y is correct.

So both statements X and Y are correct.

THINKING SKILLS
Problem solving—Word problems   Pages 88–89

Real Test 2

1 C 2 C 3 D 4 D 5 B 6 C 7 B 8 A 9 D 10 A

EXPLANATIONS

1 All entrants in the competition must be great singers and great dancers. So, if Brice is not a great singer, he cannot have entered the competition and so cannot have won.

2 Every house in Parker Street that is painted white has a green roof and every house with a green roof also has a green fence. So if a house in Parker Street is painted white it must have a green fence.

3 Magpies are black and white birds but that doesn't mean that every black and white bird is a magpie. (Peewees and currawongs, for example, are also black and white birds.) So, Statement I is not correct. Magpies are black and white birds but that does not mean that all their feathers must have both black and white. Statement II is not correct. So, neither I nor II are correct.

4 Music Theory is compulsory for anyone studying Piano, so everyone who studies Piano must also study Music Theory. But there are some Voice students who study Music Theory and do not study Piano. So there must be more students of Music Theory than of Piano. The statement 'Fewer students study Piano than Music Theory' must be true.

A, B and C might be true, but they are not the statements that **must** be true.

5 Everyone who liked romance movies also liked mysteries and everyone who liked mysteries also liked comedies so those who like comedies include all those who like romances and mysteries. Everyone who liked sci-fi movies also liked at least one of the other types so everyone who liked sci-fi must have also liked comedies. Some of the people only liked comedies. So more people liked comedies than any of the other types.

A is incorrect. More people liked comedies than sci-fi. C or D might be true but are not the option that must be true.

6 The person's claim was not correct, so if Shannon used the product carefully the chip must not have been removed. As Courtney's chip was not removed, the product must have been used carefully if the claim was incorrect.

7 Everyone in Class V is older than everyone in Class P, so if Osman is in Class P, he is younger than anyone in Class V.

A, B and C are incorrect. There is no information about the age of students in Class J compared with those in Classes B or V.

8 Fawad does not have red or white marbles. Nor does he have yellow or green marbles. So Fawad has the blue marbles. Georgia has the yellow marbles. So the sentence that cannot be true is that 'Georgia has the blue marbles'.

B is not the correct answer because it is true. Indi doesn't have the red, white, blue or yellow marbles, so she has the green marbles.

C is not the correct answer because it is true. Millie doesn't have the green or blue or red or yellow marbles, so she has the white marbles.

D is not the correct answer because it is true. Zac doesn't have the green or blue or yellow marbles, nor the white marbles, so he has the red marbles.

9 There were 2 boys and 2 girls and the youngest was a boy. So the other boy could have been born first, second or third. The possibilities are BGGB, GBGB or GGBB. In every case, the next child born after at least one of the girls was a boy.

A is not correct. The two girls might have been born consecutively, but if the other boy was born second that wouldn't be true.

B is not correct. The oldest child might have been a boy.

C is not correct. If the other boy was born third, no girl would be born after a boy.

10 'The Sapphires beat the Emeralds' cannot be true. The Pearls lost all their matches. This means that the Sapphires must have beaten the Pearls. But the Sapphires won only one match, so they did not win any other matches. As there were no draws the Sapphires must have lost their match against the Emeralds. So the statement 'The Sapphires beat the Emeralds' is not correct.

B is not the correct answer. The Sapphires' only win was against the Pearls, so the Diamonds must have beaten the Sapphires. The statement in B must be true.

C is not the correct answer. The Diamonds must have beaten the Pearls and the Sapphires. As they won exactly two matches, they cannot have beaten the Emeralds. There were no draws so the Emeralds beat the Diamonds. The statement in C must be true.

D is not the correct answer. The Emeralds must have beaten the Pearls, Sapphires and Diamonds. They were beaten by the Rubies, so they won exactly three matches. The statement in D must be true.

THINKING SKILLS
Problem solving—Numerical reasoning
Pages 92–93

Real Test 3

1 B **2** C **3** B **4** A **5** B **6** D **7** C **8** D **9** A **10** C

EXPLANATIONS

1 The 3-year-old child can get in free. The 9-year-old and 6-year-old can get in for half the single price, so $10 together. The remaining 4 people can get in on a family ticket of $25. The total price is $25 + $10 or $35.

2 There are 30 more cows than calves. Now 68 − 30 = 38 and half of 38 is 19. So there are 19 calves and 19 + 30 or 49 cows. One cow has 2 calves. So 18 cows have calves. As 49 − 18 = 31, it means that 31 cows do not have any calves.

3 There are 31 days in July. If 22 July is a Tuesday then, as 22 + 7 = 29, 29 July is also a Tuesday. 31 July will be a Thursday and 1 August a Friday. The first Thursday in August will be 7 August and 14 days after that will be 21 August.

4 Altogether there are 22 + 12 + 8 = 42 children in Year 6. If there are 2 more boys than girls there must be 20 girls and 22 boys. As 22 − 12 = 10, there must be 10 boys in 6K.

5 In the first week a weekly ticket is cheaper than 4 return tickets and one one-way ticket. So the cheapest price for the first week is $50. In the second week, return tickets on Tuesday, Thursday and Friday and a one-way ticket on Wednesday is the cheapest ticket cost. As 3 × 12 + 7 = 36 + 7 = 43, the cheapest price for the second week is $43. Now 50 + 43 = 93, so $93 is the cheapest total price.

6 Mary is 3 times Elsie's age so the difference in their ages is twice Elsie's age. But the difference is 8 years. So Elsie must be 4

and Mary 12. The sum of all their ages is 3 times Noella's age. Together Elsie and Mary must be twice Noella's age. But 4 + 12 = 16. Noella must be half of 16 or 8 years old.

7 As 234 − 41 = 193, 193 runners finished the race and were awarded yellow ribbons. Now 287 − 193 = 94. So 94 extra ribbons were awarded, meaning that 94 people also received a green ribbon. As 193 − 94 = 99, 99 runners received a yellow ribbon but not a green one.

8 From Newman's 3 plants cost 3 × $15 or $45. At Sergei's the plants will cost 2 × $20 + $10 or $50. Poppy's price is 3 × $21 − $15 or $48. Hannah's price is 2 × $22 or $44. So George will pay the least if he buys the plants from Hannah.

9 Olly should pay for 5 days from the 8th to the 12th, 1 day for the 13th, 5 days for the 16th to the 20th (paying for 5 days is cheaper than two lots of 2 day passes) and 1 day for the 23rd.
Total to pay is 2 × $25 + 2 × $10 = $70.

Date	Attend	Date	Attend
8	Y	16	Y
9	Y	17	Y
10		18	Y
11	Y	19	Y
12	Y	20	
13	Y	21	
14		22	
15		23	Y

10 As 47 − 9 − 5 + 12 = 45, there are now 45 cars and trucks in the parking lot. As there are 8 times as many cars as trucks, there are 9 times the number of trucks in the parking lot. Now 45 ÷ 9 = 5, so there are

5 trucks and 8 × 5 = 40 cars. Before the 12 cars entered there would have been 40 − 12 = 28 cars and before the 9 cars left there would have been 28 + 9 = 37 cars. So there were originally 37 cars (and 10 trucks) in the parking lot.

MATHEMATICAL REASONING
Length and area   Pages 95–98

Real Test 1

1 C 2 C 3 A 4 B 5 E 6 E 7 A 8 B 9 E 10 D

EXPLANATIONS

1 You need to find how many 1.5 m in 30 km. First, 30 km = 30 000 m, and 30 000 ÷ 1.5 = 60 000 ÷ 3 = 20 000. There will be 20 000 revolutions of the car's tyre.

2 If the perimeter is 24 cm, then the length plus width is 12 cm. This means the width is 3 cm (with length of 9 cm).

3 The length of the frame will be 4 cm before and after the 22 cm length of photograph, and the same with the width. This means the frame will be 30 cm by 20 cm. This means the perimeter is 100 cm, or 1 m.

4 As 48 ÷ 3 is 16, the triangle has a side length of 16 cm, which means the rectangle has a length of 16 cm. As 48 ÷ 2 is 24, the sum of 16 and the width is 24. As 24 − 16 = 8, the width is 8 cm.

5 The perimeter is 2 × (14 + 12) + 8 + 8 which gives a perimeter of 68 cm.

6 The rectangle had dimensions (12 + 4) cm and (6 + 4) cm. As 16 × 10 = 160, the original rectangle had an area of 160 cm². As 4 × 4 is 16, both small shapes have an area of 16 cm² each. As 16 + 16 is 32, and $\frac{32}{160} = \frac{1}{5}$, the area of the original rectangle has decreased by $\frac{1}{5}$. As $1 - \frac{1}{5} = \frac{4}{5}$, the area of the new shape is $\frac{4}{5}$ the area of the old rectangle.

7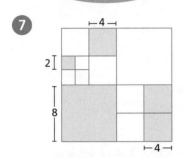

Consider the unshaded squares:
$3 \times 2 \times 2 + 4 \times 4 \times 4 + 8 \times 8$
$= 12 + 64 + 64 = 140$ cm^2.

8 Compare the perimeters of the two shapes. The perimeter of Shape B is 2 rectangle-lengths more than the perimeter of Shape A. As $60 - 44$ is 16, the length of the rectangle is 8 cm.

9 Each square has a side length of 8 cm. This means that the area of each square is 64 cm^2. As $2 \times 64 - 12 \times 8 = 32$, the area of the shaded rectangle is 32 cm^2.

10 As 40×3 is 120 the perimeter of the triangle is 120 cm. If 120 is $\frac{4}{5}$ of a number then $120 \div 4 = 30$ is $\frac{1}{5}$ of the number and $30 \times 5 = 150$ is the number. This means the perimeter of the rectangle is 150 cm. The sum of the length and width will be 75 cm. As $75 \div 3$ is 25, the width is 25 cm and the length is 50 cm.

Real Test 2

1 B 2 B 3 E 4 C 5 A 6 C 7 B 8 D 9 B 10 C

EXPLANATIONS

1 The perimeter is 20 cm, and this means the side of the square is 5 cm. If the length was 3 cm longer, then the original width was 2 cm.

2 As 2 m = 2000 mm, each side = $2000 \div 8 = 1000 \div 4 = 250$. Each side is 250 mm.

3 Each side is 0.6 cm, or 6 mm. The area is $6 \times 6 = 36$, or 36 mm^2.

4 As $6 + 4$ is 10, the perimeter is $2 \times (10 + 8)$ which is 36. As $36 \div 6$ is 6, the hexagon has side length of 6 cm.

5 The length of each side of P is 6 cm. The area is 36 cm^2. As 36×9 is 324, the area of square Q is 324 cm^2. As 18×18 is 324, the length of each side of square Q is 18 cm. As 18×4 is 72, the perimeter is 72 cm.

6 The perimeter of the new shape is the same as the perimeter of the original rectangle. As the perimeter is 44, then 10 + length = 22, which means the length is 12 cm. Now $12 - 8 = 4$ and as the squares are identical, the side length of each square is 2 cm. The area of each square is 4 cm^2, so the total area of the squares is 16 cm^2.

7 Consider squares inside the large square. The shaded area is $10 \times 10 - 8 \times 8 + 6 \times 6 - 4 \times 4$, which is $100 - 64 + 36 - 16 = 56$. The area is 56 cm^2.

8 Compared to Shape P, Shape Q has an additional rectangle, but its perimeter has only increased by 2 'widths' of the extra rectangle. As $68 - 56 = 12$, then 2 'widths' = 12 cm, and so the width of each small rectangle is 6 cm. As $6 \times 3 = 18$, the length of Shape P is 18 cm. As the perimeter of Shape P is 56 cm, the sum of the length and width is 28 cm. As $28 - 18 = 10$, the width of Shape P is 10 cm. As $18 \times 10 = 180$, the area of Shape P is 180 cm^2.

9 As 12×8 is 96 and one-quarter is $96 \div 4 = 24$, the area of the shaded section is 24 cm^2. As $24 \div 6$ is 4, the length of PQ is 4 cm.

10 The length of the rectangle is twice the width. As the perimeter is 24 cm, then length + width = 12, so the width is 4 cm. As 4×4 is 16, the area is 16 cm^2.

MATHEMATICAL REASONING
*Volume, capacity, mass, speed
and time*   Pages 101–102

Real Test 3

1 D 2 B 3 C 4 C 5 B 6 A 7 E 8 D 9 E 10 C
EXPLANATIONS

1. Change all dimensions to cm: 2000 cm by 1000 cm by 5 cm. This means 10 000 000 cm³ of rain fell, which is 10 000 L.

2. If it drips every 4 seconds, this means 15 drips per minute. This means 8 mL, 15 times a minute, 60 minutes per hour, 24 hours in a day, 7 days a week, then divided by 1000 to convert to litres.

3. As 3 × 10 = 30, Costa takes 30 mL per day. This means the medicine will last 270 ÷ 30 = 27 ÷ 3 = 9, which is 9 days.

4. Time is distance ÷ speed. This means she walks for 2 h, rests for 3 h, then walks for another 4 h. The total time is 9 hours, which means she completes her journey at 3 pm.

5. Johannesburg is 6 h behind Singapore. This means it is 9:20 pm Tuesday.

6. The difference in times is 18 h 30 min, but the time difference in the table is 5 h 30 min. This means the flight took 13 h.

7. Three-quarters of an hour is 45 minutes. From 1440 to 1500 is 20 minutes and another 25 minutes is 1525. In 12-hour time, this is 3:25 pm.

8. As 360 ÷ 2 is 180, the glass has 180 mL of water. As 180 – 40 is 140, and 360 – 140 is 220, Sophia pours 220 mL from the bottle. As 1000 – 220 is 780 there is 780 mL of water remaining in the bottle.

9. As 2.5 kg is 2500 grams, and 2500 – 80 is 2420, the four blocks have a combined mass of 2420 grams. As 2420 ÷ 4 is 605, the mass of one block is 605 grams. As 605 + 80 is 685 the display will show 685 grams.

10. As $15 - 4\frac{1}{2}$ is $10\frac{1}{2}$, Mumbai is $10\frac{1}{2}$ hours ahead of Chicago. Adding $10\frac{1}{2}$ hours on to 8:20 am gives 6:50 pm. The video call commenced at 6:50 pm and lasted 26 minutes. This means the call ended at 7:16 pm.

Real Test 4

1 D 2 A 3 B 4 C 5 C 6 C 7 A 8 E 9 D 10 D
EXPLANATIONS

1. The total mass of 3 boys is 40 × 3 = 120, and the total of 4 boys is 45 × 4 = 180. This means the fourth boy has a mass of 60 kg.

2. As 20 cm = $\frac{1}{5}$ m, then the volume = $5 \times 4 \times \frac{1}{5} = 4$. This means the volume is 4 m³.

3. From the table, Auckland is 18 h ahead of Boston. This means it is 2:20 pm Tuesday in Auckland.

4. From the table, London is 13 hours behind Auckland. This means the phone call started at 7:50 am London time, and ended at 8:02 am.

5. 112 minutes is 8 minutes less than 2 hours. From 1905, subtract 2 hours gives 1705, and then add 8 minutes is 1713. This is 5:13 pm.

6. As the middle of 150 and 300 is 225, the glass initially contains 225 mL of water. As 225 – 100 is 125, and 300 – 125 is 175, Nupur needs to pour 175 mL from the jug into the glass. The jug originally contains 1500 mL of water. As 1500 – 175 is 1325, there is 1325 mL remaining in the jug.

7. As 670 – 510 is 160, the empty glass jar has a mass of 160 g. Half of 510 is 255. As 160 + 255 is 415, the mass will be 415 grams.

8. Adding 16.5, 16.2 and 17.3 is 50, so the mass of 2 prisms, 2 cylinders and 2 cones is 50 kg. As 50 ÷ 2 is 25, the combined mass is 25 kg.

9 From 1930 Wednesday, add 9 hours is 0430 Thursday in Sydney. As 14 + 4 + 8 is 26, and 26 hours added to 0430 is 0630 the following day, Willow arrives in Sydney at 0630 on Friday.

10 The time will be 12:34. From 6:54 to 7:00 is 6 minutes, to 12:00 is 300 minutes, and to 12:34 is 34 minutes. As 6 + 300 + 34 is 340 minutes.

WRITING
Narrative response   Pages 107–109

Task 3

cross-country race; small; poor/bad/weak; nightmare; actual/real

Task 5

1 pounded

2 shoved

3 dodged

4 thundered

5 lunged

6 stampeded

Task 6

1 My body shrieked with pain.

2 I heard shouting and swearing; an enormous pile of waving arms and legs sliding around in a mud patch

3 An ear-splitting grin cracked the mud covering my face.

Task 7

1 a

2 Yes. Most of the runners fall over in the mud (paragraph 6).

WEEK 4

READING
Varied short texts   Pages 115–123

Practice Task 1

1 A **2** D **3** B **4** C **5** B **6** A **7** C **8** D **9** D **10** A

EXPLANATIONS

1 This whole extract is about the experiences of those who fly the craft—the astronauts. It is the total focus of the text. Text B refers to what the pilots do but text B is not about the experiences they have.

2 This extract describes the three main parts of a balloon.

3 This extract is all about the fear of flying. No others mention this. Extract A mentions a physical response to zero gravity and an emotional response but no psychological responses.

4 This extract refers to how people going on a ballooning trip expect to rock from side to side and feel wind and movement, and explains that this is not what happens.

5 This extract mentions that one of the strategies to combat fear of flying is to learn about how planes fly.

6 This extract refers to the challenges of being in zero gravity in space.

7 This extract emphasises throughout the skill and expertise of the balloon pilots.

8 This extract begins with an explanation about how balloons fly.

9 This extract says that balloon baskets can carry up to 24 people.

10 This extract begins with a question about what astronauts do all day and then answers it.

Practice Task 2

1 C 2 A 3 B 4 C 5 D 6 D 7 A 8 B 9 C 10 B

EXPLANATIONS

1 This extract is entirely the story of a carer. It mentions specifically how enjoyable the role is.

2 This extract focuses on how Australian mammals do a dangerous thing in going close to the roadside to feed.

3 This extract argues for humans to help other species because we have the intelligence to do so and because it is so important for all living things.

4 The carer in this extract mentions how upsetting it can be to see how humans sometimes hurt animals in the wild and gives the example of using netting in their gardens.

5 This extract states the difficulty of understanding and solving the problem with bees because there are no bees left in the colony to examine.

6 This extract argues in the last two sentences that we need to take notice because if bees are dying something is wrong.

7 This extract mentions some of the ways the researchers are experimenting to stop animals coming close to the roadside.

8 This extract is mostly about why we should help other species but it also mentions that not everyone agrees with interfering in nature.

9 This extract begins with an explanation of the moment that this person began her work as a carer, and then continues to explain how rewarding it is. It suggests but does not state explicitly, that this changed the direction of this person's life.

10 This extract is entirely an argument for intervening to protect species in danger.

Practice Task 3

1 A 2 B 3 D 4 D 5 A 6 C 7 C 8 B 9 B 10 C

EXPLANATIONS

1 This extract refers to 'the views of various writers and artists who have travelled to foreign lands in times gone by'.

2 This extract appears to be from a diary. It describes the feelings and experiences of the writer.

3 This extract begins with the feelings the writer experiences well before he or she begins the journey.

4 This extract mentions something most people would not find the most enjoyable part of travel—emerging from the airport.

5 This extract finishes with some thoughts that many a tired traveller might feel— wanting to stay in bed instead of going out to see sites and so on.

6 This extract mentions the writer's feelings about seeing a hint of the mountains through the mist and the pull this exercises on him—'I needed to see more'.

7 This extract mentions three motivations of people who go to high mountain regions.

8 This extract focuses in a significant way on seasickness.

9 This extract mentions the 'anguish on leaving family and friends', the fact that the children are the only ones enjoying the trip, and the despair the writer feels.

10 The last three sentences in this extract advise other adventurers to do what he did and go 'off the beaten track'.

Real Test

1 B 2 C 3 A 4 D 5 C 6 A 7 B 8 C 9 D 10 A

EXPLANATIONS

1 The three stories in this extract are all about the things that parents said or did. This suggests not surprisingly that we take notice of and remember these words and actions.

2 This extract in the opening line compares our memories to a 'gigantic jigsaw'.

3 This extract focuses on a survey and some facts about the age we remember from.

4 This extract is all about improving your mind and memory. We need to 'use it or lose it'.

5 This extract refers to the 'trivial' (unimportant) memories like 'the colour of a dress or the feel of a cushion'.

6 This extract explains how some people might build up memories from something that happened after they were three or four and combine it with later information.

7 This extract is about not being allowed to do what we want (e.g. wear clothes, stay in bed, avoid certain foods) so suggests we might remember these things more than the happier moments.

8 This extract mentions both family and culture as influences on how we remember.

9 This extract mentions this as one of the criteria for improving our memory.

10 The last line of this extract says that people often refuse to believe their memories are false—they are 'like gold'.

> **THINKING SKILLS**
> *Problem solving—Position and order*
> Pages 126–127

Real Test 1

1 C 2 A 3 A 4 D 5 A 6 B 7 C 8 D 9 C 10 D

EXPLANATIONS

1 Alice is shorter than Jack and Jack is shorter than Kate. So Alice must be shorter than Kate.

A and D are not correct. Either Oliver or Jill must be the shortest but there is no information about who is the shorter.

B is not correct because there is no information about who is taller out of Jack and Jill.

2 Tim is on Ellen's left and opposite Stuart. Jenny and Paul sit together between Tim and Stuart. The remaining place, on Ellen's right, is for Angus.

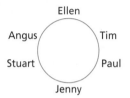

3 The person in seat 5 is not Alison, Robyn, Stephanie or Margaret, so it must be Julie. Margaret is in either seat 2 or seat 4, but Robyn is between Julie and Margaret, so Margaret can only be in seat 2. Neither Robyn nor Alison can be in seat 1, so that must be for Stephanie. There is one seat between Stephanie and Alison, meaning that Alison must be in seat 3.

1	2	3	4	5
Stephanie	Margaret	Alison	Robyn	Julie

4 Molly was born in September. Neither Louis nor Isaac can be born in July because they are born two months apart, meaning that the other would be born in September. Both Thea and James were born after Oliver, so only Oliver can be born in July.

July	August	September	October	November	December
Oliver	Isaac/ Louis	Molly	Louis/ Isaac	Thea	James

A is not correct. The statement might be true, but it is not the statement that must be true.

B and C are not correct. Thea was born the month before James. So neither Thea nor James was born in August. So Isaac or Louis was born then and the other of those two was born in October. This means that Thea was born in November and James in December.

5 The newsagency and the shop where Ruth works are not in position 4 and they are not next to each other, so they must be in positions 1 and 3 in some order. If the newsagency was in position 3 then, as the chemist is between the newsagency and post office, the post office would have to be in position 1. But that is not correct. So, the newsagency is not in position 3, it is in position 1. The bank and chemist are not next to each other, so one must be in position 2 and the other in position 4. The post office would have to be in position 3, meaning that the chemist is in position 2.

1	2	3	4
News	Chemist	P.O.	Bank

High Street

6 Oscar finished first and found the least number of items. He didn't find one, because he didn't finish in the same position as the number of items he found. He found at least two. Luke found more than Oscar, so must have found at least three. David found two more than Luke so must have found at least five. But David found the same number as the position he finished in and his lowest possible finishing position is five. So David found 5, Luke found 3 and Oscar found 2.

A and D might be true but are not the options that must be true.

C is not correct because David found 5 items.

7 Arabella is older than Pip who is older than Ted. Matilda is older than Xavier who is older than Pip. Arabella might be the oldest or Matilda might be the oldest. The statement that might not be true is Arabella is the oldest.

Neither A nor B is the correct answer because those statements must be true. Pip is shorter than Matilda who is shorter than Arabella who is shorter than Xavier.

Ted is taller than Matilda but shorter than Xavier. So Pip is the shortest and Xavier is the tallest.

D is not the correct answer because that statement must be true. Ted is younger than Pip who is younger than Arabella. Pip is also younger than Xavier who is younger than Matilda. So Ted must be the youngest.

8 The Dawsons live in the house that is furthest right and the centre house has only one occupant. Alison and Liz Elliott both live with one other person. As Alison is not named Dawson, they must live in the two houses on the left. Marshall Smith and his two children must live in the second house on the right. As there are two houses between George and Isabel Ford, neither of those can live in the centre house. So Isabel Ford must be the person who lives with Alison and Chang is the last name of the person in the centre house. George's last name must be either Dawson or Smith and the last name of Xavier and Henrietta will be the other of those two names. Peter lives between George and Victor so Peter must live in the centre house and Victor is the person who lives with Liz.

Liz Victor Elliott	Alison Isabel Ford	Peter Chang	Marshall Xavier Henrietta Smith	George Maree Dawson

Pringle Street

Pringle Park

OR

Alison Isabel Ford	Liz Victor Elliott	Peter Chang	Marshall George Maree Smith	Xavier Henrietta Dawson

Pringle Street

Pringle Park

9 Benjamin and Dylan live as far apart as possible so they must live in two of the end houses on opposite sides of the lane.

Jennifer lives at house 1 and Helen lives in either house 5 or house 6. Now, Helen has two brothers. Neither Benjamin nor Dylan has a brother, so one of Benjamin or Dylan must live directly opposite Helen. Frank and Thomas live opposite one another but cannot be opposite either Benjamin or Dylan, so they live in houses 3 and 4. Helen's brothers are not Benjamin, Dylan, Frank or Thomas. So they are Oliver and Ross. Jennifer's brother is not Frank or Thomas or Oliver or Ross and is not Dylan because he has no siblings, so Jennifer's brother is Benjamin. Dylan lives in house 6 so Helen, Oliver and Ross live in house 5.

10 Zara looks after the sheep and Rosie has the cow so the girl who looks after the chickens is Grace. John is opposite the goats so he must have the pig as the horse is opposite the sheep. The chickens must be opposite the cow. As Rosie is on the northern side, Grace is on the southern side, on John's right. So the centre pen on the southern side is John's and has the pig.

N	William/Henry	Henry/William	Rosie
↑	horse	goats	cow
	Walkway		
	Zara	John	Grace
	sheep	pig	chickens

THINKING SKILLS
Problem solving—Logic problems and contradictions   Pages 130–131

Real Test 2

1 A 2 B 3 D 4 B 5 A 6 C 7 C 8 A 9 D 10 B
EXPLANATIONS

1 Only one answer was incorrect. Connor and Mo gave contradictory answers, so one of those must be the incorrect answer. All other answers must be correct. The hoodie must be blue.

2 The person who knocked over the plant was the one who lied. Ash and Pete gave contradictory answers so one of them was the culprit. Polly must have told the truth so Pete was the culprit.

3 One girl was wrong. Nadia and Jessica gave contradictory replies so one of them is wrong. Simone must be right so their brother is 5. Jessica is the one who is wrong.

4 Three children lied and only one told the truth. Guy and Daniel gave contradictory answers, so one of them must be the child who told the truth. Everyone else lied. So Samuel lied when he said it wasn't him. Samuel sent the flowers.

5 Two answers were correct and one was wrong. If the first answer was wrong then the winning horse was Jim's Boy, but that contradicts the second answer which would have to be correct. So the first answer is correct. The winner wasn't Jim's Boy. Similarly, if the third answer was wrong there again would be a contradiction. So the answer that was wrong must be the second answer. Riverflow didn't win, but neither did Jim's Boy or Sensation as the first and third answers would be correct. So the winner must have been Pride.

6 Only one person gave a wrong answer. Celia and Bill gave contradictory replies so one of those gave the wrong answer. Douglas gave a correct answer so the time was 10:45. Celia gave the wrong answer because it was not a quarter to ten.

7 Only one person is telling the truth. If Oscar was telling the truth then Nathan wouldn't be lying and so two would be telling the truth. That is a contradiction, so Oscar cannot be telling the truth. So Nathan is lying. This means that his statement is false so Georgia is not lying. The person telling the truth is Georgia.

8 On each parcel one sentence is true and one is false. If the first statement on parcel 1 was true then the second must be false. This means that the first statement on parcel 2 is false and the second is true. The first statement on parcel 3 is true and the second is false. So the present would be in parcel 1 and it is not a book.

If the first statement on parcel 1 was false then the second must be true. So the second statement on parcel 2 is false meaning that the first must be true. The present would be in parcel 2. The second statement on parcel 3 would be true so the first would be false. So the present would be in parcel 3. This is a contradiction. The present cannot be both in parcel 2 and parcel 3. So the first statement on parcel 1 must be true.

9 One, and only one, of the sisters is the oldest. The person who makes two true statements must be the oldest. The first statement of the other two sisters must be false. So one of those sisters will make two false statements meaning that their second statement is also false. The other sister will make a true statement second so that she makes one true and one false statement. So two of the second statements are true and one is false. The second statements of Imogen and Ruby are contradictions. One must be true and one must be false. This means that Maisie's second statement must be true. Maisie has the most cars so Maisie has more than Ruby.

B is not correct because Imogen must make two false statements.

Either A or C will be correct but there is not enough information to determine which one must be correct.

10 The statements that the man drove the car every day and that he drove it only occasionally are contradictions. Only one of those statements can be true. As the man gave every person at least one true piece of information, the statement that he owned the car for three years must be true.

A must therefore be false.

Either C or D might be true, but there is not enough information to determine which must be true.

THINKING SKILLS
Problem solving—Thinking outside the square Pags 134–135

Thinking outside the square:

Real Test 3

1 B **2** C **3** D **4** D **5** A **6** B **7** C **8** A **9** A **10** C

EXPLANATIONS

1 After 4 weeks the total scores are Lincoln 14, Max 17, Jessica 13 and Thomas 15. After 5 weeks the lowest score Max could have is 17 + 1 = 18 and the highest score Jessica could have is 13 + 5 = 18. So if they all have the same total that total must be 18. To have a total score of 18, Thomas will need to score 3 in Week 5.

2 Each of the three girls begins with 20 marbles so there are 60 marbles altogether. If Ebony has 18, Sue and Michaela have 60 – 18 = 42 between them. Now Sue has 10 more than Michaela. If Sue had 10 less, they would both have the same number. Now 42 – 10 = 32 and 32 ÷ 2 = 16. So Michaela has 16 marbles (and Sue has 26).

3 Green has the most votes so the second column is green. The only possibility of two adding to the same total as green is the first and third columns, so they must be grey and lilac in some order. As more

than twice as many voted for blue than lilac, lilac must be the third column and blue the fourth. So lemon is the fifth column.

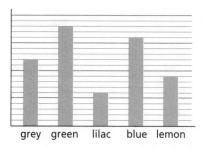

We are looking for the option that cannot be true. The numbers that voted for each are not known, but twice as many did vote for green than for lemon, so A is not the answer.

More people voted for blue than grey, so B is not the answer.

The least favourite colour was lilac, so C is not the answer.

If each division on the vertical axis is one vote, then 18 + 12 = 30 voted for green and grey together. Blue, lemon and lilac combined is 16 + 9 + 6 = 31. So the totals are not the same. This will be the case whatever the scale is on the vertical axis, so D is the answer.

4 If Tyler has more cards than Cooper then Tyler must have gained cards on his spin and Cooper must have lost cards. As Joseph has 7 cards, he has also lost cards. Tyler must have spun an even number and both Cooper and Joseph must have spun an odd number. Cooper and Joseph will both have lost 3 cards and Tyler will have gained 6 cards. Tyler will have 16 cards. (If Tyler went first and spun an even number, he would have got 2 cards from both Joseph and Cooper, so would have 14 and they would both have 8. If Joseph then spun an odd number, he would give 1 card to Tyler and 1 to Cooper. Tyler would have 15 cards, Cooper 9 and Joseph 6. If Cooper then spun an odd number, he

would give 1 to Tyler and one to Joseph. Tyler would have 16, Cooper 7 and Joseph 7.)

5 The last digit in the top number must be 5 because 5 + 6 = 11. That means that the middle digit in the top number must be 8. The digits in the sum are all different so the remaining two digits must be either 2, 4 or 7. The only possibility for the sum of the first digits is 3 + 4 = 7. The digit that is not used in the sum is 2.

6 The total time taken by each of the drivers is Nelson 78 min, Melissa 88 min, David 71 min and Shona 74 min. So David is the person who will win if he finishes well. He has a 3-minute lead over Shona, so provided he doesn't finish more than 2 minutes behind Shona he will win outright.

7 The day at the bottom of the graph has 6 symbols. As this is the greatest number it must be the amount for Wednesday or, if Wednesday is the day that is missing, for Tuesday. If it is the amount for Tuesday, then as 36 ÷ 6 = 6 every symbol would represent 6. Monday would have 24 ÷ 6 = 4 symbols. But there is no day with 4 symbols. So Wednesday is not the day that is missing. Each symbol represents 48 ÷ 6 or 8. Monday would have 24 ÷ 8 = 3 symbols. Tuesday would have 36 ÷ 8 or $4\frac{1}{2}$ symbols. Thursday would have 32 ÷ 8 = 4 symbols and Friday 28 ÷ 8 = $3\frac{1}{2}$ symbols. As there is no day with 4 symbols, Thursday is the day that is missing.

8 Ed rolls 4 so Mick gives him 4 counters. Ed has 24 and Mick 16 counters. Mick rolls 3 and so must give 3 counters to Ed. Ed has 27 and Mick 13. Morgan rolls 1 and so must give 1 counter to Mick. Morgan has 19 and Mick 14 counters. After Ed's next roll he has 29 counters, so he has received 2 more. He must have rolled a 2 and received 2 counters from Mick. Mick will have 14 − 2 or 12 counters.

9 The times on the clocks, in order, are 8:00, 8:30, 9:00, 9:30 and 10:00. In total, the four slowest clocks are 5 hours behind the clock that shows 10 o'clock. But altogether the clocks are $12\frac{1}{2}$ hours behind the correct time which is another $7\frac{1}{2}$ hours. As $7\frac{1}{2} \div 5 = 1\frac{1}{2}$, the clocks are a further hour and a half slow. The correct time must be 11:30 and the clocks are $3\frac{1}{2}$, 3, $2\frac{1}{2}$, 2 and $1\frac{1}{2}$ hours slow. The only clock that is twice as slow as any other is the one that is 3 hours slow. That is the clock that shows 8:30 and it is twice as slow as the clock that shows 10:00.

10 Sophie is to the left of at least two people, so can only be in position 1 or 2. Lily is to the right of at least two people so can only be in position 3 or 4. Sophie and Lily are sitting next to each other. So Sophie must be in position 2 and Lily in position 3. James will be in position 1 and Alistair in position 4. Now Sophie is immediately left of the 7-year-old who is somewhere left of the child in the red shirt. So Lily must be the 7-year-old and Alistair must have the red shirt. Lily is immediately right of the child in the green shirt who is right of the 8-year-old. So Sophie must have the green shirt and James must be the 8-year-old. Now the blue shirt was worn by the person immediately left of the 9-year-old and somewhere right of the child in the yellow shirt. So Lily must have the blue shirt and James the yellow shirt. Alistair is the 9-year-old so Sophie, in the green shirt, must be 10.

James yellow 8	Sophie green 10	Lily blue 7	Alistair red 9

MATHEMATICAL REASONING
Space and geometry   Pages 138–141

Real Test 1

1 C 2 A 3 B 4 E 5 B 6 D 7 E 8 C 9 E 10 A

EXPLANATIONS

1 The solid has four faces, all triangular. This means it is a triangular pyramid.

2 There are eight sides on an octagon. This means there are 10 faces on an octagonal prism.

3 Considering the shading, there are four axes of symmetry. (If there were no shaded triangles, there would be eight.)

4 The diagram has all of the features. (If it has quarter turn symmetry, it must have half turn symmetry.)

5 Austin shades six more squares.

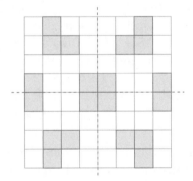

6 The solid is a hexagonal prism. There are two hexagons and six rectangles. The solid has 8 faces, 18 edges and 12 vertices. As 8 + 18 + 12 is 38, the total is 38.

7 The shape has been rotated 90° in a clockwise direction. This is the same as a rotation of 270° in an anticlockwise direction.

8 As 40 + 50 is 90, then $\frac{90}{360}$ or $\frac{1}{4}$ or 25% of the circle is not shaded. As 100 − 25 is 75, then 75% of the circle is shaded.

9 The hexagon is regular. The equilateral triangle has all sides and all angles equal. This means that each angle inside the triangle will be 60°. This means that each angle inside the hexagon is 120°. As 120 × 3 is 360, then $a + b + c = 360$.

10 S, H, I and N are letters with rotational symmetry.

Real Test 2

1 D 2 A 3 A 4 B 5 C 6 B 7 B 8 E 9 C 10 A

EXPLANATIONS

1 As the centre shape is a hexagon and there are therefore six triangles, the net forms a hexagonal pyramid.

2 The order of rotation is 5 as the shape is a five-pointed star. (The shape can be rotated through 360 ÷ 5 = 72° to produce a shape identical to the original.)

3 The shaded square will appear at C2.

4 Only B will have quarter turn symmetry. (Although A is a square, it is partly shaded, which means it will not have quarter turn symmetry.)

5 The shape in C will be on the missing face.

6 Amelia adds two more white squares and two more black squares. She adds a total of 4 squares.

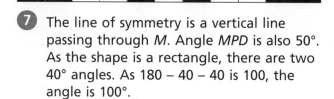

7 The line of symmetry is a vertical line passing through *M*. Angle *MPD* is also 50°. As the shape is a rectangle, there are two 40° angles. As 180 – 40 – 40 is 100, the angle is 100°.

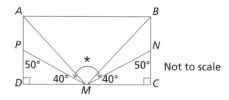

Not to scale

8 *Q* and *S* should be shaded.

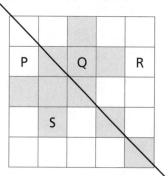

9 Alexis shades 3 more triangles.

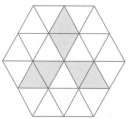

10 2 is opposite 5, 7 is opposite 10 and 18 is opposite 15. As 2 × 7 × 18 is 7 × 36 = 252, the product is 252.

MATHEMATICAL REASONING
Statistics and probability   Pages 144–147

Real Test 3

1 A 2 C 3 C 4 A 5 D 6 C 7 B 8 E 9 A 10 D

EXPLANATIONS

1 The angle for basketball was 60°. As this is $\frac{1}{6}$ of the circle, and $\frac{1}{6}$ of 120 is 20, so 20 students nominated basketball.

2 As 90° is $\frac{1}{4}$ of the 120 students, then 30 students nominated netball. One-third do not play netball. As $\frac{1}{3}$ of 30 is 10, there are 10 students who chose netball who don't play each weekend.

3 In the first group, 25% of 120 students chose netball. In the second group, 35% of 120 students chose it. The total number of students who chose it is the middle of 25% and 35%, which is 30%.

4 Bill catches the 08:14 to make the train to get to Flinders by 9 am.

5 Bruce will arrive at Cootha by 08:27, but the train stops at Gresford at 10:54.

6 As A\$100 = US\$80, then A\$500 converts to US\$400.

7 US\$80 = A\$100 = 60 euros.

8 Walk: 8, Bus: 9, Car: 5 and Bike: 3.
As 8 + 9 + 5 + 3 = 25, there were 25 students surveyed. Statement 1 is correct. Six out of 8 walkers are boys, which is three-quarters. Statement 2 is incorrect. As 6 + 4 + 1 + 1 is 12 there are 12 boys in the class. 6 out of 12, or half of the boys walked. Statement 3 is correct. This means statements 1 and 3 are correct.

9 The probability that it is green is half of 0.6 which is 0.3. As 1 – 0.6 – 0.3 is 0.1, the probability that the ball is blue is 0.1.

10 Look at the options: 18 occurs twice (6 × 3 and 3 × 6) and 24 occurs twice (6 × 4 and 4 × 6). This means these scores are equally likely.

Real Test 4

1 C 2 B 3 D 4 E 5 B 6 C 7 A 8 B 9 D 10 C
EXPLANATIONS

1 'Movies' is shown as 120° out of 360°. This means $\frac{1}{3}$ of \$18 is used for movies, that is, \$6.

2 As 360° – (80° + 120° + 90°) = 70°; Samoi saves $\frac{7}{36}$ of her allowance. In 2 weeks she is given \$36 which means she saves \$7 each fortnight, or \$14 every 4 weeks.

3 'Movies' was \$6 and now will become \$8. As \$18 = 360°, then \$1 = 20° and so \$8 is 160°.

4 It is 2781 km to Pantana and 982 km to Bullawa. The difference is 1799 km.

5 This will be the same time as Makira to

Amstrada—1.05 h, or 1 h 3 min.

6 Bullawa to Salarki (16 h), then Salarki to Pantana (38 h) totals 54 hours.

7 Pantana to Salarki (3.1 h), Salarki to Makira (1.1 h), Makira to Amstrada (1.05 h), Amstrada to Bullawa (2.15 h). This totals 7.4 hours.

8 As 6 + 4 + 6 + 3 + 7 + 2 + 3 + 1 is 32, there were 32 students surveyed. Statement 1 is incorrect. There were 6 straight-haired blondes and 3 curly-haired blondes. Statement 2 is correct. 9 students have black hair but 10 students have brown hair. Statement 3 is incorrect.

9 As $1 - \frac{1}{10} = \frac{9}{10}$, the probability of selecting a black or yellow marble is $\frac{9}{10}$. Now, as 6 is twice 3 and $\frac{6}{10}$ is twice $\frac{3}{10}$, the probability of selecting a black marble is $\frac{6}{10}$, or $\frac{3}{5}$.

10 First, 35% is $\frac{35}{100}$, which is $\frac{7}{20}$. For every 20 balls in the box, 7 are red and so 13 are blue. This means the smallest possible number of blue balls is 13.

WRITING
Persuasive text   Page 153

Task 3

1 a Secondly, wheels are especially important in food production (paragraph 3).
   Thirdly, our world would be completely different if we did not have the wheel for transport (paragraph 4).

   b food

   c transport

2 firstly, for example (paragraph 2); secondly, in fact (paragraph 3); thirdly (paragraph 4)

3 a probably

   b especially

   c completely

   d surely

SAMPLE TEST PAPER
Part 1: Reading
Pages 158–164

1 A 2 C 3 B 4 B 5 D 6 A 7 C 8 C 9 A 10 D
11 B 12 C 13 B 14 A 15 B 16 C 17 G 18 E
19 A 20 F 21 A 22 D 23 B 24 C 25 C 26 D
27 C 28 D 29 B 30 B

Extracts A and B

1 There is a lot of personal description in both texts. To get the right answer it is best to quickly scan for mention of each one—the teacher arriving on the scene, the students, the school or classroom. This scan will show you only A is correct— Extract A describes Miss Blackstone and Extract B describes Miss Temple.

2 You will find all these reasons given here for the girls not liking Miss Blackstone, but the first few paragraphs show you how much they loved Miss Faberge and sets up the contrast between the two teachers (especially line 1).

3 This is tricky as all three words refer to groups. But only one refers to the noise of a group as does 'clamour'—and that is 'tumult'. It is clear from the second part of the sentence that the 'tumult' refers to the girls talking. It is also clear in paragraph 4 that the words 'throng' and 'assemblage' refer to the group of girls itself.

4 You have to imagine the image Marianne gives and then think about what you know about warriors, witches and so on. The words 'a hat with horns' (an ancient warrior headdress) and 'saucepan lids for her chest' (battle armour) create an image of a warrior more than anything else.

5 You have to draw your own conclusions from the clues given. It is a rainy day, the children's clothes are wet and smelly, they are 'squeezed into', they 'mumble' the words and the flag looks like 'damp washing'. On top of all that, we know that one class is missing Miss Faberge terribly. The image should make you eliminate answer A immediately. And if you think about it there is no evidence the feeling is as strong as suggested in B and C.

6 Clearly the classroom described in Extract B is a different place to that in Extract A. There is plenty of evidence that the teacher who enters is instantly obeyed. Even the thought of her coming makes everyone sit down and be quiet. But there does not seem to be any fear so not B; to say it is warm and loving is a bit too much so not C; and there the girls are quiet still so not D.

7 You need to read the last three paragraphs of Extract A to get this right. If you don't read all three paragraphs you could be tricked into the other answers which are all mentioned in part. At first her stare was 'unnerving' (unsettling) but then Tracey feels 'a fear as cold as stone' (terrified).

8 The last paragraph of Extract B clearly shows the storyteller's feeling is of 'admiring awe'. The whole paragraph shows the teacher in a positive light, so the answer is certainly not fear (so not answer B). The storyteller may feel envy as she seems to be new and on her own but there is no evidence for this (so not A) and she may be astonished at the teacher's appearance and clothing but this is not the dominant feeling (so not D). She feels very warm towards this teacher.

Old Man Platypus

9 If you know that 'fragment' is a small part of something and if you think about how platypuses look, you should get this right.

10 Only line 6 is about the platypus's playfulness, so not C. Only line 8 mentions relations and friends, so not B. Although the platypus plays by himself, the poet suggests he is content, not lonely, so not A. Lines 8, 9 and 10 all relate to how special and unusual he is ('few relations', 'family most exclusive'), so the answer is D.

11 You are looking for an adjective or describing word. Poets sometimes put an adjective ('rank') after a noun ('grasses'). So the answer is A, B or C. You then have to think about what the grasses would be like under the bank and down near the roots—'smelly' seems the most logical answer.

12 Lines 8, 18, 21 and 22 should give you the answer.

13 Although the poet describes other aspects of the platypus, the emphasis is on the animal's uniqueness. The last line, in particular, focuses on this: 'In fact, he's the one and only'.

14 The whole poem reflects the poet's positive feeling towards the animal, so obviously not B. The poet might feel the feelings mentioned in C and D also, but this poem expresses mostly his respect and wonderment.

Jenolan Caves

15 This is a general introductory statement about caves and so suggests it is from the first paragraph. The sentence links to the previous sentence's mention of visitors.

16 This sentence clearly links with the previous sentence which is about the First Nations Australians' knowledge of the caves.

17 The name 'Grand Arch' links back to the previous sentence's mention of 'archways' and the following sentence giving its dimensions.

18 The words 'this cave' tell you that you need to look to the previous sentence and reference to a particular cave, which is the Lucas Cave.

19 This sentence is clearly about the formation of the cave and belongs in the paragraph which describes that.

20 Again, this sentence is about the formation of the cave but belongs at the end as it builds upon earlier geological knowledge about cave formation.

The unneeded sentence is D. While the idea stated is true—some people do find caves scary—there is no mention of this theme in the text. Also it is unlikely that you would find an informal word like 'scary' in an information report such as this.

Extracts A–D

21 This is not stated explicitly but the people who made the bad predictions are all leaders in their field, so it is possible the bad predictions affected their careers. For example, the movie producer (line 12) was not worried about the effect television might have on movies when he probably should have been.

22 This extract clearly refers to the life of great-grandparents and to the life of children now.

23 There is mention of HG Wells who is said to have imagined 'even something resembling the World Wide Web'.

24 Both the line 'I love the show because it really makes you think about future possibilities' and the final line which encourages the reader to think about the future tell you this is the correct answer.

25 This extract is mainly made up of the writer's memory of one scene in *Dr Who*.

26 This extract mentions 'immortality' twice—it is in the name of the book being discussed and in the line about some of the ideas in the book.

27 The extract says clearly that Dr Who is a time traveller.

28 This extract is all about a book written about future possibilities.

29 All the extracts except B have a question to the reader in them. A is at the very beginning, C and D end with a question.

30 This extract says in the second sentence that science fiction 'can also criticise present-day society'.

SAMPLE TEST PAPER
Part 2: Mathematical Reasoning Pages 165–171

1 B 2 A 3 E 4 B 5 E 6 D 7 D 8 E 9 A 10 C
11 A 12 D 13 B 14 C 15 B 16 C 17 E 18 A
19 E 20 B 21 B 22 C 23 A 24 E 25 E 26 D
27 D 28 C 29 B 30 D 31 B 32 B 33 C 34 D
35 C

1 From 1545 to 1600 is 15 minutes. An hour and a half is 90 minutes. As 15 + 90 + 5 is 110, Brendan has been away from home for 110 minutes.

2 There are 20 squares in the shape. As $\frac{1}{5}$ of the squares is 20 ÷ 5 = 4, then $\frac{2}{5}$ is 8 squares. As 20 − 8 is 12, there are 12 unshaded squares. Now as $\frac{1}{4}$ of 12 is 12 ÷ 4 = 3, then $\frac{3}{4}$ is 9 squares. As 12 − 9 is 3, there are 3 unshaded squares remaining. As 3 − 2 is 1, only 1 square remains unshaded.

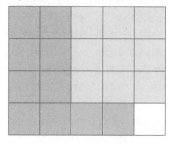

3 The four multiples are 80, 90, 100 and 110. As 8 × 9 is 72 and 72 × 11 is 792, then 80 × 90 × 100 × 110 is 792 followed by 5 zeros. The product is 79 200 000.

4 14.3 − 8.5 is 5.8. This means that the mass of the additional water is 5.8 kg. As 5.8 × 2 is 11.6 the mass of water in the filled container is 11.6 kg. Now as 14.3 − 11.6 is 2.7, the mass of the empty container is 2.7 kg.

5 S and Z do not have any line of symmetry. Statement 1 is correct. 11 letters have one line of symmetry, whereas only 4 letters have two lines of symmetry. Statement 2 is correct. A, E, I, O and U all have at least one line of symmetry. Statement 3 is correct. All three statements are correct.

6 As 64 is a multiple of 8 and 6 + 4 = 10, Ben is 64 years old. As 28 is 3 more than 25 and 2 less than 30, Jen is 28 years old. Now as 64 − 28 is 36, then Ben was 36 years old.

7 As 12 × 4 is 48, the area of Paddock *A* is 4800 m². The length of Paddock *B* is 80 m. As 48 ÷ 8 is 6, then 4800 ÷ 80 is 60, and so the width of Paddock *B* is 60 m. As 60 − 40 is 20, Paddock *B* is 20 m wider.

8 As $\frac{3}{4}$ of 60 is 60 ÷ 4 × 3 = 45, there was 45 L of petrol in the tank. As 8.5 × 2 is 17, Albert used 17 L of petrol during the day. As 45 − 17 is 28, there was 28 L of petrol remaining in the tank. As 60 − 28 is 32, Albert filled the tank with 32 L of petrol.

9 As 7 × ■ = 63, then ■ is 9.
Now, 9 + ▲ = 21 means ▲ is 12.
Finally, as 12 − 8 = 4, then ● = 4

10 Joshua needs 3 more triangles. Two of these triangles will be black.

11 Row four represents 1 × 4 = 4, 2 × 4 = 8, 3 × 4 = 12 (2), 4 × 4 = 16 (6), 5 × 4 = 20 (0) and 6 × 4 = 24 (4). This means the sequence will be 4 8 2 6 0 4.

12 From 7:40 to 10:30 there are only 3 trains that stop at Mitchells Flat. Statement 1 is incorrect. The fastest trip between Highmead and Stanhope takes 43 minutes, leaving Highmead at 09:40. Statement 2 is correct. Mercia arrives at 7:30. She should take the 7:59 train to Roughit, then wait 35 minutes and take the 8:55 train to Cranky Corner arriving at 9:10. This means it takes her 1 hour 40 minutes to get to Cranky Corner. Statement 3 is correct. Statements 2 and 3 are correct.

13 As $180 ÷ 3 is $60, each person has $60 remaining. Leah must have spent $60. For Colton, if $\frac{2}{3}$ of his money is $60, he must have spent $30. For Prue, if $\frac{3}{4}$ of her money is $60, then she must have spent $20. As 60 + 30 + 20 = 110, then $110 was spent.

14 The protractor measures an angle of 120°. As the hexagon is regular, all interior angles are 120°. The line of symmetry cuts one of these angles in half. This means the angle shown as * is 60°.

15 Multiplying 13 by 6 and adding 3 gives the total number of pieces of fruit. This is 81, which is the same as adding 39 and 42.

16 The perimeter is 36 cm, which means the length is 9 cm. This means the original dimensions were 9 cm by 5 cm. The area of the original rectangle was 45 cm².

17 As $\frac{1}{3} + \frac{1}{4}$ is $\frac{4}{12} + \frac{3}{12} = \frac{7}{12}$, then Catriona drove $1 - \frac{7}{12} = \frac{5}{12}$ of the distance. As $\frac{4}{12} < \frac{5}{12}$, Iris did not drive further than Catriona.

Statement 1 is incorrect. As $\frac{5}{12} < \frac{6}{12}$, Catriona drove less than half the distance. Statement 2 is correct. As $1 - \frac{1}{3}$ is $\frac{2}{3}$, and $\frac{2}{3} < \frac{3}{4}$, Demi and Catriona drove less than $\frac{3}{4}$ of the distance altogether. Statement 3 is correct. Statements 2 and 3 are correct.

18 As 7 + 12 + 1 + 14 = 34, all rows, columns and diagonals add to 34.

9	16	2	7
6	3	13	12
15	10	8	1
4	5	11	14

The missing number is 2.

19 There are 4 even numbers out of 6 so the probability of an even number is $\frac{4}{6}$ or $\frac{2}{3}$. Statement 1 is correct. As 2 + 4 is 6, and there is 1 six, the probability is $\frac{1}{6}$. Statement 2 is correct. As Pia spun a 2, Shaun needs to spin a 4 or a 6. The probability of a 4 or 6 is $\frac{2}{6}$, which is $\frac{1}{3}$. Statement 3 is correct. This means statements 1, 2 and 3 are correct.

20 Gabriela's number is 5 700 000 and Enrico's number is 5 679 900.

```
  5 700 000
− 5 679 900
     20 100
```

The difference is 20 100.

21 As 160 + 160 is 320, Goran travelled 320 km. As 200 + 200 is 400, Seth travelled 400 km. As 400 − 320 = 80, Seth travelled 80 km further than Goran. Statement 1 is incorrect. From 8 am to 4 pm is 8 h and 10 am to 4 pm is 6 h. As 8 − 6 is 2, then Seth was away 2 fewer hours than Goran. Statement 2 is correct. In the morning Goran stopped 10 am to 11 am which is 1 hour. Statement 3 is incorrect. Only Statement 2 is correct.

22 Use 1 cm³ = 1 mL. As the height of Tank A is 12 cm and $\frac{2}{3}$ of 12 = 12 ÷ 3 × 2 = 8, the depth of water is 8 cm. Half of the water will be a depth of 4 cm. As 20 × 10 × 4 is 800, then 800 mL is poured from Tank *A* into Tank *B*. As 1 – $\frac{1}{5}$ is $\frac{4}{5}$, then $\frac{4}{5}$ of Tank *B* must be 800 mL. As 800 ÷ 4 × 5 = 1000, then Tank *B* has a capacity of 1000 mL, or 1 L.

23 In total Stefania, Oliver and Marlon bought 3 boxes of each cereal and paid a total of $38.10.

As 3)$\overline{38.10}$, Johannes paid $12.70 for a box of each cereal.

24 As the area is 16 cm², then each side is 4 cm. The cube has 12 edges. This means the sum is 48 cm.

25 The value of the 4 is 40 000 and the value of the 8 is 80. Now, 40 000 ÷ 80 is 4000 ÷ 8 which is 500. This means it is 500 times larger.

26 Tokyo is 7 hours ahead of Berlin. At 9:05 pm Wednesday in Berlin it is 4:05 am Thursday in Tokyo. Adding a flight time of 14 hours gives 6:05 pm Thursday.

27 The four rectangles have dimensions 8 cm by 7 cm, 6 cm by 5 cm, 4 cm by 3 cm, and 2 cm by 1 cm. As 8 × 7 – 6 × 5 + 4 × 3 – 2 × 1 is 56 – 30 + 12 – 2 = 36, the area is 36 cm².

28 250 × 50 is 12 500 and then adding 250 gives 12 750. This means Leon has 12 750 mL, or 12.75 L.

29 Another 4 squares need to be shaded.

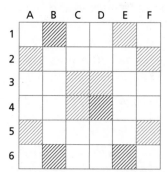

30 As the large cube is cut into 64 smaller cubes and 4 × 4 × 4 = 64, the cube has 4 layers of 4 by 4 cubes. Only the 4 inside cubes on each of the middle 2 layers will be unpainted. As 4 + 4 = 8, there will be 8 cubes not painted.

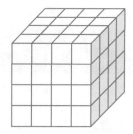

31 As the perimeter is 640 m, the sum of the length and width is 320 m. As 320 – 180 is 140 the width is 140 m. The area is 180 × 80 + 120 × 60, which is 14 400 + 7200 = 21 600. The area is 21 600 m², or 2.16 ha.

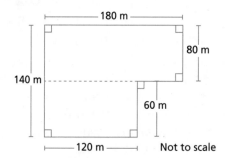

32 Keep the sequence going: 1, 3, 6, 10, 15, 21, 28, 36. This represents the handshakes for a group of 9 people.

33 Jace has 4 ☺ and 3 ★. Adalyne has one more of each sticker and has earned 10 more points. This means ☺ + ★ = 10 points. As Clementine has 2 of each sticker, she has 20 points. As 50 − 20 = 30, she needs another 30 points.

34 Row 1 (0 'sewings'), row 2 (3), row 3 (6), row 4 (9), row 5 (12) and row 6 (15). Total sewings: 3 + 6 + 9 + 12 + 15 = 45. This means it will take 45 minutes.

35 12 kL is 12 000 L. $\frac{2}{3}$ of 12 000 is 12 000 ÷ 3 × 2 = 8000, so the tank contains 8000 L of water. 10 L/15 seconds is 40 L/ minute and 15 L/10 seconds is 90 L/minute. As 90 − 40 = 50, water is leaving the tank at the rate of 50 L/minute. As 8000 ÷ 50 is 800 ÷ 5 = 160, the tank will be empty in 160 minutes, or 2 h 40 min.

SAMPLE TEST PAPER
Part 3: Thinking Skills   Pages 172–181

1 D 2 D 3 D 4 D 5 A 6 B 7 C 8 C 9 B 10 A
11 A 12 C 13 A 14 A 15 C 16 A 17 B 18 C
19 A 20 C 21 B 22 C 23 A 24 B 25 D 26 B
27 D 28 C 29 A 30 B 31 D 32 B 33 B 34 C
35 D 36 C 37 A 38 D 39 A 40 B

1 60 tickets were bought by 10 people, so the remaining 284 people bought 422 tickets. Now 422 − 284 = 138. So 138 more tickets were bought than there were people. This means that 138 people bought 2 tickets each. As 284 − 138 = 146, 146 people bought one ticket.

2 Isla's conclusion is that Ben loves eating fish for dinner. The evidence she has based this on is that he eats a lot of fish. So, for Isla's conclusion to hold, it must be assumed that anyone who eats a lot of fish must love eating fish.

3 If it is true that whoever drove the car must have known where to find the key and Jack did not know where to find the key, he could not have driven the car.

4 Ethan and Penny both rolled 4. George rolled two lower than Penny so he rolled 2 and Jeannie rolled 1. Samara's roll was 2 higher than Ben's, and as these had to be different to the others Samara can only have rolled 5 and Ben 3. This means that no-one rolled 6.

5 The text wants you to accept that one of the healthiest things you can do for yourself is go for a walk and A is the statement in the list that best expresses this. The rest of the text gives you reasons to believe this main idea, giving supporting details about different health benefits from walking.

6 The tiles are identical. The top row of the two bottom tiles can be seen so that the orientation can be seen. The bottom left tile will be top left rotated through half a turn (180°). The bottom right tile is the same as the top left.

7 There were 32 babies. 8 were added and 10 taken out. So there were then 30 babies. There were 24 teens and 10 were added. There are now 28, so 6 must have been taken out. The springers had 37, 6 were added and 5 taken out so there are now 38.

8 Dora's argument is that the Wildlife Clinic needs a mobile van. The statement that wildlife carers in some areas do not have access to a vet is further evidence of the need for a van, so most strengthens this argument.

9 If anyone who found the needle in the haystack must have had both perseverance and keen eyesight, then it follows that anyone who does not satisfy both requirements cannot have found the needle. So, if Dermot does not have perseverance, he cannot have found the needle. A is not correct because you cannot say it **must** be true. Dermot might have keen eyesight but still not have found the needle. C is not correct because you cannot say it **must** be true. Dermot might have perseverance but still not have found the needle.

10 The given pieces must form the outside of the square. The missing piece must fit with those pieces. The only piece that will fit with the third of the given pieces is A.

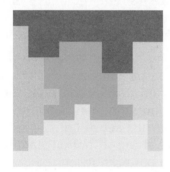

11 Sam's conclusion is that Fang's mother daydreams all day. The evidence this is based on is that Fang's mother is an author. So, for Sam's conclusion to hold, it must be assumed that all authors daydream all day.

12 Kirby has lost the least points, 10, after three rounds. The next lowest is 16. If anyone who has lost 16 loses none in the fourth round, they can finish on 16. Kirby will definitely win provided she loses fewer than 6 points in the next round. So the maximum number of points that Kirby can afford to lose is 5.

Competitor	Round 1	Round 2	Round 3	Total
Walter	9	1	6	16
Paige	4	7	5	16
Anne	8	6	7	21
Cooper	2	13	4	19
Olivia	7	4	6	17
Kirby	3	5	2	10
Osman	12	3	1	16
Shae	5	4	8	17
Matt	1	2	15	18
Sylvia	6	8	3	17

13 Barney's plot is at the left end and Lloyd's carrots are next to that. Lloyd's fence is not blue (Barney's), orange (corn) or yellow (Stefan), so it is red or green. The red fence is to the right of the green fence so Lloyd's fence is not red, it is green. Rafael's and the red fenced plot are two apart. So one must be on the far right and one in the middle. Neither of these is Stefan with his yellow fence, so the red fence must be around Jock's plot and be the one in the middle. Jock grows beans so beans are grown in the middle of the row.

Barney	Lloyd	Jock	Stefan	Rafael
Blue	Green	Red	Yellow	Orange
Peas	Carrots	Beans	Broccoli	Corn

14 No information is given about the meaning of a light that is on continuously, so Locky's reasoning that the battery **must** be fine is incorrect. Olivia's reasoning would also have been incorrect if she had said the battery **must** be about to run out, since there could be a number of reasons for the light being on continuously. However, Olivia said the battery **might** be about to run out. So her reasoning is correct since,

in the absence of further information, that could be one of the reasons for the light being on continuously.

15 Norbit's mother is arguing that the new farmers' market should not continue because it takes business away from local shops that serve the local community. If the market supports local farmers and creates a sense of community, that also serves the local community. So statement C undermines and weakens her argument.

16 In both the minutes positions the horizontal bars are lit up, so each digit has one of the vertical positions not working. The third digit across can only be a 2 in the first time shown, so it is the top right position that is not working. The final digit could be a 3 or a 5. In the second time shown the top right position is lit up, so it is the top left that is not working. The final digit in the first time was a 5, so the clock showed 8:25. Nine minutes later it is 8:34. Six minutes after that will be 8:40.

The clock should show ⊟⊟:⊟⊟ but would show ⊟⊟:⊟⊟.

17 Livvy's conclusion is that there's nothing wrong with skipping class to go to the mall. The evidence she bases this on is that other students do it all the time. So, for Livvy's conclusion to hold, it must be assumed that there is nothing wrong with doing something if other students do it.

18 Both people use correct reasoning. They both acknowledge the things they need to learn and do to be successful hair stylists. Travis thinks he could probably learn time management skills and if he does then he has a good chance of being successful. Sybilla is sure that if she tries hard to be a better listener, she could be a successful hair stylist. Both use correct reasoning to allow for situations where they might not be successful.

19

Mon.	Tues.	Wed.	Thurs.	Fri.
3			6	
	11	12	13	14
17		19	20	
24	25			28

Tia could buy a fortnightly ticket for the middle two weeks, but daily tickets for the 2 days in the first week and 3 days in the last week. Total cost = $40 + 5 × $7 = $75.

20 It cannot be true that Hermione will not be allowed to participate in the excursion because she has fulfilled the two criteria required. She has saved the money that her parents required, and she has passed the teacher's requirement of either achieving an excellent result in the end-of-term test and/ or the major assignment.

21 Ariana has correctly reasoned that the lights can be adjusted to allow for anticipated traffic conditions such as school hours. She has not specified that the particular set of lights is set up because of the school on Hamilton Street. Quentin has acknowledged the traffic light adjustment coinciding with school hours but the Hamilton Street school he mentions is north of the lights and the lights only allow four cars through that way during school hours so his reasoning that the lights are adjusted specifically for that school is incorrect. There may be bigger schools in the other direction or other reasons for the lights to operate the way they have been programmed.

22 The object could be three spheres, which would give side view X or three cylinders which would give side view Y.

23 The argument is intended to sell a range of skin care products. It uses the claim of expertise and science in the area of skin care to persuade readers/listeners to purchase the products. Lucie claims that

'You need to look after your skin and the best way to do that is through our range of protective and nourishing Love Your Skin products'. Option A is a recommendation to protect the skin by using the all-important sun protection ingredients. This strengthens the argument that the products protect the skin.

24 2 April is a Wednesday. So adding 7 each time, 9, 16, 23 and 30 April will also be Wednesdays. Without considering the Sunday shows, there will be 4 shows in each of the first 3 weeks, 3 shows in the week that includes Anzac Day, Friday 25 April and 1 final show in the following week. That is a total of 16 shows. Adding the two Sunday shows gives 18 times that the play will be performed.

25 Every shrub that was in flower had a wren and no shrub with a wren also had a parrot. So, if a shrub is in flower, it must not have a parrot.

26 The information tells you that Claire has already been approved to compete in the individual events at the nationals but she will still compete in the state trials. If she finishes in the top two at the trials, she will automatically enter into the team competition (as well as compete individually).

27 The book states that cucumbers need plenty of water in summer, but that doesn't mean that the only reason they don't grow well is lack of water. The book also states that they will grow successfully in full sun but that doesn't mean that they need lots of sun to grow well.

28 There were 12 bicycles and tricycles altogether and 29 wheels. If there were 12 bicycles there would be 12 × 2 = 24 wheels. As 29 – 24 = 5, there were 5 more wheels so there must have been 5 tricycles. Now 12 – 5 = 7 so there were 7 bicycles.

29 To mend the cloth a piece 4 squares across and 5 down is needed. So, the pieces in each of the options need to be rotated one-quarter of a turn (90°). There is one arrow in the middle row that must point left and one in the bottom row that points right.

30 Toby had the fastest time. Keith had the slowest time. Jenny's time was slower than Joel's which was slower than Sally's. So Sally must have had the second fastest time. The statement that Sally did not have the second fastest time cannot be true.

A is not the correct answer because that statement must be true. Joel did have the third fastest time.

C and D are not correct because those statements might be true.

31 If the vaccine is working then anyone who was vaccinated should not have caught the disease. As Zara caught the disease, she needs to not be vaccinated in order for the vaccine to be working. As Mikey was vaccinated, he needs to not have caught the disease for the vaccine to be working. As April was not vaccinated, it will not matter whether or not she caught the disease as far as the effectiveness of the vaccine is concerned. As Jai did not catch the disease, it will not matter whether or not he was vaccinated as far as the effectiveness of the vaccine is concerned.

32 The argument is that a healthy diet which consists of a range of real foods is the best way to get all the nutrition you need and it's too easy to overdo it with supplements. The statement that most strengthens Huw's argument is that 'Some supplements can cause an imbalance of minerals in the body that can be detrimental to good health'.

33

Stallholder	Price	Price for 12
Helen	$2.10 each or 2 for $4.00	6 × $4.00 = $24.00
Louise	$2.50 each or 3 for $5.00	4 × $5.00 = $20.00
Neil	$2.40 each or 4 for $7.00	3 × $7.00 = $21.00
Gaynor	$2.20 each or 5 for $8.00	2 × $8.00 + 2 × $2.20 = $20.40

34 The number for red is double the number for green. As none of the columns are double the height of another, either red or green must be the colour left out. The smallest column must be yellow and represents the number 10. The difference between the number for blue and the number for green is 10, but that is not the difference between the other two columns. So the missing column must be green.

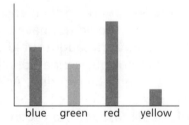

blue   green   red   yellow

35 This statement provides additional evidence that weakens the argument which is in favour of the convenience and ease of online supermarket grocery shopping. Don't be tricked by C. This statement is a restatement of the statement that 'the convenience [of online supermarket shopping] outweighs any negative consequences such as being delivered bananas that are either too ripe or too

unripe', and so does not provide additional evidence to weaken the argument.

36 If the car was blue, the second statement of both Max and Susan was true so their first statements must be false. That would mean that Susan caused the incident and Julie caused the incident. Only one of them caused the incident so those first statements cannot both be false. The false statements must have been that the car was blue. So the car was not blue. Julie's second statement is true so the first must be false. Max caused the incident.

37 The number who have read *Purple Fields* includes all those who have read *Meanderings*, which includes all those who have read *Grace*. All readers of *Road to Rio* must have also read *Purple Fields* or have read only *Road to Rio*. As more people had read only *Purple Fields* than had read only *Road to Rio*, then more people overall must have read *Purple Fields* than *Road to Rio*.

38 The text wants you to accept that every child should read *Alice's Adventures in Wonderland* for all the numerous reasons listed.

39 The text argues in favour of table tennis as an option for sport at school. In his argument Shaun identifies two potential problems: the purchase cost of equipment and working out where to store the tables. Option B answers his concern about the costs. Option A concludes that there is nowhere to store the equipment. This weakens Shaun's argument. Without a storage location, Shaun will have no chance of arguing his case to the school.

40 Pieces II and IV are used.

Your parents or teachers can use these checklists to give you feedback on your writing. The checklist they use will depend on the kind of writing you did. They might use points from more than one checklist to give you feedback.

Checklist for writing a description

Did the student:

- ☐ orient the reader to the scene, and suggest a persona for the writer?
- ☐ give some details about the scene using vivid adjectives or other language?
- ☐ include imagined sounds and smells as well as sights?
- ☐ express his or her own thoughts and feelings about the scene?
- ☐ comment on the atmosphere of the scene?
- ☐ use correct and appropriate grammar, punctuation and spelling?

Checklist for writing a recount

Did the student:

- ☐ orient the reader to who, what, where and when?
- ☐ choose only important events to write about?
- ☐ include at least some interesting detail?
- ☐ add personal comments about what happened?
- ☐ use time words and expressions to help the reader follow the order of events?
- ☐ write a concluding comment?
- ☐ use correct and appropriate grammar, punctuation and spelling?

Checklist for writing a narrative

Did the student:

- ☐ write at least one sentence to orient the reader and capture his or her attention?
- ☐ include an event that gives interest to the story and makes it worth telling?
- ☐ resolve the story in some way?

- ☐ use vivid, interesting images to describe people, things and activities—for example, through verbs, adjectives and similes?
- ☐ use correct and appropriate grammar, punctuation and spelling?

Checklist for writing a persuasive text

Did the student:

- ☐ introduce the topic/question and state his or her overall opinion?
- ☐ give strong arguments to support his or her opinion?
- ☐ develop his or her arguments using facts or examples?
- ☐ use signpost words to help the reader follow his or her arguments?
- ☐ write a conclusion summing up his or her opinion?
- ☐ use correct and appropriate grammar, punctuation and spelling?